MAYA CHILDREN

MAYA CHILDREN
Helpers at the Farm

Karen L. Kramer

HARVARD UNIVERSITY PRESS
Cambridge, Massachusetts
London, England
2005

LIBRARY OF CONGRESS CATALOGING-IN-PUBLICATION DATA
Kramer, Karen.
  Maya children : helpers at the farm / Karen L. Kramer.
      p.   cm.
  Includes bibliographical references and index.
  ISBN 0-674-01690-4 (alk. paper)
    1. Maya children—Mexico—Yucatan (State)—Social Conditions. 2. Maya children—
  Mexico—Yucatan (State)—Economic Conditions. 3. Mayas—Agricultural—Mexico—
  Yucatan (State) 4. Mayas—Mexico—Yucatan (State)—Kinship. 5. Sustainable
  agriculture—Mexico—Yucatan (Mexico : State)—Economic conditions. I. Title.

F1435.3.C47K73 2005
305.23'089'97427—dc22

                                                          2004059661

CONTENTS

FOREWORD

James L. Boone and Jane Lancaster

One of the great watersheds in human history is the marked increase in population growth rates that occurred at the end of the Pleistocene as a consequence of the adoption of food production and sedentism. Virtually the entire habitable surface of the Earth was colonized by humans in what amounts to little more than the blink of a paleontologist's eye. In the Holocene epoch that followed, coinciding with global warming, the widespread adoption of domesticates, and increased sedentism, the near-zero growth rates that characterized most of the Pleistocene began to rise, ultimately resulting in the population of a little over six billion in which we find ourselves immersed today. The development of social inequality, the formation of civilizations and states, and the far-reaching technological advancements that are now both the boon and the bane of our existence all follow from the exponential increase in human population size and density that accompanies the development of cultivation and animal husbandry. Why were growth rates so low when essentially all humans alive were foragers? Why did growth rates increase during the Holocene? These questions have been in the forefront of anthropological inquiry since the beginning of the discipline.

A common explanation for this increase in growth rates has always been that circumstances associated with food production and greater sedentism allowed for higher fertility rates than had been possible during our long history as foragers. Over the past decade, however, empirical studies and simulation analyses have revealed that the relationship between the mode of subsistence and fertility is more complex than had previously been realized. In 1988 Campbell and Wood published a cross-cultural compilation of total fertility rates (TFRs) for seventy forager, horticulturalist, and intensive agricultural societies from the contemporary ethnographic record that showed that there were no significant differences in TFRs across subsistence practices. Hewlett (1991) published a similar analysis of forty mobile and sedentary foragers and pastoralists that found slightly higher fertility rates among pastoralists, although the difference was not significant. In 1993 Bentley et al. published an extensive critique and reanalysis of the Campbell and Wood study, presenting a new cross-cultural comparison of fifty-seven forager, horticultural, and intensive agricultural groups. Bentley et al. (1993a, b) used a subset of the Campbell and Wood sample, excluding populations with high levels of sterility and also attempting to correct for the inflated sample size resulting from the inclusion of nonindependent cases (ethnic groups that were closely related). Their results showed that intensive agriculturalists had significantly higher fertility rates than either foragers or horticulturalists. Interestingly, however, horticulturalists showed slightly lower fertility than foragers in the sample, although the difference was not significant.

Bentley et al.'s finding that intensive agriculturalists have higher fertility than foragers, but that horticulturalists do not, strongly suggests that the development of sedentism or food production *alone* does not account for the historical increase in fertility per se. More important, however, all three subsistence groups show considerable variation in fertility, and subsistence regime by itself remains a poor predictor of fertility. Yet if agriculturalists have a significantly higher mean TFR, this result requires an explanation. Available evidence suggests that significant increases in fertility do not occur until dependence on agriculture is well established. Therefore changes in the household energy budget resulting from reorganization of the relative contribution of men, women, and children may turn out to be a more promising explanation for increases in fertility that occur with the adoption of agriculture.

Human families have a finite time and energy budget out of which various activities associated with survival, maintenance, and reproduction must be funded. From this perspective, time and energy expenditures are commonly subsumed under two categories: somatic effort, comprising the time and energy spent in survival and maintenance; and reproductive effort, comprising the time and energy expended in the production of offspring. The more time and energy that must be put into acquiring and processing resources to support the existing household, the less time and energy is left over for reproduction and rearing additional children. The total number of children that a family can successfully raise should be directly affected by the net efficiency of the subsistence regime.

Subsistence intensification, which is the process by which the amount of time or energy required to produce and process food increases relative to net return (Brookfield 1972), thus raising the labor cost per unit of food. Typically this occurs when items are added to the diet that require more time to harvest or process to render them edible, or when cultivation techniques are adopted that require more ground preparation and maintenance. In either case, subsistence intensification results in decreased individual labor efficiency: an individual expends more energy for each calorie acquired or produced. The payoff to intensification is that more calories per unit area of land become available, making it possible for more individuals to survive and reproduce on less land. If individual efficiency (labor per unit of food) declines under intensification, holding other conditions equal, it seems reasonable to expect that fertility would actually decrease, not increase, since parents are putting more time and energy into food production relative to the production of offspring. Bentley et al.'s (1993a, b) data on the relative TFRs of foragers, horticulturalists, and intensive agriculturalists support this somewhat counterintuitive proposition in the sense that horticulturalists on average have about the same or even a slightly lower TFR than foragers.

But the prediction that fertility ought to decline with increased subsistence intensification is not borne out. The fact that it is not—at least with respect to intensive agriculture—raises an interesting question: how can parents working at a lower individual efficiency afford to support yet more children than parents under less intensive subsistence regimes?

One possibility is that in agricultural regimes children contribute substantially to household production. This is the basis of Caldwell's "wealth flows" theory of fertility. Caldwell (1982) argues that shifts in social and economic structure, and specifically in the economic cost of producing children, precipitate changes in the demand for children. Part of the cost of children is the extent to which they do or do not contribute to household production. A number of ethnographic studies have examined the issue of the economic value of agriculturalist children's work and have found that these children work hard and contribute substantially to household production. Few researchers, however, measure the net value of children's work—that is, how much children produce relative to how much they consume—in quantitative or comparable terms, an issue that forms the central theme of this book. Thus, though it is apparent that children in subsistence agriculturalist settings work hard, the question of whether they ever produce more than they consume while they are still in their natal households has never been answered. This is a critical question on which Karen Kramer focuses. If children do not produce more than they consume, then the motivation to increase household production by increasing the number of offspring cannot account for the observed increase in completed family size among agriculturalists compared with horticulturalists or foragers.

Further, it is not a foregone conclusion that just because children work hard they are net producers. Kaplan's (1994, 1996, 1997) analyses of the relationship between production and consumption for three groups of horticulturalists and foragers (Machiguenga, Piro, and Ache) found that, among all three groups, children provide only 20 percent to 25 percent of the calories that they consume before the age of 18 and that they do not become net producers, producing more than they consume, until their early twenties, after they already have children of their own.

Under these conditions, having more children would decrease, not increase, total net household production. Of course any contribution that children make reduces the amount of subsidy someone else, usually parents or other kin, has to make and helps to underwrite the children's own cost. As Kramer shows us in this book, however, unless children produce more than they consume, the desire for more children cannot be explained in terms of an increased parental demand for children's labor. Her analysis of the relationship between age-specific production and consumption for a group of modern Maya agriculturalists addresses the central question: Does the economic potential of children help to explain the relatively high fertility of humans in natural fertility populations?

Kramer further shows that parents' work alone is not sufficient to meet the labor demands of their large households. It appears that older children's labor is helping to meet the mounting labor demands of the household as younger children are added to the family.

More than a case study of a group of agriculturalists, Kramer provides a framework that looks beyond the traditional classification of agriculturalist and forager to define children's economic value. Because the level of children's economic contributions crosscuts these classifications, knowing whether a child is an agriculturalists or a forager is not in itself very informative in predicting the helping behavior of children. The analysis and data Kramer presents suggest that parents only have enough time to support about four children. In situations where the reproductive rate exceeds this level of fertility, as it does in most natural fertility populations regardless of the mode of production, children's contributions may be an alternate or additional means to maintain the relatively short birth intervals characteristic of human reproduction.

How does one take all these abstract ideas and cold hard facts and turn them into a book that does justice to a village full of people whom one has come to care deeply about over a year or more of fieldwork? This is a problem that every scientifically oriented anthropologist must face. Readers of this volume will find that Karen Kramer has done a splendid job not only of exploring one of the central questions about the human experience but of evoking the lives and experiences of her Maya subjects.

ACKNOWLEDGMENTS

The day my field partner and I arrived in the village of Xculoc, strangers looking for a research location, the village spokesman asked us, "How long are you going to stay?" This became a standing exchange with villagers, changing in tenor over the following year from disbelief, to quizzicalness, to lament. The Maya graciously provided not only shelter and a community in which to work but also a home, an aspect of fieldwork I had not expected. More lasting than the data that we collected, the Maya's gift of friendship, humor, and the beauty of their families is something for which I will always be thankful. They never seemed to weary of the endless questions or the hoisting, weighing, measuring, mapping, noting, and photographing of various aspects of their lives. Their seeming lack of annoyance for the long hours I spent sitting in their houses—following them around as they worked in their milpas (maize fields) or in the forest, or with trepidation asking about yet another large insect—was remarkable. In very fond memory and abiding appreciation of the people of Xculoc, *dios bo'otik*.

Doing fieldwork in a remote location cannot be accomplished without the help of many. Foremost I would like to thank Christopher Dore, without whose support through the Xculoc Ethnoarchaeological Project and knowledge of the Puuc region this research would not have been possible. Vitaliano Canul Pat spent numerous hours as liaison, informant, and translator and greatly facilitated our work in the village. Assistance was also generously provided by many local residents in surrounding towns. Among them, Don Miquel Uc Medina and his family, as well as George and Janet Cobb, helped us through many field logistics and kept us linked to the world outside.

Much of the methodological and theoretic development presented here benefited from conversations with my advisor Hillard Kaplan, who spent long and patient hours helping me to clarify my field methodology and distill my analysis. I am also thankful for the input of John Bock, a student of Kaplan's as well, whose interest and expertise concern children and who has contributed much to bringing the behavioral ecology of children to the fore. I am deeply grateful to the members of the Department of Demography at the University of California, Berkeley, for their support in my postdoctoral study. I owe much to Ronald Lee, who has been very generous as a mentor and a collaborator. Ron fostered rich interdisciplinary insight into the Maya case and contributed substantially to the analytic formulation presented here.

My advisor James Boone affably fielded a multitude of questions and helped me to work out many details of logic. I greatly appreciate Jane Lancaster's gracious assistance and readiness to provide scholarly guidance. Her research on primate juveniles and females has been of great inspiration to me. Both Jim and Jane were integral in initiating and bringing this book project to fruition.

I am indebted to Lewis Binford, who inspired my initial pursuit of anthropology and who taught me the importance of staying focused on variability. I thank Edward Bedrick for his statistical advice and Garnett McMillan for his patience as a sounding board. Thank you to James Boone, Jane Lancaster, John Bock, Aisha Kahn, and Russell Greaves for their comments on previous drafts. Special thanks to Kate Niles for her editorial assistance, and to my editor at Harvard, Michael Fisher. Tonnya Norwood and June-el Piper provided invaluable assistance and support. Their attention to detail was critical to the completion of this project.

I offer much appreciation to my friends, family, and husband, without whose stalwart support and, importantly, humor, writing this book could not have been accomplished. I am thankful for my association with the many graduate students and faculty at the University of New Mexico, University of California at Berkeley, and SUNY Stony Brook who, bound by their appreciation of anthropology, spawned provocative dialogue among diverse subdisciplines and perspectives.

The initial data collection phase of the fieldwork was supported by a National Science Foundation Dissertation Improvement Grant awarded to James Boone and Christopher Dore. Additional funding was provided by the Tinker-Mellon Foundation and the University of New Mexico. I gratefully acknowledge Ronald Lee, the support of the National Institute of Health/National Institute of Aging, the Mellon Foundation, and the Center for the Economics and Demography of Aging for funding subsequent phases of this research and analysis.

Finally, special appreciation to Mark Twain, who aptly pointed out that "only a fool can spell a word one way," a sentiment reflected by the Maya, who taught me that there are many ways to look at the world.

MAYA CHILDREN

INTRODUCTION

O ne of the striking observations that came out of my initial field-work among the Maya was that even though from a young age children spent long hours working, parents did not have enough time in the day to support their families. This book addresses the seeming contradiction that although children are expensive to raise and consti-tute a net cost throughout the duration of time they spend living in their natal households, they nonetheless play a crucial economic and repro-ductive role in underwriting the cost of large families. The key lay in deciphering the effects of children as both consumers and producers, and in the timing of children's economic contributions across the demo-graphic life cycle of the family.

There are as many ways to look at the economic lives of children as there are ways in which anthropologists collect data to make observa-tions about the people they study. Qualitative observations provide many descriptive details, background information, and provocative anecdotes that inspire research directions and are important to breathe life into how we present the people we study. Quantitative data collec-tion involves systematically making repetitive observations about the same set of variables. Compiled, these quantitative observations allow us to consider not only that two things are different but also how much they differ—both within a study group and across groups—and, thus, form the basis for comparative analyses. No one method tells the whole story. In this case, the research is concerned with cross-cultural variation in the duration of offspring dependence and the relationship between the economic role of children and family size, an issue that is comparative and quantitative in nature. Although skepticism periodically emerges over the perfunctory and impersonal nature of quantitative methods to explain cultural phenomena, if anthropologists seek to make comparative statements, at the most fundamental level we first have to be able to compare different kinds of apples and how these relate to different kinds of oranges. My choice of analytic framework and field methodology was in many ways guided by my interest in collecting empirical, quantitative data that were comparable with other time-allocation studies.

That said, one of the challenges of writing this book was to craft potentially belabored discussions of methods and results so they would be accessible to a broad readership. On the one hand, I take the perspective that quantitative methods are the most programmatic means to comparative research. On the other hand, in doing so it is easy to lose sight of the very people whose lives we seek to study. To balance these two viewpoints, my goal here is to build a compendium of Maya children's work in the context of an ethnographic presentation of Maya economic life and reproductive life history.

Most empirical studies have shown that children, regardless of mode of subsistence, require considerable time and resources to support. The Maya are no exception. Recognition that human children spend a relatively long period of time as dependents has spawned recent interest in anthropology, demography, and economics about who supports them. What seems clear through this discussion is that children rely on a range of social options. Whether mothers, fathers, grandmothers, siblings, extended kin, or governments help to support children depends on subsistence economics, social organization, the timing of births, and levels of fertility and mortality schedules. This book focuses on children's economic lives from a number of analytic perspectives with the purpose of asking what role children themselves play in underwriting fertility.

Because I set out to explore in detail children's helping behavior I necessarily have limited my focus. Doing so has illuminated some of the questions yet to be fully answered: How do we model the differential helping effects of children, older adults, and nonfamily members on raising dependents cross-culturally? And, how do fertility and mortality schedules affect the status and contribution of helpers? As new data are incorporated and techniques developed, I expect some fine-tuning will be made to the conclusions drawn here.

While this book is about the specific Maya village of Xculoc, in the lowland forests of the Yucatan Peninsula, Mexico, it is not intended as a unique case, nor is it meant as a generalization of the economic value of agricultural children as essentially different from some other mode of subsistence. A tendency within anthropology and disciplines that draw on anthropological data is to use often-studied hunter-gatherers as exemplars of all hunter-gatherers or often-studied groups of agriculturalists as representative of all agriculturalists. The very asset of ethnographic examples is that they are windows into the range of human diversity rather than being representative of cultural norms. What anthropology brings to the human behavior table is the study of diverse, small-scale populations. As we have learned about many aspects of hunter-gatherers, new studies continue to demonstrate that they express vast behavioral variation and, consequently, purported norms about hunter-gatherers rarely hold lasting relevance. The same is true of agriculturalists. The Maya represent one expression of children's helping behavior in the cross-cultural continuum of subsistence and reproductive ecology.

Some may ask why we need another study. Recent time-allocation research among hunter-gatherers has provided provocative insight into the complex relationship between subsistence ecology and children's work. Subsistence economies—by which I mean those economies with little involvement in the labor market or national economy—whether they be of hunter-gatherers, agriculturalists, or pastoralists, are quickly transitioning. This study of the Maya increases the diversity of subsistence populations, especially agriculturalists, for whom we have detailed and individual data. The study of small-scale societies offers a very different insight into demographic transitions than is possible with aggregate, national-level data and augment our understanding of the interaction between economics and reproductive ecology in pre-market systems. Establishing an empirical baseline for this predemographic-transition community will provide a vantage point from which to view the future effects of modernization on demographic processes, both in the Maya region and in natural fertility populations elsewhere.

Structure of This Book

This book is organized into three general sections. The first section is an overview of the theoretic, historic, and methodological issues surrounding the role of children as helpers. The second section provides a background to the Maya, and the third presents the analysis of Maya children's economic contributions and the implications of those findings to fertility. The overview section is divided into two chapters. Chapter 1 places children as helpers within the context of cooperative breeding and addresses the theoretic interest in children's economic behavior and its relationship to fertility in both the behavioral ecology and economic literature. Chapter 2 situates Maya children's subsistance and economic activities in a comparative framework as a way to think about the variation in children's economic contributions. As a background to the Maya study, Chapter 3 positions the Maya in their physical and historical landscape with emphasis on those aspects of their subsistence, household organization, and the village's relationship with the national economy that affect the economic lives of children. Chapter 4 outlines the field methodology used in collecting the reproductive history and census data and then describes demographic fluctuations across the Maya family life cycle and historical demographic trends. Chapter 5 outlines the field methods that were used to collect the time-allocation data.

After establishing this background, the analysis is staged in three steps that address whether children's economic contributions enable mothers to maintain relatively short birth intervals and large families. Each chapter builds on the previous analytic outcome. My goal in doing this is to clarify and offer a suggestion to rectify the ongoing methodological debate that surrounds children's economic value. By approaching children's work from a number of analytic perspectives, the economic contributions of Maya children are cross-culturally comparable to a variety of other research, and the strength of the conclusions does not rest on any one demonstration of patterning but on several convergent analyses.

To descriptively situate the economic lives of Maya children, first I examine the time the Maya children spend working (Chapter 6). What are their economic contributions? What kinds of work do they participate in, and how much time do male and female children allocate to various productive tasks? In the second step, I consider the duration of children's economic dependence (Chapter 7). What is the age patterning of their production relative to their consumption? At what age do Maya children achieve economic independence? And how does the Maya pattern compare with different food production systems? In the third analytic step, I look at children's help from the parents' perspective (Chapter 8). What is the net cost to raise Maya children? Is the net flow of wealth, as has been traditionally predicted, from children to parents? Are children a net economic cost or an asset? Or is the timing of children's help across the family life cycle a more relevant approach to explain why Maya parents can afford large families? Does the surplus production of teenage children enable their parents to continue childbearing during family life-cycle stages when parents themselves may not have sufficient time and resources to support their family?

The final analytic chapter evaluates the effect that a change in helping behavior and labor efficiency has on the constraints of leaving home and the age at first birth (Chapter 9). How does a change in labor efficiency through the introduction of laborsaving technology affect how children spend their time? What effect does this have on the helping behavior of young women and the age at which they leave home and begin families of their own? Chapter 10 summarizes the results, looks at the contributions of older adults, and readdresses the success of the Maya strategy for raising large families. The Postscript discusses the very recent changes in Xculoc and the implications of those changes to future economic and reproductive options.

Because this book draws from both economic and behavioral ecology perspectives, certain key terms that are familiar to one discipline but not necessarily to the other are defined or clarified in endnotes rather than in the body of the text. For parsimony's sake, I often refer to the specific Maya who are the subject of this study simply as the Maya. In doing so, I am not intending to make generalizations about modern-day Maya villagers as a whole. Where appropriate, I use Bolenchen Maya in reference to the geographic region of the Yucatan in which they live or Xculoc Maya in reference to the village in which they live. It is important to point out that when the data were collected for this book, the villagers of Xculoc grew nearly all the food that they consumed and were minimally involved in wage labor, cash cropping, or the national Mexican economy. Because of this, their subsistence base is not directly comparable to those of several well-documented and frequently referenced studies of agriculturalists in Bangladesh, India, and elsewhere who do cash crop and who buy a much greater portion of the food they consume. The time-allocation and demographic data used here were principally collected during 1992 and 1993. During subsequent fieldwork in 2001 and 2003, it became apparent that the village was becoming more incorporated into the national Mexican economy, not through greater involvement in wage labor but through an increase in maize production. These economic changes no doubt in the future will affect many aspects of the lives of children discussed herein.

– 1 –

Children as Helpers at the Nest

Humans have remarkably diverse ways of raising children to be successful adults. Reflecting the range of social and ecological environments in which we live, in some cases, children are schooled for years, while in others, they learn while working and contribute to their well being from a young age. In some cases, children help to support their siblings or extended kin aid in absorbing the costs of raising children. In others, mothers or parents alone support their children. In some socioecological environments, parental investment in children's training, education, and health is significant; in others, it is less so.

Humans also express a great deal of variability in the number of children they have and in the survival of those children. In recent decades, family size has reached historic lows in Europe, North America, China, Japan, and urban areas elsewhere but remains high in many other communities, as it has among the Maya about whom this book is written. The total fertility rate in Mexico, for example, fell from 6.8 to 2.8 between 1960 and 2000 (Wilkie 2002:208). Yet during this same period of time, in a rural Maya village, fertility stayed at pretransitional levels, with mothers having a median completed family size of 7.3 in 2000.[1] Much attention has been given to the modern demographic transition—the unprecedented trend toward declining fertility and mortality rates during recent centuries—and the relationship between small families and the increasing cost of supporting modern-day children. Yet, we know comparatively less about how parents meet the challenge of raising large families in pretransitional economies.

Life History's Challenge to Mothers

Human life history has evolved such that short birth intervals make it possible for mothers to bear more offspring over their reproductive

careers than can other closely related primates. Not only can human
mothers have children in relatively rapid succession, but many more of
those children are also likely to survive into adulthood. This means
that human mothers are in the unusual position of supporting multiple
dependents of various ages simultaneously. Caring for children of different ages would, perhaps, be fairly straightforward if they all benefited from the same kinds of time and energy expenditures. Under such
circumstances, mothers could spend more time in the same suite of
activities as their number of dependent offspring increased. However,
mothers are posed with an allocation problem. Infants, young children, and older children all require different kinds of care. Infant survival is dependent on mother's milk. Young children—whose dental
and digestive maturation is incomplete, yet whose brain growth is
calorically demanding—are dependent on specialized, calorie-rich, yet
easily digestible and low-volume food (Bogin 1999a, 2002).[2] Older
children, in contrast, consume adult foods and other resources, and
often require investments in training and education.[3] Childhood in
many ways is an extension of infancy in that young children are not
yet able to procure the specialty foods they need and must rely on provisioning from others for their survival. However, from the point of
view of the mother, there is one significant distinction. Weaning of
young but still-dependent children allows mothers to physiologically
prepare to bear another child since they are not energetically constrained by lactation (overview in Low 2000, chap. 6; Small 2001;
Zeller 1987).

The transition to self-care and economic independence is a protracted, though variable, process, during which children continue to
develop and mature, taking on the order of twenty years to reach
reproductive maturity and be able to initiate independent reproduction—much longer than other closely related primates of similar size
(Appendix Table 1.1).[4] Consequently, throughout their reproductive
careers, mothers are faced with how to provide high-quality child care
to unweaned children without forgoing their economic activities to
feed older children (Hames 1988; Hewlett 1991; Hill and Hurtado
1996; Hill and Kaplan 1988; Hrdy 1999; Hurtado et al. 1992; Lee
1979; LeVine 1977; LeVine et al. 1988; Panter-Brick 1989). These
attributes of human life history—short birth intervals, the allocation
problem of caring for multiple dependents of different ages, prolonged

dependence, and late age of initiating reproduction—link together in creating a demand for cooperative breeding among humans and an opportunity for children as helpers.

Behavioral Ecology and Economic Approaches to Children's Economic Contributions

Children's development has captured the attention of scholars from diverse perspectives. Concern with the economic lives of children is nestled in this much-broader interest and issues from two main theoretic domains: behavioral ecology and economics. In both disciplines, children's economic contributions were peripheral to the study of fertility, and who helps to underwrite the cost of raising children, until they vaulted into focus when a conundrum arose within each of these paradigms. In behavioral ecology, this focus emerged in explaining why in some species' offspring stay in their natal home and delay reproduction. In economics, children become important to place high fertility within the framework of rational decision making. Since then, both disciplines have contributed substantially and in different ways to our cross-cultural appreciation of the relationship between children as helpers and parental fitness.[5]

The Evolutionary Puzzle of Helping

Cooperative breeding has long been recognized by biologists as a reproductive strategy and social system in which nonparental members of the social group help to support offspring (Emlen 1984, 1991; Skutch 1935, 1987).[6] Although relatively uncommon, cooperative breeding has been documented across diverse taxa, predominantly among some 2–3 percent of bird species and 2 percent of mammals—primarily species of wild canids, mongoose, and rodents and several species of primates, including humans (Brown 1987; Emlen 1984; Krebs and Davies 1997; Solomon and French 1997; Stacey and Koenig 1990; Trivers 1985).[7] The terms *helpers-at-the-nest* and *helpers-at-the-den*, often used to refer to cooperative breeders, point to its relative rarity across taxa.[8] In these species, nonparental helpers may guard young from predation when parents are absent, help forage for food to feed young, defend territory boundaries, or build and clean nests.

Among primates, dependence on help to raise young is best viewed as a continuum across species, from rare incidences of nonmaternal assistance to committed cooperative breeding (overview in Mitani and Watts 1997; Nicolson 1987). Among most species of primates, young are transported by older individuals until they are capable of sustaining their own locomotion. Although helpers may also groom and protect infants, carrying is the focus of allomothering research in primates because it is both a clear form of parental investment and energetically demanding of mothers (Mitani and Watts 1997). Infants usually ride on the backs of their mothers, but situational carrying by older siblings, related adults, and unrelated members of the troop is referenced both anecdotally and quantitatively across a wide range of primate species. In its extreme case among tamarins and marmosets (small South American primates), help in carrying infants allows mothers to forage more efficiently and reallocate energy from carrying toward lactation and the production of young (French 1997; Koenig 1995; Koenig and Rothe 1991; Tardif 1997).

Two kinds of general questions have emerged out of the cooperative breeding literature. From the vantage point of the parent, the research question often posed is whether helpers really help. The weight of evidence across cooperative breeders evinces that mothers with helpers have better success in raising young, either by reducing offspring mortality or by enhancing fertility (Emlen 1991; Emlen and Wrege 1991; Moehlman 1986; Wiley and Rabenold 1984; Woolfenden and Fitzpatrick 1984). For example, among tamarins and marmosets, allomothering appears to be of direct reproductive benefit since mothers who receive help have shorter birth intervals and produce infants who grow more rapidly (Goldizen 1987; Mitani and Watts 1997; Ross and MacLarnon 1995).[9] In humans cross-culturally, parents commonly rely on the help of others to raise young. The roles that children, grandmothers, and extended kin play in subsidizing dependents have been documented across a breadth of disciplines (Hawkes et al. 1997; Ivey 2000; Kramer 2002). Turke's (1988, 1989) seminal study among the Ifaluk (Micronesian islanders) first introduced human cooperative breeding to anthropology. Ifaluk girls are valuable helpers to their mothers. Using time-allocation data, Turke showed that mothers who bore female children early in their reproductive careers had greater completed fertility than if their firstborn children were boys. Of the other relatively few empirical studies that place human reproductive strategies in the framework of cooperative breeding, some show that helpers alleviate constraints on mothers' time but are less conclusive whether helpers have a direct effect on maternal reproductive success (Bove et al. 2002; Flinn 1988). Others are aimed specifically at the effects of infants on mothers' time and fertility (Bereczkei 1998; Hames 1988; Ivey 2000).

The second question central to cooperative breeding pivots on why helpers should help. From the vantage point of the helper, studies among birds, mammals, and primates seek to understand the evolution of the seemingly paradoxical behavior of why offspring delay or even forgo their own reproduction by staying in their natal home and committing their energy and resources to another's reproductive success. Prior to the articulation of inclusive fitness theory (Hamilton 1964), there was no satisfying way to explain helping, which was seen as an enigmatic expression of altruism. Hamilton's rule, which articulates the conditions under which altruism and cooperation might evolve, predicts that helping behavior among kin will be favored when $rb > c$, where r is the coefficient of relatedness, b is the benefit to the recipient, and c is the cost to the helper (overview in Dugatkin 1997). The benefit of helping is estimated by its effect on some proxy of inclusive fitness, which can be defined as "the sum of an individual's contribution to the next generation through the effects of an individual's actions on genes identical by descent in other individuals" (Low 2000:327).

Hamilton's rule, along with its reformulation by Brown (1975), provided a heuristic framework to view helping as an adaptive behavior by formulating a means to weigh whether the benefits accrued by helpers compensate for the cost of their help (Brown 1974, 1987; Emlen 1991; Vehrencamp 1978; but see Jamieson 1989; Jamieson and Craig 1987; McKenna 1987 for alternative positions).[10] Helpers may benefit directly by learning skills that enhance their own survival and future success in raising young of their own, or indirectly, through increasing their inclusive fitness by augmenting the reproductive success of a close kin.[11] That helping incurs inclusive fitness benefits is supported by the correlation noted in several species of cooperative breeders, including humans, between the degree of genetic relatedness of the helper and the amount of care they provide (Denham 1974; Hames 1988; Ivey 2000; Skutch 1987; overview in Emlen 1991;

Koenig and Mumme 1990; but see Clutton-Brock et al. 2001 for review of studies that do not show an association).[12] If an individual is sexually mature, whether to stay and help or go and breed hangs in the inclusive fitness balance of alternately helping to support siblings or one's own offspring. But herein lies a knotty problem: What if the helper is not sexually mature?

Why helpers help is often enmeshed in the question of why they stay. Sexually mature offspring may stay in their natal territory or group if leaving incurs the risk of mortality, predation, or not finding a mate. Evidence generally supports the view that among cooperative breeders, sexually mature offspring delay their own reproduction when constraints exist either on mating opportunities or on the availability of the resources and/or territory necessary to compete for mates and successfully reproduce (Brown 1987; Emlen 1982; Stacey and Koenig 1990; Woolfenden and Fitzpatrick 1984). Likewise, in human studies, the postponement of marriage and low marriage rates have been associated with ecological constraints on the accessibility of land or wealth necessary for reproduction (Boone 1988; Clarke 1993; Clarke and Low 1992; Strassman and Clarke 1998). Because delayed dispersal of sexually mature young from their natal group is often assumed to be critical in setting the stage for cooperative breeding in birds and animals (Brown 1987; Mumme 1997), it is sometimes inferred that when children delay marriage and reproduction beyond sexual maturity, they act as helpers (Crognier et al. 2001, 2002; Voland et al. 1991). But the benefits to stay do not necessarily explain why helpers help. For example, among fork-marked lemurs who live in competitive environments, offspring may remain in their natal territories following sexual maturity. The gains to offspring survival appear sufficient for parents to tolerate the delayed dispersal of their young, even though offspring do not help and the increase in group size raises feeding competition and compromises the nutritional status of parents (Schülke 2003).[13]

Two related points are important here. Although delayed dispersal is commonly associated with cooperative breeding in animals, segregating the issue of helping from staying is important in humans, since helpers may not be sexually mature. Among humans, juveniles commonly provide help, as do sexually mature siblings, fathers, older adults, and in some cases, unrelated adults who have offspring of their own. Importantly, depending on the helper's developmental and reproductive status, the costs and benefits of helping involve very different tradeoffs and explanations (Appendix Table 1.2). The centrality of delayed dispersal in the cooperative breeding literature perhaps overshadows the potential low-cost help of children, for whom the expensive cost of delayed reproduction is obviously attenuated. Although emphasis has been placed on the indirect benefits of helping through kin selection, recent research suggests that this focus may eclipse the positive direct benefits to the helper. Clutton-Brock (2002) points out that the cost of helping may be overstated, especially when the benefits to the helper's survival are high. This point has clear implications for humans, since children often begin to work before they are sexually mature. The concentration here is on children as helpers, who—because they may not be sexually mature—present new challenges to placing humans within the framework of cooperative breeding.

Children's Economic Value: The Irrationality of High Fertility?
In the economic and demographic literature, the interest in children's economic activities was launched out of a different kind of problem. When economists and demographers began to focus on the fertility decline characteristic of the modern demographic transition, it became clear that global population growth was occurring at disparate rates in different parts of the world. While fertility had dropped substantially in developed regions, it remained high in many parts of Africa, Asia, and Latin America. This discrepancy was puzzling and spurred discussion about the economic rationality of high fertility (overview in Cain 1982; Lindert 1983). What concerned economists and demographers was the questionable link between poverty and high fertility. Did population growth inhibit economic development or was it, instead, a vector to economic gain? The economic costs and benefits of children became seminal to the theoretic connection between children's labor and fertility made by Becker and Lewis (1973), Caldwell (1977), and Lee and Bulatao (1983).[14]

Concomitant with this theoretic link was a burgeoning of empirical, quantified data on children's economic value. Rather than providing resolution, however, this proliferation illuminated the breadth of cross-cultural variation in children's economic contributions, and the question of whether large families are economically irrational remained unresolved. While economic positions generally state that the demand for children fluctuates with economic opportunity (Lee and Bulatao 1983; Szreter 1993), the connection between children's help and fertility is an ongoing debate, in part because of differences in the methodological definition of children's economic value, which is a unifying theme throughout the analytic section of this book.[15]

Children's Economic Value and Fertility

Behavioral ecology and economics each place a strong emphasis on the relationship between resources and fertility. Both disciplines start from the proposition that time and resources used toward one purpose cannot be simultaneously vested in another. Further, if parents have a finite time and resource budget out of which various competing expenditures must be funded—taking care of themselves as well as providing food and other resources to older children and primary care to younger children—each additional child diminishes the time and resources available for other children. Consequently, decisions are made between alternate expenditures. This principle, canonical to the key life history tradeoff of parental investment in the quantity versus quality of offspring (Lack 1968; Smith and Fretwell 1974; Trivers 1972), is also fundamental to a similar tradeoff developed in the economic literature (Becker 1975; Becker and Lewis 1973; Caldwell 1978; Easterlin and Crimmins 1985; Handwerker 1986).

Both disciplines model the quality/quantity tradeoff in terms of maximization, albeit different measures of maximization. Although the principle of maximization is commonly misunderstood to be an empirical description of the world, it is a heuristic expectation from which to observe variation and measure deviation. This yardstick from an evolutionary point of view is fitness maximization and, from an economic point of view, utility maximization, which is expressed as a measure of satisfaction or value of children to parents. These differing assumptions affect the formulation of the questions asked and perhaps explain why contributions made in one discipline all too often remain opaque to the other. Although the two disciplines diverge in terminology and what they seek to explain, both behavioral ecology and economic approaches to the quality/quantity tradeoff find importance in the cost of raising children and the recognition that children's helping behavior is closely related to fertility (Becker 1981; Blurton

Jones 1989, 1993; Caldwell 1983; Handwerker 1986; Lee and Bulatao 1983; Lindert 1980).

The perspective taken here is planted in both traditions. Resting on the principles of natural selection, cooperative breeding offers a robust framework in which to formulate questions about the relationship between helpers and fertility, while economic and demographic approaches provide the supporting methodological tools to analytically articulate that relationship. The folding together of these disciplines renders a productive and quantitative means of assessing the effect that children's economic contributions have on parental labor demands and fertility.

Human Juvenility and Children's Value as Helpers

One conspicuous feature of primate life history in general, and of humans specifically, is the protracted period spent following weaning, when young continue to grow but have not achieved sexual maturity. Several related traits that distinguish human juveniles from the young of other species are important to children's roles as helpers and to placing humans in the framework of cooperative breeding. For most mammals, parental support ends at weaning. Among nonhuman primates, parents may assist juveniles, let them forage in close proximity, confer protection, provide agonistic support, or help negotiate their social position. Carrying and grooming may continue situationally during the transition from weaning to full independence (Altmann 1980; Nicolson 1987). But nonhuman primate juveniles once fully weaned are on their own when it comes to food (for exceptions in callitrichid primates, see Bales et al. 2000).

Human juveniles, in contrast, are not self-feeders (do not provide their own food) and continue, in many cases, to be fed, and given shelter and other resources, often throughout the two decades of their growth and development (Kaplan 1994, 1997). Yet at the same time, dependent non-sexually mature children also often work. That is, human juveniles often become producers before they are independent. In addition to childcare, the critical activity that juveniles in many subsistence economies both contribute to as well as are dependent on others for, is food provisioning. For example, a Pumé boy living as a forager on the llanos of Venezuela is successful at bringing home a catch of fish, fish that he shares with his siblings. But, he also depends on shores of processed plant food and larger game from others (Greaves n.d.). It is this nature of the human feeding niche and mix of dependency and assistance that underscore the potential for cooperative breeding.

Defining Juvenility

Juvenility, a shared mammalian trait, has been defined in several general ways.[16] Developmentally, juvenility is a time of relatively slow and prolonged growth (overview for human growth and development in Bogin 1999a; Ellison 2001; Worthman 1993). From a life history perspective, the juvenile period is bracketed by weaning and sexual maturity.[17] From a demographic point of view, not being fully grown incurs a high survival cost, with juveniles having the highest mortality rates outside of infancy relative to adult mortality rates (Charnov 1991; Janson and van Schaik 1993; Pereira and Fairbanks 1993; Worthman 1993).

Whether viewed as a developmental, life history, or demographic stage, the age at sexual maturity is tied to one of life history's central tradeoffs—the benefits of continuing to grow, countered by the probability of not surviving to reproductive age (Bronson 1989; Kozlowski 1992; Roff 1986; Sibly and Calow 1986; Stearns and Koella 1986). Since an age-related relationship exists between body size (strength) and resource production—traits that confer a survival and reproductive advantage— growing longer and delaying age at sexual maturity when growth rates drop off can be beneficial. However, since the probability of dying also increases with age, continuing to grow incurs the risk of not surviving to reproduce and recouping the investment in development.

Because physiological constraints affect growth rates, larger mammals spend a longer period of time growing and reaching sexual maturation than do smaller mammals (Bronson 1989; Charnov 1993). But the scaling of growth trajectories is slower in primates compared with other mammals of similar size (Harvey et al. 1989a; Harvey and Clutton-Brock 1985), such that a lemur, baboon, and gorilla grow along a slow-to-fast continuum, but do so at a slower rate than a mouse, dog, and elephant (Fleagle 1999:71).

Because delaying reproduction carries an expensive fitness cost, and juvenility is a dangerous time to be alive (Pereira and Fairbanks 1993), the function of an expanded juvenile stage presents a challenging life history problem. Competing explanations of the selective pressures that conditioned this feature of primate life history stress the importance of mortality, size, and learning but deviate in where the emphasis is placed and in the direction of the causal arrow in the sequence of selective forces.

Taxa with shorter adult life spans benefit from a shorter period of growth and reproducing at a younger age, whereas taxa with longer adult life spans have more to gain from growing for longer periods and delaying sexual maturity. This payoff structure represents a continuum across taxa, with an invariant relationship between adult mortality and age at sexual maturity (Charnov 1993; Kozlowski and Wiegert 1986, 1987). One explanation for the prolonged human juvenile period is that it is a function of the late age of sexual maturity being stretched along by a prolonged adult life span (Blurton Jones and Marlowe 2002; Hawkes et al. 1998; O'Connell et al. 1999; overview in Alvarez 2000). Children spend time learning during the juvenile period, but learning itself is not invoked as a special selective pressure to explain the late age at which sexual maturity is reached. Thus the length of the human juvenile period is where it is supposed to be, given adult life span (Blurton Jones and Marlowe 2002).

From the point of view of size, however, explaining the length of the juvenile period is more problematic. Because large-bodied primates grow slower and longer than predicted by allometric rules, competing explanations have focused on the selective forces that precipitate expanded juvenility in light of mortality risks.

Having a large adult body size is advantageous in lowering predation rates and adult mortality and in improving chances of surviving short-term fluctuations in food availability (Pagel and Harvey 1993; Pereira and Fairbanks 1993; for size tradeoffs in humans, see Bogin 1999a; Ellison 2001). But it is spending the time to grow large that is troublesome. The longer juveniles spend not being fully grown, the longer they spend in a period of elevated mortality risk. Because juveniles are novices at finding food, they spend more time foraging and are less efficient at getting food than adults. If juveniles grow slowly, they consume fewer daily calories. For primates who live and feed in social groups, suppressed growth rates appear to be an opportune risk-adverse strategy for coping with conspecific foraging competition (Janson 1990; Janson and van Schaik 1993; van Schaik 1989).

Juvenility is often viewed as a kind of "phenotypic limbo" (Pagel and Harvey 1993:28), a life stage during which an individual bides his or her time growing until large enough to reproduce. But it can also be time well spent if learned behaviors reduce a juvenile's own risk of mortality, improve chances of survival as an adult, or increase the production of resources necessary for reproduction (Janson and van Schaik 1993). The idea of being both large and competent has been championed by many (Fairbanks 1990; Lancaster 1971; Munroe and Munroe 1994 [1975]; Pereira and Altmann 1985; Weisner 1987). If the goals of juvenility are first to survive it and then to be able to reproduce successfully at the end of the period, juveniles who spend the time learning social and subsistence skills that affect mortality rates and future birth rates are more likely to be better survivors and reproducers.

Time for learning is also embedded in many ideas about why humans spend such a long period as juveniles (Worthman 1993). The benefits of learning are amplified when they increase future fitness. Investment in development and learning augments children's abilities to exploit the complex human feeding niche, subsistence technology (Kaplan et al. 2000), and social interactions (Dunbar 1998, 2003). These skills enhance adult productivity, which confers a reproductive advantage in competently being able to support offspring. The delayed payoff of prolonged growth and learning is strengthened by the length of the life span, since the return to investment can be realized over a longer period. From this point of view, the long human juvenile period coevolved with other life history features in response to a shift in feeding ecology to calorie-rich, but difficult-to-procure, resources (Hill and Kaplan 1999; Kaplan et al. 2000).

Although a debate surrounds the reasons why humans spend a conspicuously long period as juveniles, the fact that the juvenile period is long is not contested. The role of juveniles as both producers and consumers, the late age of human sexual maturation, and the attendant expansion of juvenility—to well over a decade—have important implications for the potential of cooperative breeding.

A Need and Opportunity for Cooperative Breeding

In comparing life history traits of human and nonhuman primates, certain characteristics of prolonged human juvenility become transparent that further a demand and opportunity for help to raise young. Until weaning, infant growth across mammals is dependent on maternal physical condition. After weaning, growth among most nonhuman primates is independent of its mother. But weaned children are dependent on someone else for their sustenance, and consequently their growth, for much longer.

While mothers with both a nursing infant and older dependent children have an increased demand on their time and resources, the cost to the mother of the children's dependence is diluted if they help. Because juveniles are not yet fully grown, sexually mature, or competing for mating opportunities, while there may be energetic costs to help, tradeoffs with health risks, and the opportunity cost of learning, training, and schooling, juveniles do not compromise their own reproductive success by helping (see Chapter 2). Besides the benefit of helping to support their siblings, the help that juveniles provide may be especially low cost for another reason. Because juveniles are both dependents and workers, self-feeding and helping may be closely aligned activities.

Although the magnitude of the complexity of the human feeding niche is debated, from the point of view of a child trying to make it on his or her own, it is complex. Children participate in some subsistence tasks much more easily than others, and depending on the particular feeding niche, children may be successful in procuring some of the resources they need as well as some of those resources in excess of their own consumption needs, while other foods and critical resources may be inaccessible. Where children live in safe environments with easy-to-obtain foods, they may spend considerable time collecting fruit or shellfish—snack foods that are an ideal package size for children and require little processing. Under these circumstances, children may contribute substantially to their caloric intake (Bliege Bird and Bird 2002; Blurton Jones et al. 1989, 1997; Draper and Cashdan 1988; Kaplan et al. 2000; Lee 1979). In other environments, children may rely on others for labor and resource subsidies until they are much older.

Children's economic dependence not only varies generally across subsistence ecology, it also varies across tasks in any one subsistence regime. All human diets incorporate a diverse suite of plant, animal, and in many cases, aquatic resources. Children may provide all of the calories for some of the foods they eat but may be unable to access other food. Among the Central Australian hunter-gatherers, for instance, children are successful at capturing small game such as reptiles and rodents but depend on others for processed plant foods and larger game (Gould 1980).

Across latitudes, many of the foods incorporated in the human diet require processing—butchering, cracking, hulling, winnowing, shelling, leaching, pounding, grinding, or cooking—to be edible, tasks that small children are incapable of and juveniles, depending on the particular task, may not have the strength and skills to accomplish. Besides processing, in many environments dependence on stored food for at least part of the year is critical to solve overwintering and hyperseasonal constraints in resource availability or in predictable annual resource shortfalls. Storage may require boning, drying, and salting, as well as specialized tools, structures, and containers. In most human environments, survival minimally entails investment in food processing, proficiency at storage and tool manufacture, and reliance on shelter and clothing technology, activities that may be beyond the grasp of a child's ability, and only under extreme and rare circumstances does a child live on his or her own and concomitantly fund all of the tasks necessary for survival. Even in environments that are less demanding from a child's point of view, the benefits of an economy of scale that come from participating in a larger production unit may be essential to a child's survival.

Because of their small size and lack of experience, dietary independence of juveniles comes at a high cost. The juvenile period has been described as "a selection funnel into which many enter and few pass through" (Lancaster 1991:5). As such, the benefits of reducing juvenile mortality are high, from both the child's and the parents' perspectives. Because human juveniles fall short of where they need to be as providers, they have much to gain from maintaining their dependence. Although a juvenile no doubt benefits from the continued care of a parent, why parents prolong their investment can appear deceptively simple. On the one hand, the cost of prolonged parental investment is compensated by gains in offspring survival (Kaplan et al. 2000; Lancaster and Lancaster 1983; Worthman 1993). Extended maternal investment, on the other hand, constrains mothers from investing in further reproduction. Consequently, if an offspring is dependent on its mother for a long period, the fitness gains made through reduced mortality can be countered by long birth intervals and lowered lifetime fertility—the life history scenario of the great apes. Maternal constraints on providing care to multiple children of different ages are not just a problem for modern mothers but extend into the hominid past. Several lines of evidence suggest that some form of allomaternal care had to be in place before mothers consigned to producing long-term dependent offspring, and that the level of dependence and level of commitment to cooperative breeding morphed over time (Hrdy 1999, in press).

Juveniles in all likelihood were self-feeders in our ancestral past, since humans are the only species today who are not. At some point in hominid evolution juveniles came to depend on others for at least part of their survival. Provisioning juveniles allowed humans to exploit new food resources and expand into habitats they could not otherwise live in if juveniles were self-feeders (O'Connell et al. 1999). It is often tacitly assumed that as provisioning of children extended further into juvenility, their self-support decreased in step. In those ecological situations where it does not—where juveniles were able to provision themselves to some extent or provide child care or other forms of help—children's contributions can have a positive effect, alleviating maternal time constraints. The protraction of childhood, a distinct human developmental stage, and the feasibility of the short birth intervals of two and half to three years characteristic of modern natural fertility populations, are likely to have occurred fairly recently—following the emergence of *Homo erectus* (Bogin 1999; Smith and Tompkins 1995). During childhood (from weaning until the eruption of permanent teeth), children grow slowly and, because of their immature dentition and digestive tracts, rely on specialty foods, foods that they are too small or inexperienced to procure and process on their own.[18] The push toward subsidizing children then may have become punctuated at several points, notably with geographic expansion and with the further shortening of birth intervals that followed the protraction of childhood.

The Anatomy of Help

Although helpers have been shown to enhance parental fertility across many species of cooperative breeders, the jury remains out for humans. Some studies position children as positive economic assets. Others dispute the fact that children's assistance augments parental fertility. How do we rectify, for example, the common-sense view that agriculturalists have many children because they are needed to work on the family farm with the empirical findings that "the average child is a net drain on household resources" (Lee and Bulatao 1983:241)? A number of studies in both economic and the anthropology literature have found that agricultural children make substantial contributions to the household and are an economic benefit (Cain 1977; Kasarda 1971; Munroe et al. 1983, 1984; Nag et al. 1978; White 1975). Other studies find that, to the contrary, agricultural children are a cost to their parents (Lindert 1983; Vlassoff 1979). And still other studies show that children are a negative net cost (Lee 1994a, b, c; Lee and Kramer 2002; Mueller 1976; Skoufias 1994; Stecklov 1999; Turke 1988, 1989).[19]

These differences illustrate one of the central methodological concerns of this book and of situating children in the context of cooperative breeding—how to define help and helpers. Does help consist of any contribution that a child makes to his or her well-being? Or is help only the surplus that children produce beyond what they consume that can be transferred to support other dependents? Uncovering whether helpers actually help is methodologically perplexing and analytically unresolved because of two related traits discussed in the previous section. Juveniles are not economically independent, and children—even very young children—are both consumers and producers. Because of the complexity of human subsistence ecology, resources are transferred, or shared, across individuals of different ages and sexes.

Even though children receive assistance from others throughout much, if not all, of their growth and development, children may also contribute to their own economic well-being as well as help support their siblings. A ten-year-old, for example, may spend considerable time harvesting maize. He consumes some of that maize, but so do his siblings. He also does not immediately consume the maize he harvests but, rather, only after it has been leached, soaked, ground into meal, and processed into tortillas—tasks his older sisters perform. Child care is another well-documented example wherein children who are young enough to receive child care also, in turn, help care for their younger siblings (Bledsoe 1995; Bove et al. 2002; Ivey 2000; Munroe and Munroe 1994 [1975]; Weisner 1987; Weisner and Gallimore 1977).

Because children often start to work before they are independent, the distinction between self-care and help can be elusive. If a girl spends several hours processing maize and preparing food, how do we distinguish between that portion of her work that serves her own well-being and that portion that contributes to subsidizing her siblings? While how to quantify this dual aspect of children as both dependents and workers has been ardently debated in the economic literature, the anatomy of help has itself remained largely unaddressed in the behavioral ecology literature. Answering questions about whether helpers really help involves two parts. First, are children actually helping? Second, is the effect of helping on parental fertility positive? Although helpers appear to have a positive effect on parental fitness in other species of animals, it must be recognized that economics, the discipline that has dissected and agonized over how to define children's economic value, is divided in its findings. It is perhaps not unexpected that estimates of children's economic value vary widely given the ecological and social diversity among the study groups that have been the subject of this research. However, identifying any real variation is obscured because of differences in how children's economic value is evaluated.

Some studies use the time that children spend working, others use their net value (the balance of how much children work and how much they consume), and others use wealth flows (intergenerational transfer of resources from parents to children or vice versa). Each of these studies measures something quite different about the economics of childhood and its relationship to parental fertility. To begin to rectify these disparities, this study applies each of these different analytic vantage points to one study population. With time-allocation data used as the common currency, Maya children are progressively followed through each of these analytic perspectives in order to determine the most appropriate measure of evaluating whether helpers really help.

Because this book focuses on the changing status of children as workers and dependents and the effect of that dynamic on subsidizing parents' continued fertility, it places an emphasis throughout on timing: the timing of births, the timing of consumption, the timing of production, and the timing of demographic and economic pressure across the family life cycle. Through the process of maturation, children pass from being net consumers to net producers. The timing of that transition influences parents' time and reproductive budgets in two important ways. First, any economic contribution that children make offsets their cost and the amount of subsidy that someone else has to make. And second, the production surplus of older children can be transferred to help underwrite the cost of continued childbearing when parents themselves may not have sufficient time and resources to support their growing number of dependents.

Relevance of the Maya Study

Since the question of whether helpers really help is one that concerns the economics of juvenility, this book distinguishes between juvenile dependence and sexual maturity, which do not necessarily covary in humans. In both labor-market and some preindustrial populations, children may rely on their parents after they reach sexual maturity, marry, and even have children of their own (Kaplan 1996).[20] Yet, in other preindustrial populations, children may be self-supporting at a relatively younger age, and the timing of sexual maturity and economic independence may occur in close sequence. An Arctic hunter-gather, an Australian forager, a Maya agriculturalist, and an American postindustrial child vary widely in their ability to care for themselves and in their dependence on someone else for food, shelter, protection, and education. Given the ecological diversity of the human habitat, variation in children's economic participation is not surprising, but it is of interest because of its effect on the competing demands of parents having to support younger and older children simultaneously and, ultimately, on the number of children parents can afford to raise.

Recent time-allocation research among hunter-gatherers has provided provocative insight into the complex relationship between subsistence ecology and children's work (Bliege Bird and Bird 2002; Blurton Jones et al. 1989; Blurton Jones et al. 1994a, 1994b; Blurton Jones and Marlowe 2002; Bock 2002a; Draper and Cashdan 1988; Hawkes et al. 1995; Kaplan 1997). It is evident from this research that children's economic value may be similar across some groups of hunter-gatherers and agriculturalists, while among other groups of hunter-gatherers it more closely resembles that of modern children. These similarities and differences are evidence not of a single set of behaviors dictated by general subsistence but of a range of social and economic dynamics, and they suggest that we look beyond the general mode of subsistence to hone the question of whether helpers really help.

This book builds a case about children's helping behavior and the role that children play in subsidizing the cost of their parents' continued reproduction. The Maya are an ideal population to study how parents meet the challenges of raising multiple dependents for a number of reasons. First, Maya parents do not participate in financial markets and have limited options for reallocating resources from net producers to consumers across the family life cycle. Because of this, many of the confounding problems associated with economic flow across large social units, or from institutions, are attenuated, and the reallocation of help within the family can be more closely observed. Second, the Maya maize economy is supported by many tasks in which coresident children regularly, productively, and safely participate from an early age. And third, the Maya have large families, and throughout much of their marriage union, Maya parents have multiple dependents living at home.

Although this book is about a group of subsistence agriculturalists, the questions addressed here about the role of children are more broadly applicable to natural fertility populations, whether foragers, pastralists, agriculturalists, or representing mixed economies. Not only does the level of children's economic contributions crosscut these classifications, fertility levels do as well. It is individual data and small-scale studies that give us a window onto the variation and complexity of demographic processes and the role of children as an alternate or additional means to maintain the relatively short birth intervals characteristic of human reproduction.

– 2 –

Sources of Variation in
Children's Time Allocation

Children transition from full dependence on others to independence. Given the ecological diversity of their habitat, humans, not surprisingly, do not have a species-specific age pattern of economic maturation. Rather, the timing of when children become helpers, self-feeders, and economically independent is ecologically driven and highly variable cross-culturally. The economic maturation of children is guided in certain ways by developmental maturation, which has been under selection for tens of thousands of years. Gains in body size shape children's capacity for physical strength and cognitive ability. But within the evolved constraints of growth and development, the age patterning of children's participation in economic activities varies cross-culturally. Because children's economic maturation is not specifically tethered to a developmental stage, its variation more directly reflects subsistence, ecological, and social diversity rather than the outcome of natural selection, per se.

Researching the role that ecology and subsistence play in conditioning the age patterning of children's work across human populations has a lengthy intellectual precedent (Boserup 1965; Clark and Haswell 1967; Munroe et al. 1983; Whiting and Edwards 1988; Whiting and Whiting 1975). How people make their living has an obvious link to variations in the economic contribution of children, since subsistence, at its simplest, delimits the kinds of tasks that children can perform. We may suspect, for example, that the economic contribution of children, and especially young children, among circumpolar hunter-gatherers who subsist predominantly on large game and have complex hunting, housing, storage, and clothing technologies will be very different from children in the Australian Central Desert who subsist largely on grass seeds, fruits, nuts, and small reptiles and have minimal clothing and shelter technologies.

Yet the relationship between subsistence ecology and children's economic participation is far more complex than previously thought. Many authors have noted that lower-latitude hunter-gatherer children may help support themselves at relatively young ages by foraging for easy-to-obtain foods such as fruit (Blurton Jones et al. 1989, 1997; Draper 1976; Draper and Cashdan 1988; Hawkes et al. 1995; Kaplan 1997; Kaplan et al. 2000; Lee 1979). However, children's participation in economic activities also varies considerably within a general subsistence regime. A comparison of the !Kung and Hadza, two groups of hunter-gatherers who live on the savannas of sub-Saharan Africa, shows that Hadza children contribute significantly more to their caloric intake than do !Kung children (Blurton Jones 1993; Blurton Jones et al. 1989, 1994a,b). Both !Kung and Hadza children could forage for fruit. The health risks associated with foraging—heat stress, lack of water, the presence of large predatory animals, and distance between fruiting trees and camp—have a negative effect, however, on the probability of child survivorship and limit the foraging options of !Kung children relative to Hadza children, whose environment presents far fewer risks to unsupervised children. In addition, resource characteristics affect team return rates of mothers and children and the extent to which !Kung and Hadza children spend time in processing and foraging activities. Children's economic participation, thus, may express a range of variation within a general subsistence regime, and simply knowing whether a child is a hunter-gatherer or an agriculturalist, or even what kind of hunter-gatherer, may not in itself be very informative in predicting the economic role of children.

The ecological conditions that affect differences in foraging patterns between !Kung and Hadza children illuminate some of the sources of variation that contribute to cross-cultural differences in children's work effort. These studies make the important point that the extent to which children acquire their own food is conditioned not only by the subsistence base and the kinds of economic roles available to children but also by the constraints associated with children's participation in those tasks. Both of these factors are rooted in socioecology, which importantly crosscut norms of subsistence classifications. To comparatively situate Maya subsistence, three sources of variation—task difficulty, how children learn, and health risks—are discussed as being relevant in determining cross-cultural differences in the age patterning of children's work.

Constraints on the Time Children Spend Working

The age patterning of children's work reflects the outcome of how children spend their time, which they can broadly spend in three competing ways—learning, working, or in leisure. Why children work at all and do not opt to spend all their time in leisure, play, rest, or other diversions is an interesting problem, for which two general types of explanations have been offered. First, children work because of inclusive fitness benefits incurred by helping to support siblings, to whom they are closely related (Emlen 1984; Hamilton 1964; Russell and Rowley 1988; Turke 1988, 1989). And second, since children are at a competitive disadvantage, it is in their best interest to cooperate with their parents (e.g., "Rotten Kid Theorem," Becker 1981; Bock 1999, 2002b; Clutton-Brock and Parker 1995 for nonhumans). Though parents may leverage how children spend their time and may have in mind an optimal amount of help they desire from their children, children also assess the benefits of their labor and may have a different appraisal of the help they want to give. Most parents experience this conflict daily. The resolution of this conflict of interest, or the actual amount of work that a child does and for how long, should reflect some compromise between the parents' and child's conception of the optimal workload. Whether the extent to which children actually work is closer to either the parents' or the children's optimum is unknown and is an area of study that has not been theoretically developed. However, it seems reasonable that the more work benefits both the parents and the children, the less parent/offspring conflict will arise, and the less reluctance will occur on the part of a child to meet parental demands for his or her work.

Starting from the perspective that parents leverage how their children spend time, this chapter looks at sources of variation in children's economic contributions across subsistence ecologies. Although parents benefit from their children working, because any contribution children make to their own well-being allows parents to divert at least some of their time and energy to other ends, certain constraints limit children from spending all their time working.

Task Difficulty
Bock's (1995; Bock and Johnson 2002) research among African children presents a useful heuristic framework in which to think about

task difficulty. Building on this work, each task has some minimal level of skill and strength that has to be met for an individual to spend time at that task.[1] Skills can be acquired in three general ways: through general age-related gains in cognitive ability, through learning while working, or through formal training and education. Strength may also be acquired through age-related gains in body size and developmental maturation or, in some cases, by working at the task itself or through special training. Although each task may require some combination of these means to acquire skill and strength, the process of growth and development underlies the age patterning of children's work. Not unexpectedly, age—as an assay for body size and cognitive development—has an often-noted covarying relationship with children's productivity. Differences in growth trajectories, although they vary among individuals and from population to population, are not, however, expected to be a significant source of cross-cultural variation in children's economic contributions. For example, growth trajectories are probably not sufficiently different to explain why a fifteen-year-old Piro teenager depends on someone else for most of his calories (Kaplan 1997), while a Bangladesh teenager does not (Cain 1977). These differences are more likely due to the particular suite of subsistence tasks, and the benefits and costs of children's participation in them, rather than to divergent growth trajectories.

Ranking Maya Subsistence Tasks

Children can participate in some kinds of subsistence tasks more easily than others. To position Maya subsistence in terms of difficulty, domestic and field tasks are qualitatively arrayed along the dimensions of skill and strength (Figure 2.1). Task skill is ranked based on the level of cognitive ability, training, or instruction necessary to successfully perform the task. Caloric expenditure is used as a proxy to rank task strength and the physical demand of performing tasks (Astrand 1971; Durnin and Passmore 1967; Montgomery and Johnson 1977; Ulijaszek 1995).

Few tasks that the Maya regularly perform are ranked as having high levels of either skill or strength. Hunting, beekeeping, and planting are exceptions in requiring knowledge of animal behavior, plant ecology, travel through the jungle (in some cases, long distances), and the use of specialized equipment. Other than planting, field tasks are repetitive

High Strength

Cutting
Firewood

Grinding Maize
Water Collection
Shelling Maize

Low Skill   Washing   **High Skill**
                Shelling Maize
                   Processing Maize   Hunting

                                                            Beekeeping

                                                                Planting

                                Weeding
                    Cleaning   Harvesting

                                            Food Preparation

                            Child Care   Making Tortillas
                Feeding Animals
                    Errands   Sewing

Low Strength

Figure 2.1 Common Maya field and domestic tasks ranked by skill and strength.

and easy to perform. In traditional slash-and-burn agriculture, the ground is prepared by felling hardwood trees with a machete, which requires considerable upper-arm strength and dexterity. But since the introduction of fertilizers and tractors over the past decade, old-growth forest is now less commonly felled, and ground preparation entails cutting and then burning stands of weeds and scrub, which are either pulled by hand or cut using a small, curved machete. These more manageable tools—unlike the long, straight-blade machetes used to fell trees and cut firewood—are used safely by children from a young age (see page 29). Maize is harvested by slitting the husk open with a small tool, often a sharpened nail, pulling back the husk, and removing the ear of corn—a repetitive task requiring neither skill nor strength

Figure 2.2   Maya brothers harvesting maize.

(Figure 2.2). Hauling water, washing clothes by hand, and processing maize involve lifting and carrying heavy loads. Likewise, shelling maize and grinding maize require little skill but are rigorous in their demand for upper-arm and hand strength. Sewing, food preparation, and making tortillas demand little strength but require dexterity, patience, and concentration. Feeding animals and running errands are simple tasks that young children are able to perform. Although the Maya maize-based economy is comprised of primarily unskilled, repetitive tasks, what is important about task difficulty in limiting the time children allocate to those tasks is not skill or strength level, per se, but whether a child learns while working at the task or needs to be trained a priori.

How Children Learn
Modeling the time children spend learning versus the time they spend working is complex and theoretically unresolved. One framework for thinking about this tradeoff and its effect on cross-cultural differences in children's work effort is concerned with how children become productive adults. Nested in what is traditionally framed as the quality/quantity tradeoff is a proximate set of parental tradeoffs that weighs the benefit

that parents receive from a child's help versus the delayed payoff of investing in a child's learning and skills (Bock 1995; Bock and Johnson 2002; Kaplan 1996). This tradeoff has been formalized through the concept of embodied capital (Becker 1981, 1993; Bock 2002a; Kaplan 1994, 1996; Kaplan et al. 1995; Kaplan and Lancaster 2000). Parents invest in a stock of embodied capital that may include food and other resources that contribute to their children's physiological development, maintenance, and health but that also includes providing their children with skills, training, access to social status, and alliances. Educating children a priori is demanding both in terms of the cost to finance training as well as in the time children forfeit from engaging in productive work (Caldwell 1976; Hardwerker 1986; Parsons and Goldin 1989).

Reflecting variation in the complexity of subsistence strategies, the benefit of training and educating children at the expense of forgoing their help is greater in some cases than in others (Bock and Johnson 2002). No doubt the training necessary to become a successful adult is very different for a Maya farmer, an Alaskan Nunamiut hunter-gatherer, and a twenty-first-century American teenager, and we would expect parents to adjust their investments accordingly. In today's postindustrial world, where children are educated (albeit to varying degrees) before they go to work, this tradeoff is fairly straightforward, since time spent learning is not time spent working. But the tradeoff becomes opaque in situations where learning is embedded in work.

If how children learn to become economically competent adults is seen as a continuum distinguished at one end by formal education and training and at the other by learning while working, Maya subsistence is at the latter end of that continuum. Maya children participate in most field and domestic tasks without having to spend a long period, or any time, being trained. A child is expected to learn while working as long as the benefit of his or her participation does not exceed the cost of potential resource loss. For example, a seven-year-old boy is able to discern what part of the stalk contains an ear of corn, open the husk, and remove the ear. Even though he may frequently be distracted, break his concentration to play, and later return to the task, if he misses an ear of corn, it can be picked another day. In another example, young Maya children often help their older siblings and parents shell maize, which requires a fair amount of hand strength. Although a young child may haphazardly shell an ear of corn, picking off only loose kernels and putting the ear back in the pile for a parent to finish, little is jeopardized. In both cases, the risk of resource loss is low.

For most tasks, Maya children learn as they work because the risk of resource loss is minimal. But there are exceptions. Planting, for example, involves punching a sharpened stick into the ground, dropping a few seeds into a hole, covering it, and moving on. Planting appears to be a relatively easy task that a ten-year-old has the physical ability to readily accomplish. Yet, although children are capable, planting is one task that is performed only by adult males. Planting is obviously critical to maize production and to household survival, and if a crop is improperly planted, the risk of crop loss is high. Formal training is brief, but being successful at planting requires concentration, attention to detail, and the ability to gauge environmental cues so as to appropriately schedule planting—general cognitive skills that accumulate with age. Other than planting, most field work and domestic tasks have a low risk of loss, and children work while learning rather than being trained a priori. Regardless of skill level, no task in the suite of Maya subsistence activities requires formal education.

At the time of this study, villagers had no opportunity to work in jobs that required an education, and parents benefited little from forgoing their children's work and sending their children to school beyond the primary schooling young children receive in the village. The limited amount of training necessary to be successful at maize production, coupled with the unavailability of skill-based wage labor, result in a low payoff to parents who forgo their children's work and formally educate or train them.

Health Risks

Regardless of how capable children are of participating in a task, they are not expected to do so if it compromises their survival and safety. Pennington and Harpending (1988) distinguish between children's health risks that are dependent and those that are independent of parental investment. The implication of this distinction is that the constraint on children's participation in work increases as the probability of illness or accident varies positively with their participation in work. These risks are greatest for young children, who are the most susceptible to environmental health hazards. Among the Maya, health risks present less of a constraint on how much children work than on where they work. The village itself is a safe domain for children, who once they can walk, are free to roam throughout the village, in and out of neighbors' houses. Meticulously cleared of vegetation, the village is devoid of many tropical pests that are especially dangerous to young children. Domesticated pigs are unpenned and wander in the village, eating any garbage that vermin would otherwise feed on. Importantly, although young Maya children may participate in seemingly unsupervised work, most village members are related, and an aunt, uncle, grandparent, parent, adult sibling, or cousin is always in close proximity if needed.

The forest is a different matter. The tropical forest presents many health risks to children—snakes, killer bees, army ants, and numerous other stinging insects and toxic plants. Although Maya children grow up hearing folklore and cautionary tales about these pests and know how to avoid many potentially hazardous situations, young children rarely go alone into the forest or to fields and seldom accompany adults during forest activities such as beekeeping and hunting.

The Effect of Family Composition on Children's Help

Task difficulty, how children learn, and health risks limit the extent to which children of different ages work. These constraints help to explain why children's work effort differs across subsistence economies. However, these factors, which for the most part are constant across the Xculoc population since all village members make their living as subsistence maize farmers, are not likely to explain differences in the economic contribution of two Maya children of the same age. Family composition, though, is likely to affect variation in the amount of time two children of the same age spend working. If an eight-year-old girl who can carry water, but not very easily, from the village spigot to her household's cistern has three older sisters, she is unlikely to participate in the task, since it is more efficient for her sisters to allocate time to the task while she does something else. But if the eight-year-old girl is the eldest daughter and her mother's only helper, she is much more likely to spend time at the task, even if she has to struggle to carry only half a pail of water.

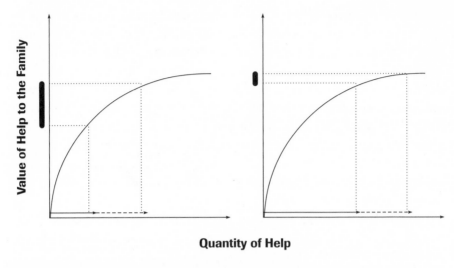

Figure 2.3 Schematic relationship between the marginal value of help and family composition: The vertical axis shows the value of help provided by all family members. The dashed arrow along the horizontal axis is the amount of help provided by one child, and the solid arrow is the amount of help provided by other family members. The value of help is related to the amount of help through the utility curve. The solid black bar beside the vertical axis represents the child's marginal value of help. In Family A little help is provided by other family members, and in Family B much more help is provided by other family members.

One way to illustrate the effect that family composition has on the time a child allocates to work is through a model of the marginal value of help—or the additional value of a person's labor when added to the work already provided by other family members (Kramer and McMillan 1998). Whether or not the eight-year-old girl in the above example helps to haul water will be determined in part by the value of that help to her family. Figure 2.3 shows the schematic relationship between the marginal value of help and family composition. On the vertical axis is the value of help provided to the family by its members. The dashed arrow along the horizontal axis refers to the amount of help provided by, in this case, an eight-year-old girl, and the solid arrow shows the amount of help provided by other family members. The value of help is related to the amount of help through a utility curve. The solid black bar shown beside the vertical axis represents the marginal value of help given by the eight-year-old girl. Two family situations are depicted. In Family A on the left, little help is provided by other family members, as might be the situation if the eight-year-old had no sisters to help her haul water. In this case, the marginal value of the eight-year-old's contribution is considerable when compared with the situation in Family B on the right. In Family B, other family members allocate much more time to the task, as might be the situation if the eight-year-old had three older sisters. In this case, the marginal value of the eight-year-old's help is much less. Her assistance hauling water may not be critical, and she may be asked to do another task at which she is more efficient. The marginal value of help is one way to schematically illustrate the effect that family composition may have on the variation in work effort among children of the same age.

Return Rates, Time Allocation, and Maya Children

Work effort is characterized not only by the time spent working but also by how efficient one is at a task. Efficiency, or productivity, is often expressed as a return rate, or the amount an individual produces divided by the time he or she spends in the activity. How quickly a child's efficiency reaches that of an adult—or the rate of increase in return rates—is determined in part by the magnitude of a task's difficulty and the extent to which skill or strength play a role. If a task requires strength but little skill, once children are strong enough, they may achieve high return rates relatively quickly. For example, once a thirteen-year-old girl has the muscular development to carry water from the communal spigot to her *solar* (household compound), the increase in her return rate attributable to skill acquisition is probably fairly imperceptible.

If, however, a task is skill-dependent, a number of scenarios are possible based on whether children learn by working. If children do not learn while working and delay spending time on a task until they have matured, once they do begin spending time on the task, again they may achieve maximum return rates fairly quickly. But if children learn while working and begin to help out as soon as they are strong enough, improvement in efficiency is expected as they get older. When young children harvest maize, they are able to successfully harvest at a similar rate as their older siblings, but only over short bouts. Typical of young children, they are easily distracted, and their attention wanes quickly. Even for very easy tasks, there is some lag time before young children achieve adult return rates. But why they become more productive with age has spawned provocative debate about the role of learning in the evolution of the juvenile period, a debate related to the question of the evolution of prolonged human juvenility and whether sexual maturity is delayed while children learn to become competent adults.

Recent experimental studies have shown that age, body size, and strength covary with return rates, but practice at a task (a proxy for measuring the effects of learning) does not. These results suggest that general gains in body size and strength, not practice and learned skill, are predominantly responsible for the increase in return rates across age (Blurton Jones et al. 1997; Bird and Bliege Bird 2002). For example, among the sub-Saharan Hadza, males and females show no difference in their efficiency at digging tubers with respect to the time that they spend practicing (Blurton Jones and Marlowe 2002). Yet other experimental studies have shown that for some tasks, such as processing grain or cracking mongongo nuts, return rates do improve with experience and practice (Bock 1995, 2002a). Discerning between the effects that learning versus gains in body size have on increased return rates with age is further complicated by the payoff for young adults to increase their efficiency as they begin to have children of their own (Bliege Bird and Bird 2002).

In other words, do reproductive-age adults work faster, harder, and at higher return rates relative to children because they have young to feed or because they are more experienced, stronger, and better able to concentrate? These experimental data demonstrate that, for some tasks, the increase in efficiency is explainable by gains in body size, a process largely completed by sexual maturity, whereas for other tasks, the positive effects of learning may extend beyond age-related gains in body size. Importantly, variation occurs, and this variation appears to pattern with socioecology, the kinds of subsistence activities available for children to participate in and the constraints involved with their participation.

How much time an individual spends at a task and how efficient he is at that task have been theoretically linked through opportunity costs, or the forgone benefit to an individual to invest in one activity and not another (Hames 1992; Winterhalder 1983). An opportunity cost is high

if an individual engages in a task at which he or she is not very profi-
cient rather than allocating time to a task in which he or she has a high
return rate. Conversely, an opportunity cost is low if an individual participates in a task at which he or she is efficient rather than in a task for
which the person achieves a low return. Much of what we know empir-
ically about the relationship between return rates and time allocation
has benefited from the experimental data. More broadly, what we
know comes from general economic principles.

One of the payoffs of a high return rate is that more of a good can be
produced in the same amount of time, or the same amount of a good
can be produced in less time. If an individual does not benefit from producing more of the good once he or she has reached an adult rate of
return, the time invested in a task will also plateau, or even decline.
Whether a worker produces more of the good or does something else
with the time saved depends on the economy. In the Maya case—or any
economy in which there is little venue to exchange, surplus, or bank
resources—little economic benefit accrues from producing a good
beyond what is needed for consumption. The implication is that as
return rates increase, the time allocated to a task may stay the same or
actually decrease. For example, if a Maya girl starts to grind maize at
age 12, it may take her an hour to grind the 2 kilos that her family consumes each day. But as she becomes more efficient, it may take her only
half an hour to grind the same amount. Since ground maize is not marketable, there is no benefit for her to grind more than the 2 kilos of
maize, and she may spend less time grinding maize as her return rate
improves.

The time spent in a task may also decrease as the opportunity costs
of competing time expenditures shift with age. Child care is a good
example of this. It has been anecdotally noted that teenagers spend less
time caring for their siblings than do their younger brothers and sisters, presumably because they spend their time in more difficult tasks
that their younger siblings are not able to perform (Weisner and
Gallimore 1977; Whiting and Edwards 1988).

Strength requirements limit the time young children allocate to many
tasks. For other tasks, strength requirements can be modified so that
young, inefficient children can spend time at the task. Even though a
seven-year-old girl is not strong enough to carry the 7.5 liter bucket
usually used to haul water, she may be given a small pail and help her

Figure 2.4 Young Maya boys transporting maize from the milpa to the village with their father and uncle.

mother. Similarly, adults can transport 35 to 40 kilo sacks of maize from the fields to the village either on the back of a bicycle or by carrying the sack with a tumpline. Children cannot negotiate these heavy loads but may help by carrying what they can in smaller sacks (Figure 2.4). For other tasks, such as grinding corn or chopping wood, no means exists to accommodate a child's strength limitation, and children allocate no time to these tasks until they are strong enough.

From the above examples, it is most efficient for an adult, who can haul a 40 kilo sack of maize, to transport maize from the milpa to the village. And it is most efficient for the mother, who has a much higher return rate, to haul water. Yet children rarely return to the village empty-handed, and many little girls do help their mothers haul water. Even though young children are less efficient than their older siblings or adults, little or no opportunity cost accrues when they help, since there are few competing ways in which they can spend their time; thus, the opportunity cost to engage in a task may be low even though an individual is not very efficient. A necessary condition here is that a child is able to learn while working rather than being skilled a priori.

While return rates and time allocation are measurable and, consequently, are a comparable means for discussing variation in children's
helping behavior, other aspects of a subsistence ecology may affect how
much time children allocate to work. Hawkes et al. (1995), for example,
point out that where food processing occurs relative to where consumption takes place affects both mothers' and children's return rates and
time allocation. A child may be able to perform a task—procure the
resource—but if other risks are high there may be no benefit to bringing
them along to help. Young Maya children are capable, even if they are
less productive than a teenager, of harvesting maize. Even though there
are plenty of other tasks only older children can do, young children do
not perform all the harvesting because of other constraints. Travel
through the forest to the milpas is risky for young children, and scheduling problems may arise in arranging for someone to accompany them.
Their inability to transport maize back to the village, more than a kilometer away, or to convey important information about crop condition,
or the benefit of young children staying in the village and spending their
time in other ways, may all limit the time young children spend harvesting maize and performing other easy tasks.

Several points can be drawn from the above discussion. First, the opportunity cost of performing one task rather than another should generally
decrease with age, since an older child will tend to have high return rates
for a wider variety of tasks. Second, if task difficulty affects the age patterning of return rates, it should also affect the opportunity cost of time
allocated to competing activities. The easier subsistence tasks are for
children to perform, the broader the age range of children who can perform a breadth of tasks. Third, maize subsistence appears to present
little constraint on Maya children's participation in work along these
three sources of variation. Importantly, Maya children learn while
working at most tasks. Together these factors are expected to strongly
condition the age patterning of when and how much children help.
    Within the framework of these constraint criteria, maize subsistence
falls out at one end of what might best be seen as a continuum of task
difficulty, how children learn, and health risks. Within the village itself,
these constraints are not likely to vary much among individuals, since
the subsistence base is similar across families. However, family composition is expected to be a source of individual variation among children

of the same age. Because of the unavailability of skill-based jobs, parents benefit little from forgoing the time children spend working and investing in their training or education. In the not-distant future, however, the payoff structure with regard to schoolchildren may be very different.

It is important to emphasize that the case is not being made that the low cost of Maya children helping exemplifies the general condition of children or of agriculturalists. Rather, constraints on children's participation in work are expected to vary with the specific suite of subsistence tasks. A child may learn while working at some tasks, whether he or she is a hunter-gatherer, an agriculturalist, or a modern-day American. Meriam (indiginous Melanesians) and Hadza children spend considerable time foraging (Bliege Bird and Bird 2002; Blurton Jones and Marlowe 2002, respectively). As among the Maya, the foraging tasks in which they participate are learned with little a priori training and, presumably, involve little risk of resource loss and health insult. In other hunter-gatherer or agricultural economies, constraints on child's work may operate in the other direction (Bock 2002a). Variation in children's work effort is expected to reflect a task-by-task and a subsistence-ecology-by-subsistence-ecology set of constraints rather than to be determined by the mode of production, per se, or to have changed in a linear fashion through time.

– 3 –

Situating the Maya

The Maya have a long and diverse history in the Yucatan Peninsula, reflected not only in a rich archaeological record but also in the many hamlets and villages where present-day Maya live. The data presented in the following chapters were collected in the small, remote Maya village of Xculoc in the Bolonchen Hills region of the Yucatan Peninsula.

The Yucatan is a vast, partially emerged, limestone and dolomite formation seated on a granitic foundation. Uplifted from the surrounding coastal plain during the Pliocene, the peninsula eroded into various karstic landforms. The Puuc and the Bolonchen Hills punctuate the otherwise topographically homogenous Yucatan Peninsula, marking the transition from the flat plain to the north and the uplands farther to the south (Figures 3.1, 3.2). The Puuc, a low fault ridge, trends southeast roughly following the present-day border between the Mexican states of Yucatan and Campeche. South of the Puuc ridge are the Bolonchen Hills, a region of low but steep and densely vegetated conical hills that are the residual forms of a long process of limestone solution. Over time, rainwash eroded the slopes, carrying soils that then accumulated in basins among the hills. Xculoc is situated in one of these sediment-rich valleys.

The calcareous nature of the Yucatan's limestone deposits, the peninsula's topography, the lack of running surface water, and the limited distribution of water-catchment features have in many ways shaped both the pre-Columbian and modern-day Maya settlement of the Bolonchen region. Although the Yucatan receives substantial precipitation, rainwater rapidly seeps through the porous limestone and collects in underground channels. When exposed to water, the limestone caprock becomes soluble. These solution depressions vary from cathedral-size underground caverns to small, shallow hollows in the limestone surface. Cenotes form when the caprock overlying a subterranean water channel

Figure 3.1   The Yucatan Peninsula. See Figure 3.2 for highlight of box.

collapses, leaving a deep, steep-sided sinkhole that fills with water. Legend surrounds these murky recesses, which are abundant sources of groundwater in northeastern Yucatan but are absent in the Puuc and Bolonchen Hills. Domestic water is locally available only from more modest depressions and pools, called *aguadas* and *chaltuns,* where water collects during the rainy season.[1] A number of these features have been found close to Xculoc and remain important backup water sources.

In a landscape void of streams, rivers, and other permanent water flow, these natural basins provided the only source of domestic water until the 1800s, when the interior of the Yucatan was colonized by the Spanish, and deep wells were excavated through the caprock to the

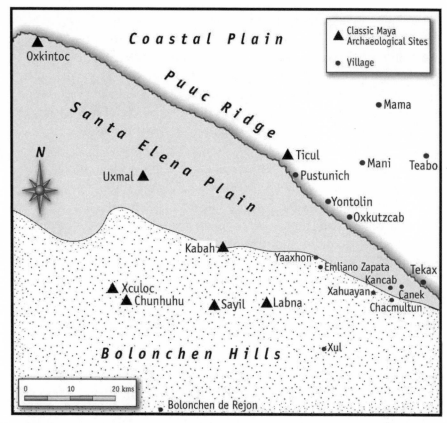

Figure 3.2 The Puuc and Bolenchen regions of the Yucatan Peninsula showing modern-day villages and several of the larger Classic Maya archaeological sites. Xculoc is both an archeological site and a modern village.

underlying water table. Following the political upheaval of the Mexican Revolution and the abandonment of the haciendas, the Maya rebuilt their villages around these reliable water sources.

The Historical Landscape

Although an archaeologist in the future may excavate little that would temporally distinguish a present-day *solar* (household compound) from one occupied several hundred years earlier—plastic buckets, planed lumber from a stool or table, strands of manufactured yarn, perhaps a plastic comb or radio battery—political perturbations from the greater social and economic sphere have long shaped the lives of the Maya *milpero* (farmer). Caught in the competitive fray between pre-Columbian Maya polities and elites, followed by the influx of European conquistadors, religious zealots, colonial entrepreneurs, revolutionaries from central Mexico, and now the increasing influence of the national economy on local subsistence, the wake of history has left its mark. Yet, throughout, the tenacity and resilience of the Maya *milpero* have been remarkable.

Sedentary swidden agriculturalists were making their living across the Yucatan Peninsula by late in the first millennium BC. During subsequent millennia, periods of population aggregation, the attendant acceleration of social stratification, vying among elites for political control, and feats in monumental architecture were followed by periods of population dispersal and hiatuses in building development. These cycles have been partially attributed to large-scale fluctuations in rainfall patterns and dependable water availability (overview of pre-Columbian Maya archaeology in the Puuc region in Dunning 1992). Compared with the archaeological attention given to civic-ceremonial centers and the architectural and artistic accomplishments of the Maya, much less is known about pre-Columbian domestic households and the lifeway of the farmer who lived on the periphery of these centers, supplying them with food and labor.

One exception is the archaeological survey of the area surrounding the Puuc Classic site of Sayil, not far from Xculoc (Sabloff et al. 1984, 1985; Sabloff and Tourtellot 1991; Tourtellot et al. 1989). Archaeological sites excavated in the hinterlands surrounding Sayil's civic center bear a striking resemblance to household spatial organization and vernacular architecture in a modern-day Maya village. While the Sayil project illuminates our picture, much of what we can gather about the everyday life of the pre-Columbian Maya farmer is drawn from ethnographic accounts written after Spanish settlement in the 1500s.

Due to the intrepidity of the Maya and to the Yucatan's geographic, political, and economic isolation, Spanish colonization—unlike elsewhere in Mexico, where it occurred fairly rapidly—was a protracted process in the Yucatan. The first recorded European contact, in 1511, was an unplanned landing, which left most of the shipwrecked sailors dead. In the years that followed, several brief landings and skirmishes occurred along the Yucatan coast. Francisco de Montejo, lured by

Hernando Cortés's success toppling the Aztecs in central Mexico, was granted permission to conquer the Yucatan. Seeking to establish a provincial capital, Montejo took the Maya city of Tihó, renaming it Mérida in 1542. Five years later, the Maya besieged Mérida but, after five months of fierce battle, were vanquished. One of the more chilling windows into the conquest era is the portentous tale of the central pyramid of Tihó going down, stone by stone, as the Spanish church is being raised stone by stone. Until recently, scholars have traditionally marked the establishment of Mérida as the beginning of colonial rule, but as this tale signifies, the dismantling of Maya culture was not a decisive event, but a stone-by-stone process (Moseley 1980; Restall 1998).

With the founding of Mérida as the colonial capital, hostility escalated between the Maya and Spanish. By the mid-1540s, Franciscan friars had begun to arrive in the Yucatan. In 1562 Fray Diego de Landa, in a self-fashioned inquisition to purge Maya idolatry, imprisoned and tortured thousands of Maya, killing several hundred people and burning twenty-seven of the Maya codices. The Spanish court, alarmed by Landa's ecclesiastic zeal, exiled him to Spain, where he wrote his *relación*, or account, of the indigenous people of the Yucatan. This constitutes the earliest Maya ethnography.

The Spanish system of *encomienda*—to extract labor and tribute from indigenous communities—was not new to the Maya *milpero*, who had a long history of paying tribute to rulers and elites. However, its successful implementation by the Spanish was contingent on the cooperation of Maya leaders to assuage tension between farmer and ruler. Many early clashes between the Maya and Spanish resulted from usurping the involvement of Maya elites and preemptively instituting a system of *encomienda* (Restall 1998). These conflicts were met in some cases with the forced relocation of the Maya into aggregated towns to facilitate administration of tribute payments (Cook and Borah 1974).

As throughout the New World, European diseases had a severe impact on indigenous mortality and greatly overshadowed lives lost to warfare. Smallpox, lethal to native populations, reticulated through the population, having its greatest demographic impact in the early decades of the 1500s, prior to the first colonial census. Estimates vary widely, but a population reduction of 50 percent to 90 percent during the first half of the sixteenth century is likely (Borah and Cook 1969:181; Denevan 1976:40; Restall 1997:174).[2] Yet, despite losses due to disease and famine, the Maya remained persistent in trying to retain their independence and were successful to some extent. The Yucatan was economically peripheral to colonial interests in central Mexico and South America and, throughout the nineteenth and much of the twentieth centuries, remained politically isolated from the rest of Mexico. The ratio of Spanish to indigenous people was (and is) much lower in the Yucatan than in other parts of Mexico, and the assimilation of the Maya populous, although it certainly progressed, wavered over the following centuries. Yet Maya opposition was not necessarily unified. Maya leaders, struggling with interregional conflict, were caught in the middle. Deferential to maintaining their own political advantage, sustaining their elite status depended on cooperating with the very hand that sought to subjugate them (Restall 1997, 1998).

Large-scale henequén (sisal hemp) and sugarcane production during the nineteenth century galvanized the stronghold of colonial economic transformation. Commercial plantations in the Yucatan produced large export crops of henequén, a valuable fiber on the world market. The henequén plantation came to represent a totem of wealthy landowners and debt peonage that was the established political and social order of the Yucatan during the nineteenth century. An estimated 800,000 hectares of Maya farmland in the Yucatan had been transferred into private ownership by the mid-1800s (Patch 1993). And in 1847, three centuries after contact, tensions culminated in the Caste War. Although this protracted struggle endured for twenty years, the Caste War did not mollify the grip of hacienda and plantation land ownership, and the mid-1800s were some of the most successful years in the henequén market. While henequén production withstood the Caste War and continued through the Mexican Revolution, many of the sugar plantations, primarily located in the eastern part of the state, were destroyed during the conflict and not reestablished (Mosely 1980).

Grounded in agrarian reform, the Mexican Revolution began as a series of localized rebellions and skirmishes that found national unity only some years later. In 1915 the revolution was just arriving in the Yucatan when the first watershed decree calling for the return of alienated native lands was signed in Mexico City. The restoration of native lands was formally declared in the 1917 Mexican constitution, although this did not occur in the Yucatan until 1937, when President Lázaro Cárdenas, showcasing his collective ejido land-tenure system, enforced the return of hacienda and plantation holdings to Maya villages. Each village was conceded land on which to build its village as well as surrounding country for crops, pasture, and woodland. Ejido lands as initially written into law could not be owned, inherited, sold, or rented, and their dominion resided within the village collective. The insoluble protection of the ejido was reversed as a contingency of the North American Free Trade Agreement (NAFTA), however, and ejido lands can now be relinquished if a community so decides.

The Maya *milpero* has outlasted centuries of fluctuations in population aggregation and dispersion, conflict among Maya chiefdoms, Spanish subjugation, Christian inculcation, and now the inroads of the national labor market economy. Since the devastation in population immediately following initial contact, the Maya population wavered at under 250,000 until it began to steadily increase after 1900. In visiting Maya villages today, one is struck by continuity through the changing faces of political power.

The Village

Not far from Xculoc, on the south side of the Puuc ridge, are several large, well-documented Classic Maya civic centers (roughly AD 250–900). As the crow flies, Uxmal is 20 kilometers to the north, Sayil 20 kilometers to the east, Kabah 20 kilometers to the northeast, and Labna 28 kilometers east (see Figure 3.2). A number of lesser-known and difficult-to-access archaeological sites—Almuchil, Chunhuhu, Kalakhuitz, Xcochkax, and Xpostanil, among others—are within 10 kilometers of the village. Yet perhaps most mysterious are the numerous vestiges of undocumented, unnamed ruins hidden in the forest surrounding the village. Upon being asked what Xculoc farmers think about these great stone edifices that from an archaeologist's perspective mark their link to a past grandeur, they explained that they were built during the time of slavery.

At the edge of the village, entwined in undergrowth and protected by a dense population of ticks, is a Classic Puuc Maya site with contiguous courtyards, platform mounds, a pyramid, ball court, and portal vault. This site is discussed in Stephens and Catherwood's two-volume tome of site descriptions and illustrations (Stephens 1993 [1841], 1996

[1843]) compiled during their travel through the interior of Mayaland in the mid-1800s. Many details about the lives of the Maya farmers whom they encountered are included in their archaeological descriptions. One of them describes their visit to the site that lies at the edge of Xculoc. Stephens notes the necessity to find food and water for his expedition but does not mention a Maya village in close proximity. Neither was Xculoc mentioned in the census record of eighteenth-century towns, although the document is incomplete (Patch 1993). Around the turn of the twentieth century, a rancho was built, presumably as a ranching post to graze cattle in the nearby savanna grasslands (which Stephens mentions as the best he had found for grazing his horses).[3] Maler (1902), who returned to document the site fifty years after Stephens's initial visit, writes that Maya houses were near the site, although these may have been associated with the rancho, rather than referring to the Maya village of Xculoc (Dore 1996). Following the Mexican Revolution and the demise of the hacienda system, the Maya relocated their villages near the then-abandoned wells that had been excavated by the Spanish. Two such wells are in the village of Xculoc, and as with many of the Maya villages in the area, Xculoc is built amid the ruins of the nineteenth-century rancho.

When asked, the elders of the village agree that when they were growing up sixty years ago, Xculoc was much smaller, a village of a dozen or so households. Given its oral history, the size of the village, the distance between the milpas and the village, and the best dates for the rancho, Xculoc has probably been established in its present location since the early part of the twentieth century (Dore 1996).

Whether there were henequén or sugar plantations in the area is unknown. But given that most of the well-documented plantations were located in the wide, flat, and drier coastal plains to the north and east, and that the region surrounding Xculoc is hilly and circumscribed by small, irregular valleys, if commercial colonial agricultural production occurred near the village, it was probably at a much smaller scale than elsewhere in the Yucatan.

The physical character of Xculoc, as of many villages in the region, aptly reveals the varied and lengthy story of the Maya. One of the first Spanish documents written in the 1500s about the Maya includes a map of the Yucatan marking the boundaries of the Maya polities during the early contact era. The name given to the area around Xculoc is a surname common to many villagers. The jagged outlines of ruined temples palisade the hilltops above the maize fields. Carved blocks scavenged from the pre-Columbian structures that surround the village are still used to build the foundations of present-day houses. The dilapidated stone walls of the abandoned rancho shade young men playing ball during hot afternoons. Women gather nightly to sing Catholic hymns in one of the rancho's storerooms that has recently been roofed and whitewashed. You can now buy a Coca-Cola, albeit warm, at the village *tienda*. Importantly, the well provides a steady source of water.

The present-day Maya population in the Bolonchen region is dispersed and sparse compared with many other rural areas of the Yucatan. What follows is a description of the village as it was when the initial research was conducted in 1992–1993. Changes that have occurred since then are described in the Postscript. The several other small villages within 10 kilometers of Xculoc are accessible by foot paths and two-track roads. Xculoc is isolated, for the most part, from vehicular traffic, although several times a year a truck may drive into town selling chairs and tables, vegetables, or other goods. The village is a five-hour walk or a two-hour bicycle ride from the closest paved road, where villagers can catch a ride to several market towns 40 to 60 kilometers away. Local lore tells that killer bees destroyed the last horse the year before my initial fieldwork in 1992–1993. Although many households now own a bicycle, which has a burden limit of about a 35 kilo sack of maize, exchange between remote villages and market centers is limited by the long distances.

At the time of this study, the village had no electricity or running water. As in many rural villages in the late-1970s, a gas-powered water pump and maize mill were introduced as part of a government development project. Until the pump was installed, water was arduously drawn from a 50 meter deep well using ropes and buckets. The pump, however, is frequently broken, and then women return to hand drawing water from the well or collecting water from natural *chultuns*. Hand-cranked mills replaced manos and metates to grind maize about seventy-five years ago. Subsequently, two gas-powered mills, or *molinos*, were installed in the late 1970s. Women can now get their daily corn ground at the *molino* for about 20 cents. Most households

still have a hand-cranked mill and use it when the *molino* is not func-
tioning or when a household does not have the cash to pay for its use.
Manos and metates are now used to grind only herbs and spices.

Until the late-1990s, Xculoc did not have a clinic, though health-care
providers did come to the village a couple of times a year to vaccinate
children. The Mexican government is vigilant of cholera outbreaks, and
officials regularly visited the village. Malaria has not been a problem in
this area for the past two decades. Other than child immunization,
however, health care is not readily accessible due to transportation and
cost limitations. Although a few free clinics operate in the larger towns,
health care is, by and large, not free.

The village *curandero,* or traditional herbal practitioner, died some
years ago, and no one has taken his place. Though villagers seem well
informed about the herbal and medicinal uses of forest plants, many
folk remedies are being replaced by a greater reliance on Western med-
icines. When children run high fevers, parents are adamant about
wanting to take them to a town where a doctor or pharmacist will
administer penicillin, which is routinely injected for undiagnosed ail-
ments. The long-term and potentially serious implications of overad-
ministered antibiotics in these situations has been well documented
(see, for example, Ewald 1994). In the case of an emergency, the one
vehicle owner in the village is solicited to take someone to the doctor.
Prior to his owning a truck, villagers tell of carrying the sick on litters
the 18 kilometers to the paved road, where they could hitch a ride to
a hospital. Yet despite their remoteness and the lack of modern facili-
ties, villagers are well nourished and in general good health.

Maya parents are interested in having their children learn to read and
write, and 99 percent of school-age children (ages 6 to 12) are sent to
the rustic primary school when classes are in session. On many morn-
ings, mothers bathed and dressed their children for school, but school-
teachers only infrequently traveled the long distance into Xculoc, and
classes were rarely held. Consequently, there was little conflict between
school and work. When in session, classes were taught in Spanish and
met for four hours a day. In spite of the erratic schedule, most children
learn to read and write in Spanish. Older children are eligible to attend
boarding schools in towns some distance from the village. These
schools, however, are not free, and very few children are sent to them.
Children's higher education is probably not more widely pursued,

because schooling provides few benefits associated with increased economic opportunity due to the community's isolation and limited need for skilled wage labor.

All villagers speak Yucatec Mayan as their first language and use it exclusively when speaking to each other. When asked, 54 percent of villagers said that they also spoke Spanish (Dore 1996), which compares with 91 percent in the state of Yucatan (INEGI 1991b: *cuadro* 8, p. 80). Men and children are somewhat more fluent in Spanish because of their exposure to it when performing wage labor and in school, while women, and especially older women, are more limited in their use.

Village politics operate on many levels. Formally, an appointed *comisario*, or major, oversees village civic activities, and an ejido *comisario* facilitates the allocation of agricultural lands. Maintenance of the village is delegated by the *comisario*, and villagers are obliged to participate in community projects, called *fagina* or *communidad*. Several times a year, women gather to sweep the village, quite literally, from end to end. As their *fagina*, men clear the scrub and vegetation from the trails and two-track roads that run in and out of the village or participate in small construction projects.

Although seemingly isolated, the village is impressively tied to the regional and state government through the municipal seat in Bolonchen, about 40 kilometers to the south. Men actively maintain political contact with the government through village-organized committees, and committee officials spend considerable time at meetings in Bolonchen. A dozen such committees, primarily concerned with agrarian interests, were documented during the 1992–1993 fieldwork.

On many occasions the affiliation of villagers to the larger social sphere would come up in the course of conversation. If asked, "What do you consider yourself?" after some deliberation, their most common response was, "Soy Católico." Although villagers are linked to the outside political sphere, the response was never, "Soy Mexicano" or "Yucataco" or "Maya."

The majority of villagers identify themselves as Catholic, although a few families report affiliation to a Protestant Evangelical sect that has been gaining presence in the Yucatan since the 1950s.[4] Only once during a year of fieldwork did I see a Catholic priest in the village; he had come to officiate at a wedding. Villagers rarely have the opportunity to attend Mass, and perhaps one copy of a Bible can be found in the village. Although they participate in certain Catholic rituals, little indoctrination into dogma and moral code is apparent. As a community project, a storeroom of the abandoned rancho was converted into a small chapel, a simple room with a nineteenth-century wooden statue of San Isidro, the patron saint of the farmer, and an old painting of the Virgin of Guadalupe. Women bring flowers and candles and gather in the evening to sing. The men congregate as well, not in the chapel, but standing outside in a guard line several men deep, watching the women. As throughout much of Mexico, the Virgin of Guadalupe, who most likely has her genesis as much in Aztec as in Catholic heritage, is the focal point of many gatherings and processions. Villagers participate in many saints' feast days and the Day of the Dead, as well as traditional, community, and familial celebrations throughout the year.

The history and ethnography of the Yucatec Maya enjoy a prolific literature.[5] A number of these ethnographic studies were recorded in the earlier part of the twentieth century and give a rich backdrop to conditions prior to the influx of the labor-market economy. Some of the most well known are Press's (1975) work in the village of Pustunich, Redfield and Villa Rojas's (1934) work in Chan Kom, and Ryder's (1977) study in Pencuyut. Although there are many similarities between these traditional Maya villages and Xculoc, even at the time when these ethnographies were written, those towns were much larger and closer to urban centers, and their populace was much more involved in wage labor and the market economy, than were the residents of Xculoc during my research.

Household Composition and Economics

Radiating out from a large central plaza, the village is laid out in *solars,* or household compounds, that may have one to several residential, cooking, and storage structures (Figure 3.3). At the time of this study, all dwellings were traditional wattle-and-daub, packed-earth floor, pitched-roof structures. Each *solar* is surrounded by a meticulously maintained rubble wall. Although *solars* vary in size, most have large yards with animal pens, a latrine, herb and vegetable gardens, and work areas.

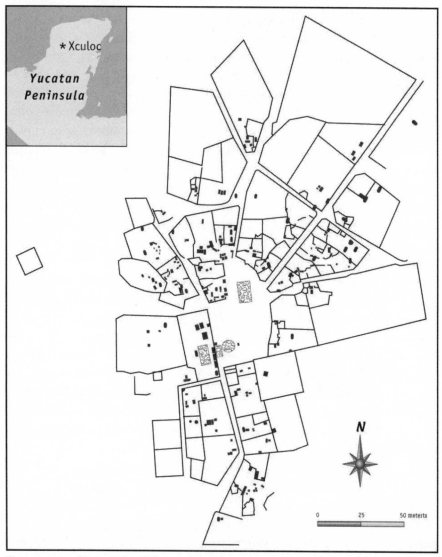

Figure 3.3   Plan view of Xculoc showing central plaza, household compounds and structures (source: Adapted from Dore 1996).

A *solar* is home to a household. A household is defined here as a discrete commensal and economic group, the unit in which production and consumption occur. As villagers often said, "Those who eat together, work together." Each household grows its own food and finances the labor to provision the household. In other tropical or cash-crop agricultural systems, labor demands may peak at various times during the agricultural cycle—when felling new forest or when garden products are harvested to be taken to market for sale. During these periods of higher labor demand, labor may be pooled or exchanged across households. However, this is seldom the case in Xculoc for a number of reasons. Field preparation, weeding, and harvesting are all tasks that occur over a several-month period, minimizing peaks in the demand for labor (see the description of an annual agricultural cycle later in this chapter). Other than the occasional sale of small quantities of maize and honey, the Xculoc Maya do not cash crop and harvest only a small amount of garden product at a time as daily needs require. Only rarely are nonhousehold members asked to assist in milpa activities. On these occasions, reciprocity is direct, in the form of either labor or cash payment.

Tools and other items are commonly borrowed across households, but food seldom is. Families often eat together, but they were rarely joined by nonhousehold members. An exception is the formalized exchange of food that occurs at midday when equal-size portions of food are exchanged between related households. Mothers give children a small bowl of their midday meal, which they deliver to a related household. The food is received and the bowl refilled with something from the second family's own pot. Most often, the food exchanged is a bowl of cooked black beans. Such sharing appears to be a symbolic gesture, with no net transfer, and may serve to reaffirm familial obligations that are drawn on during periods of resource scarcity.

In 1992–1993, the 316 residents of Xculoc (162 males and 154 females) lived in 55 households, of which 82 percent (45) were nuclear families—a mother, father, and their children. In another 18 percent (10) of households, a widowed mother or father (4), a granddaughter (1), or an older unmarried sibling (2) lived with the nuclear family. In three cases, a recently married son, his wife, and their young children shared a *solar* with his natal household (in a separate sleep structure). In these extended families, everyone in the household eats together and cultivates one milpa. Household size ranges from 4 to 11 adults and children and has a mean of 7.13 individuals.

The Subsistence Base

All households plant fields and cultivate maize and the vast majority of other foods that they consume. Although maize contributes 75 percent to 85 percent to the diet, the Maya have a delicious and varied traditional cuisine (see Appendix B for a complete food list).[6] The principal crops of maize, squash, sweet potatoes, and peanuts are grown in milpas in the open savannas 1.6 kilometers from the village. Many families also maintain kitchen gardens in their household compound, where they grow a variety of citrus, avocado, banana, and papaya trees and numerous other fruits and vegetables. Herbs, spices, and flowers are grown in small, raised beds called *trojes*. Domesticated turkeys, ducks, chickens, and pigs are raised for occasional consumption, and hunted animals include deer, peccary, coati, wild goat, armadillo, and various birds. Gathered plants tend to be medicinal, except in years of extreme drought when *ramon*, or breadfruit, was traditionally gathered.

Aside from food that is grown, raised, or hunted, small quantities of maize (1 to 3 kilos a day for about 15 cents per kilo) may be exchanged at the two village stores for a few commodities such as cooking oil, candles, eggs, rice, and sodas.[7] Maize may also be exchanged to use the *molino,* a charge of about 20 cents a day. Some families report the one-time sale of a large quantity of maize (2,000 to 6,000 kilos) in the fall. Much of this surplus maize goes immediately to repay bank loans for fertilizers and pesticides, which were introduced into farming practices in the year prior to this data collection. Corn has a relatively low market value, and once these loans are repaid, little cash remains.[8] Other than corn, no crops are cultivated for sale.

Twenty percent of village households maintain beehives and report selling honey.[9] Of these eleven households, the mean annual sale was estimated by the head of household to be 200 kilos (range 25 to 400 kilos), which in a market town can be sold for about 80 cents a kilo. Beekeepers report that, at most, 50 kilos of honey can be harvested a month during the season from late winter through spring.

In many households, adult males may work from time to time for wages. Young men, from about age fifteen to when they marry, may travel to urban areas for short periods of time to find wage labor, most often construction work. If several sons in a household are over the age of fifteen, usually only one works in part-time wage labor, while the others stay in the village cultivating their milpa. If men are gone for the week, they return to the village on the weekend. Married men from time to time will also participate in wage labor to finance the purchase of household items. Rather than traveling to a city, when available nearby, men may assist farmers in the larger surrounding villages for a wage.

In 25 percent of households, no member participated in wage labor over the course of a year's study, and the household subsisted solely on the crops they grew, domestic and hunted animals, and for some families, the additional small income from honey sales. In the other 75 percent of households, at least one male engaged in wage labor at some point over the course of a year's study. In those households that did participate in wage labor, male wage laborers spent a median of 24 percent (range 7 percent to 85 percent) of their days working for wages. Minimum wage in Mexico at the time of the study was about $3.60 a day. During the course of my fieldwork, the government sponsored two community projects for which men were paid. A basketball court was built in the town plaza and a swath of jungle was cleared from the paved road to the village for an electrical line that was to be installed later that year (but which never was). Women and younger children never participate in wage labor or other income-producing enterprises.

Access to Market Goods
Although most food is grown, villagers do purchase some basic non-food goods, medicine, and medical care with the income from honey sales and wage labor. Machetes are invaluable tools, and every family owns a couple. Other tools are often borrowed among related families and are in constant circulation. Many households own a bicycle, a gun, and a cement wash basin.[10] Some houses are now roofed with corrugated tar paper rather than the traditional palm fronds or grass. Women no longer construct men's clothing, which is purchased or obtained some other way. After reaching adolescence, all women in the village wear traditional huipils, which they sew and elaborately embroider with cloth and yarn that is bought in market towns. Most women have a manufactured *robozo* (shawl) and perhaps a piece of gold jewelry and a pair of shoes that are worn on special occasions. A

very few (three) women own a treadle sewing machine, but most women sew and mend their clothing by hand. Each household has an assortment of metal and plastic buckets, clay *ojos,* metal pots, bowls, and utensils. Most women now use commercial sponges rather than ziricote leaves to wash pots. Many, but not all, households have a table and one or two chairs. Hammocks are often bought rather than woven, and most families have one or two blankets for cold nights. Although there are a number of radios and two televisions in town, in order to operate a television someone must carry a car battery on the back of a bicycle to a market town, where it can be charged. Needless to say, televisions are infrequently operated, and the only time I saw one on, or even visible, was during the Olympics.

Agricultural Conditions

Climatic conditions in central Yucatan are characterized by a long season of very hot and humid weather from April to September, followed by a cooler and a somewhat drier season from October to March. Most of the 1,100 millimeters (43 inches) of annual rain falls during summer convection storms, but tropical hurricanes also contribute significant moisture during autumn.[11] During the summer many consecutive days have highs well over 100° F.[12] Humidity is high during the summer rainy season and can reach the point of saturation. Relative humidity measured at noon throughout the field season had a mean of 65 percent, with a range of 40 percent to 97 percent (Dore 1996).[13]

The vegetation in the Yucatan Peninsula grades generally with an increase in rainfall from almost desertic conditions on the north coast to a rain forest in the south and southeast and varies locally with drainage patterns and the length and severity of the dry season. In the Bolonchen Hills, the low tropical rain forest is broken by intermittent stands of secondary growth and savanna grasslands. In many parts of the Yucatan Peninsula, where agricultural intensification has resulted in shortened fallow periods and incomplete succession cycles, mature climax forest has been replaced by large tracts of thickets, scrubs, and brambles. This is less the case in the Bolonchen region, where the lack of surface water and the steep haystack hills historically precluded large-scale agricultural production, and population aggregation may never have been what it was (and is) elsewhere in the Yucatan. Around the village of Xculoc, replacement of forest by scrub is limited to the broad valleys where agricultural fields are now repetitively planted.

Xculoc's ejido—communally held lands allocated to the village following the Mexican Revolution—encompass some 5,211 hectares. Each household has access to these communally held agricultural lands and maintains milpas both in broad valleys within half an hour's walk from the village and in several other locations in order to minimize the risk of crop failure due to the vagaries of geographically spotty rainfall. While it may not be the case in the future, (at the time of the initial study) competition for arable land, or for forest resources such as firewood and beehive locations, was not evident from either interviews with villagers or observed land use.[14]

Although much of the Yucatan is described as having thin and poor soils, the Bolonchen Hills region has exceptionally iron-rich deposits, which in places are up to several meters thick. Reflecting the warm and moist tropical climate, the limestone parent material, and the comparatively recent origin of the Yucatan land surface, local soils are characterized as calcareous, relatively poor in manganese and potassium, and as having a high base saturation (often 100 percent) and pH levels between 7 and 8. Regional farmers recognize many types of soils based on their productivity and suitability to support specific varieties of maize. Tractors were introduced into farming practices during the early-1990s, and since then farmers have shifted from cultivating on the hill, or *witz,* slopes to cultivating the *kancab* soils, a red, loamy clay deposit, on flat valley floors (Dunning 1992).[15] Most households also maintain fields 20 kilometers from the village, where they cultivate maize in *ekbum,* or black soil, which is considered more productive.

Villagers traditionally practiced slash-and-burn agriculture, where a tract of *witz* slope was cut and burned, the cleared plot was cultivated for one or two growing seasons, and then the plot lay fallow for fifteen to twenty years. Prior to the introduction of tractors, fertilizers, and drought-resistant varieties of maize in the 1990s, villagers did not cultivate in the valley floors because of the limited water retention in hard, clayey soils. Although water retention on the rocky *witz* slopes is sufficient for cultivation, farmers report that the labor investment in felling new forest restricted their annual maize yields. By contrast, the time savings in crop preparation was substantial when they shifted to cultivating on the valley floor. Although the once-unusable valleys are transformed into arable land through the use of tractors, fertilizers, and new varieties of maize, farmers also comment that older varieties of maize had a longer storage life than newer varieties, which become infested with insects after only several months of being harvested. In 2003, a few farmers had resumed planting traditional varieties of maize. Plots on the valley floors are now being annually reused, and little new forest is felled. The well-documented relationship between shortened fallow periods, decrease in productivity, and increase in weeding effort (Johnson and Earle 2000; Pingali and Binswanger 1987; Ramakrishnan 1992) is presumably ameliorated through the use of tractors and fertilizers, since farmers interviewed in 1992 and again in 2003 did not report a reduction in crop yields over the past ten years.

The Annual Agricultural Cycle

In the late spring, April and May, each household spent several days cutting the underbrush that had grown up in the fields, leaving it to dry for several days before burning. In more densely populated areas, thick clouds of smoke usher in the beginning of the burning season. During the 1992 to 1993 field season, the Xculoc fields were burned in early June (Figure 3.4). Burning removes the secondary growth and controls insects and other vermin, but perhaps most importantly, the resulting

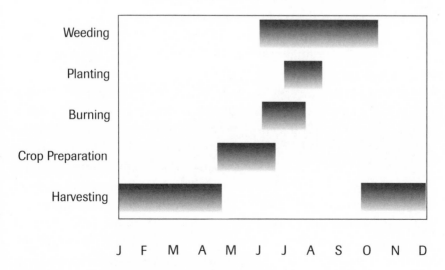

Figure 3.4 The annual Maya agricultural cycle.

Figure 3.5   Maya farmer planting maize with a digging stick.

ash rejuvenates the soil by returning nitrogen and other minerals to it. Ash, however, can easily be washed away by the heavy Yucatan rains. Therefore, it is optimal to plant prior to the full onset of the rainy season so that the minerals in the ash have a chance to penetrate into the soil. Burning must be well timed, and each household decides when to burn, depending on their evaluation of the wind, which facilitates a complete burn, and the coming rainy season.

Milpas are planted after the onset of the rainy season, but the specific timing varies substantially among households. The earliest planting dates during the 1992 growing season were in mid-June and the latest at the end of August. The male head-of-household plants the seed, assisted by a son. The planter uses a tall, sharpened, wood digging stick to punch the ground every several steps, or every 75 to 100 centimeters (Figure 3.5). He drops several seeds into the 10 centimeter deep hole, covers the hole with dirt, and moves on. Rows are about a meter apart and are scrupulously kept straight by running out a string the length of the row, which the assistant keeps taut and helps to move from one row to the next. Although a large number of maize varieties are grown throughout the Bolonchen region, three types of maize—*maíz blanco, maíz amarillo,* and *maíz medio rojo*—were being grown by local farmers at the time of this study.

Villagers report a high incidence of crop failure—four to six out of ten years—which at first seemed untenable considering the dense tropical forest that surrounds the milpas and the substantial annual rainfall. Later it became clear that timing the planting to the rainfall cycle is a very tricky scheduling decision. It is preferable to plant after a rain, when the ground is moist but not saturated, so that the seeds will germinate but not rot. The beginning of the rainy season is interrupted with a short dry spell that lasts several weeks. Planting ideally should occur just prior to this dry spell, when conditions are propitious for the young seeds. But, if the rains do not resume within several weeks, the young plants die of drought. Even though the 1992 to 1993 season produced a fruitful harvest, a number of families lost their first planting because they had planted too early, and the rains resumed later than they had anticipated. These families did successfully replant their fields, and almost all families spent some time reseeding to replace individual plants. The key, then, to the high crop failure rate is not the lack of rainfall but the timing of this short, fickle dry period at the beginning of the growing season—which in drier years would have had more disastrous results. In good years, sufficient maize is produced to get through most bad years.

Squash is often planted among the maize plants. Squash is primarily grown for its seeds, which are ground into a highly caloric paste, similar to a nut butter, used in cooking. The flesh is rarely eaten, and then only when the young plants first ripen. Some families also plant peanuts and sweet potatoes in their milpa plots.

Plots are typically weeded several times during the growing season, though weeding effort varies greatly from family to family. Some plots become overgrown, while others are meticulously maintained. The earliest harvest dates recorded during this field season were mid-September, when *elotes*—corn on the cob—were picked. This young corn, eaten with salt, chili, and lime, is greatly anticipated. After the early corn is harvested for immediate consumption, the remaining corn, and the majority of the harvest, is left on the stalk to dry. Steggerda (1941), among other ethnographers (Press 1975; Redfield and Villa Rojas 1934; Smyth 1988), in his comprehensive treatment of milpa practices reports that after the initial harvest of *elotes*, the stalks are bent over to allow the ears to dry for about a month before being harvested and brought to town for storage. However, this is not practiced in Xculoc. Instead maize is harvested as a household's needs demand throughout the winter and spring. Every day, or on several days, a family member(s) goes out to the fields to harvest what the household will need for the coming days. Some families crib off a section of their house and store large quantities of corn; others store smaller quantities (fewer than 80 kilos) in sacks.

Crop Yields

Households cultivate a mean area of 2.5 hectares of maize per year ($n = 52$; range 1.0 to 5.5 hectares). When interviewed, villagers reported that one hectare is for subsistence and the other hectare is for sale, backup, or storage, although some deviation from this occurs given the actual range of field sizes. The high rate of crop failure as reported by villagers illustrates the importance of growing surplus crops. Redfield and Villa Rojas (1934), in their early ethnographic study, recorded many details about agricultural practices and found that the average farmer in Chan Kom cultivated between 2.5 and 3.0 hectares.

Crop yields were estimated at the end of the growing season by sampling maize production in 10-by-10-meter plots in twenty milpas. The number of plants and the number of ears per plant were recorded for each plot, yielding a mean density of 3,380 ears per hectare. The mean weight of an ear of maize, with and without the cob, was then measured, giving an average annual crop yield of 5,700 kilos of maize per hectare (with cob; 4,300 kilos without cob).[16]

These mean crop yields are considerably higher than estimates reported by earlier ethnographers. Press (1975) estimated a yield of 1,680 kilos of maize per hectare. Wiseman (1978) found that in the Peten region (wetter on average than the Yucatan), average yields were 1,600 kilos per hectare,[17] and Redfield and Villa Rojas (1934) reported even lower yields: 1,470 kilos per hectare. A number of factors could contribute to the higher yield estimate from the Xculoc data. Press's estimates are for a more populated region further north, where soils are poorer and, all else being equal, are likely to be less productive. From interviews, local farmers felt that 1992–1993 was a bumper crop. Importantly, the ear weights were taken soon after the initial harvest and are for fairly fresh corn, not well-dried corn. Maize varieties also can differ substantially in size. The yield estimates given here are for *maíz blanco, maíz amarillo,* and *maíz medio rojo,* which are relatively large varieties. By the 1990s, many farmers were planting these hybrid varieties, which they report are much more productive. Crop yields from these earlier studies are likely for criollo maize (traditional maize varieties), which Xculoc farmers report to be much less productive. And lastly, the four studies cited above do not detail the methods used to derive yield estimates and so may not be directly comparable.

To an outsider, the Maya may appear poor, but unlike many other subsistence farmers, they do not experience a seasonal hungry time, and their child mortality is very low, with 95 percent of children surviving to age 15—the importance of which cannot be overstated. The Maya do not see their own lives as impoverished, in part because they are seldom exposed to materially wealthier sectors of the population. As in any community, status distinctions are recognizable among individuals and households. But what is striking about Xculoc, and perhaps about other subsistence farming villages in rural Yucatan, is that status differences are not parlayed into differential access to productive land—a farmer's baseline resource. The low competition for land can be attributed to three historical factors. First, only now is the population density of rural Yucatan returning to what it was prior to European contact. Sustained low population density over the past several hundred years was coupled with an absence of large-scale agricultural production in this part of the Yucatan. Much of the interior of Yucatan remained peripheral to widespread colonial economic interests, unlike in the Chiapas highlands to the south, where coffee production developed in the nineteenth century, or on the plains to the north, where henequén plantations displaced many Maya farmers.

Second, the institution of ejido land tenure following the Mexican Revolution deeded the village what has been ample land to sustain their population. Ejido lands, by law, are not heritable, eliminating a traditional venue for competition and wealth stratification among agriculturalists.

And third, the long distances and lack of transportation to market towns diminish individual incentive to produce agricultural surpluses for trade or exchange. More corn did not buy greater access to material wealth.[18] While this may be changing, these historical factors mollify individual competition for arable land, which has important consequences in minimizing variance in health, nutrition, and wealth among villagers. Needless to say, the population is rapidly increasing, the national economy is becoming ever more accessible, and ejido rules are now changing—communal land is no longer mandated to be held in perpetuity by the village. No doubt competition for productive land and economic opportunity will be a consequence of these changes in the near future.

— 4 —

Maya Families

Many demographic changes occur as Maya families mature. Marriage unions form, and sometime later, a child is born. Firstborn children become productive workers while their mothers are in their childbearing years. Later-born children are still young when their older siblings marry, leave their natal households, and begin families of their own. Parents age and become grandparents while they still have several dependent children living at home. As children enter and leave the family through births and marriages, not only does the number of children living at home fluctuate over the duration of a marriage, but so does the ratio of young children, who consume little and produce even less, to older children, who consume more but also produce more. Because both consumption and the capacity for work vary across the life course, as the family moves through its life cycle, consumption demands and labor supply are determined not only by family size but also by the age structure of the family.

It is this dynamic process of family maturation and shifting consumer demands and labor supply that Chayanov (1986 [1925]) recognized in his pioneering work on rural farmers' household production. Chayanov's insight provides a heuristic framework with which to track demographic changes in Maya family composition. In this chapter, Maya reproductive histories and census data are used to construct a picture of changes in demographic pressure over the life cycle of a Maya family. These data are then used to place the village in the context of past and current fertility trends.

Collecting Demographic Data

At the onset of the project, each *solar* (household compound) was mapped and family members interviewed to collect demographic, economic, and anthropometric information. Mapping and interviewing not only allowed my field partner and me to get to know the people of Xculoc and the spatial and social organization of the village but also gave villagers an opportunity to appraise us and ask questions about the project. During the household interview, village members were asked their age and birth date as well as the ages and birth dates of their parents, siblings, and children. In the case of deceased relatives, age at death and a death date were requested. When children were too young to provide this information, their mother or father did. Questions were also asked about marital status, date of marriage, languages spoken, education, religious affiliation, household economics, and farming practices. Mothers and fathers report similar information about the number and ages of their children, presumably because men and women cohabit, marriages are lifelong, and kin terminology discriminates between biological and social parents. To ensure the anonymity of participants, village members were assigned a number for subsequent identification during data recovery and analyses. Interviews were conducted in Yucatec Mayan through the assistance of a translator, who interpreted responses into Spanish as necessary.

The household survey was designed with the goals of producing a census for the village and generating reproductive histories for village mothers. The census was used to establish the age and sex structure of the 316 village members.[1] Reproductive histories were built around mothers and include their birth date and the birth dates and death dates, if applicable, of their children. Only live births (defined as live parturition) were included in the tabulation of a mother's children. Infants who died very young were included in the tally of children, but miscarriages were not. Fifty-seven mothers were living in the Xculoc at the time of the initial household survey. They and their children were directly interviewed to collect birth and death information. The reproductive histories of an additional twenty-seven deceased mothers were culled by interviewing their children and siblings who were living in the village at the time of the survey. With this information, family histories could be assembled going back several generations.

Aging the Population
Constructing reliable age/sex distributions and reproductive histories depends on collecting accurate age data. Because only a very few vil-

lage members have written birth certificates issued at the time of birth, a number of steps were taken to improve the accuracy of the age estimates.[2] First, all members of the household, not just the head-of-household, were interviewed. Although this is a lengthy process, and redundant in some respects, an individual is usually a better purveyor of his or her own age and other demographic information than someone else, especially in a large family. All family members gathered during the household survey, and on several occasions as a mother or father listed the ages of their children, a daughter or son would interject, "No, I'm not thirteen, I'm fourteen." Collecting family histories from everyone, not just the head-of-household, gave several estimates of a person's age and made us aware of cases where further questioning was needed.

Second, as a check for situations where people guessed at or were uncertain of their age, individuals were asked both their age and their birth date. Many people reported both without hesitation, although younger people were more likely to know their complete birth date (month, day, and year), while older people tended to know only their birth year. When an age and a birth date were not congruent, and the disparity could not be resolved through further discussion, age is used as the closest estimate of how old a person is. Not long after we started the household interviews, it became clear that most of these discrepancies arose because the interviewee derived his birth year by subtracting his age from the interview year rather than the interview date. The potential bias introduced from correcting by age when this situation arose is an overestimate of an individual's age by a maximum of twelve months.

Third, villagers consistently listed their children and siblings in ranked birth order from oldest to youngest, providing a cross-check for conflicting, unknown, or forgotten birth date or age information. Ranking siblings and children by birth order reflects information about the relative age of family members and has been shown to be a valuable technique to improve age estimates in populations that do not have either calendric measures or written records of absolute age (Hill and Hurtado 1996; Howell 1979; Pennington and Harpending 1993).

Last, because marriages tend to be between village members, most adults have siblings, parents, or adult children living in the village. This was especially valuable when very old people did not know both their age and birth date. If an older person's assessment of his or her age appeared incorrect when compared with his or her age as reported by siblings or children, the self-reported age tended to be an overestimate. Some people simply thought of themselves as old and insisted that they were 75 or 80 no matter how the question was posed. In the event that an age was clearly an overestimate, the age assigned to the individual was based on the person's birth rank and age as reported by his or her siblings or children living in the village.

The census data were re-collected in 2001, and the age and birth date of every individual were again recorded. In the majority of cases, the birth dates given in the 1992–1993 census and the 2001 census were the same, suggesting that people do know their age or, at any rate, that they consistently give the same estimate. The certainty of the birth date data was ranked for each mother and her children. In analyses where age is important, such as age at first birth and birth intervals, those mothers with problematic birth date data were eliminated from the sample.

Constructing Accurate Reproductive Histories

To construct accurate reproductive histories the researcher must be confident that a count has been made of all the children ever born to a mother. This is of less concern for younger mothers than elderly mothers, who may be less likely to report deceased children, especially if they died very young. Unaccounted-for children underrepresent both women's fertility and the incidence of infant and child mortality. Deceased children may be missed because of recall error, the interviewer not stating the question clearly, or cultural norms prescribing avoidance in speaking about the deceased. The Maya, however, are forthcoming in talking about deceased family members and, when asked to list their children and siblings, consistently do so in ranked birth order that incorporates deceased family members. Parents included infants who had died very young in their ranked listing, but not miscarriages, although we did not ask for this information. Parents did not hesitate when asked about the age at death but were often less certain about death dates, especially if the death occurred some time ago. Although the Maya are not reluctant to talk about deceased relatives, bias always will err in the direction of underreporting deceased children.

A mother's children who lived in the village were accounted for through the census, and their age and birth date information was collected firsthand. Because the marriage pattern is largely endogamous, few adult children were living elsewhere and not enumerated in the village census. In those cases where an individual had emigrated, his or her age and birth date information was collected from relatives who did live in the village, so they could be included in their mothers' reproductive histories.

The Family Life Cycle

Young men and women are modest, but not bashful, around each other, although they rarely have the opportunity to interact. Young women are in the perpetual company of others and are always accompanied when they go to the milpa to work in the fields or into the forest to cut firewood. The only time young women are seen alone is when they carry maize to the *molino* to be ground or haul water through the village streets. Young men and women live, work, and eat in their parents' household until they marry, in their late teens to early twenties.

Among couples in the current population, the mean age at marriage is 21.6 for males ($n = 46$; range age 16 to 33) and 18.7 for females ($n = 50$; range age 15 to 29). Marriages are stable and monogamous, lasting until a partner's death (see Chapter 3 for more about marriages). Of adults living in the village, none reported being divorced as his or her marital status. Widows and widowers were usually well into their fifties or sixties when they lost their spouses, and they rarely remarry. In the village at the time of the study, only two middle-age parents with dependent children had deceased spouses. The widower remarried during our field stay, and except for the widow who did not remarry, all other mothers still in their childbearing years were married.

No illegitimate children were documented when the reproductive histories were collected. Though monogamy is the socially sanctioned marriage system, paternity of course is difficult to ascertain. The seeming adherence to monogamy may reflect a number of factors, among them the cost to Maya mothers with many dependents of participating in extramarital liaisons and jeopardizing their husbands' help and resources. Upon marriage, young women tend to, but do not always, move into their fathers-in-law's households, where the married couple lives until they have cleared their own plot of agricultural land and have built their own *solar*, usually after the birth of the first or second child. Husbands and wives share the same house, jointly discuss many household decisions, and appear to enjoy affable marriages and family relations.

Marriages overwhelmingly occur between village members, and very few villagers marry a spouse from another village or leave the village to marry. To document the flow of marriage partners in and out of the village, the village residents were asked during the household interview, where they had lived prior to living in Xculoc. Of married adults, 97 percent were born in Xculoc (three females and one male were born elsewhere). Males and females are equally likely to find marriage partners. There is some incidence of male and female bachelorhood. Of the village residents over the age of 30, 8 percent (three) of women and 9 percent (four) of men are unmarried.

Couples do not have access to modern contraception, and a child is usually born within the first year of marriage. The median age at first birth since the mid-1970s is 19.5 (Kramer and McMillan 1999). During the first six months of a child's life, infants are breast-fed on demand, and mothers and babies are inseparable. Sometime after they are six months old, babies begin to be fed a supplemental maize gruel (mothers do not use store-bought baby food or formula). Children are fully weaned when they are about two years old, when mothers are often pregnant with another child. A few mothers asked about birth control. When pressed why they wished to know, women said they were curious about a contraceptive pill that could delay births, rather than expressing a desire for smaller families per se.

Figure 4.1 plots the length of birth intervals between children. The sample includes all mothers alive in the village at the time of the survey (*n* = 57). Because many of these mothers are still in their childbearing years, the number of mothers in each birth interval decreases with parity (Appendix Table 4.1). Complete birth dates (month, day, year) were reported for 74 percent of the 265 births (births one to seven only) included in the birth-interval sample. When a child's birth age and birth year were known, but the month and day unknown, a midyear birthday was given. Across births one to seven, the median birth interval consistently varied between 2.0 and 2.2 years, with a range of 1.0 to 7.0 years.

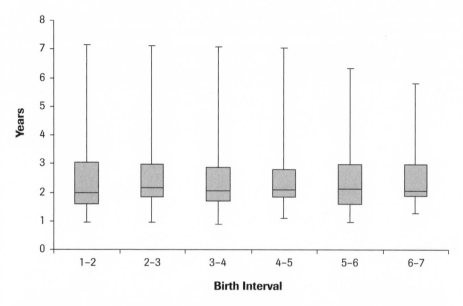

Figure 4.1 Birth-interval length for Maya mothers (*n* = 265 births for 57 mothers), showing minimum, first-quartile, median, third-quartile, and maximum values.

Completed Fertility in the Current Population

Given the size of the village, the sample of women in five-year, or even ten-year, age groups who gave birth during the field year is not sufficient to calculate a standard cross-sectional total fertility rate (TFR). However, completed family size can be derived from the age-specific fertility of Xculoc mothers. Median family size for mothers age 46 and older (*n* = 19) is seven children, with 75 percent of mothers having had eight children (Figure 4.2; Appendix Table 4.2). This level of population growth, while not sustainable in the long term, has been feasible because only now is the local Maya population recovering to pre-European-contact population levels.

Of the nineteen women in the village age 46 and older, all had given birth. Some incidence of childlessness is seen among younger reproductive-age women, however. Of the fifty-five women in the current population who have been married for more than five years, 5 percent (three) have no children. This probable primary sterility is within the range (3 percent to 5 percent) that Bongaarts and Potter (1982) report as normal in well-nourished, natural fertility populations.

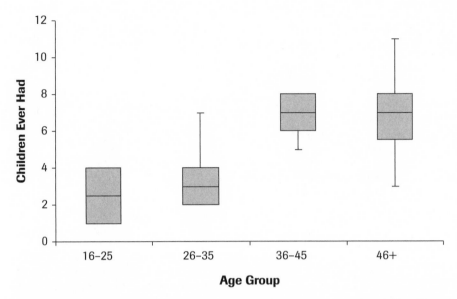

Figure 4.2 Age-specific fertility (number of children ever born) for Maya mothers (*n* = 57), showing minimum, first-quartile, median, third-quartile, and maximum values.

Child Mortality

When the number of live births (Appendix Table 4.2) is compared with the number of surviving children (Appendix Table 4.3), the incidence of child mortality (deaths to children under the age of 16) is markedly low in Xculoc. Of the 284 births to the 57 living mothers, 12 deaths were reported for children under the age of 16.[3] About a third of those were from Duchenne muscular dystrophy, which afflicts one extended family.[4] Though the sample size is small and conclusions speculative, this means that about 95 percent of village children survive to age 16. This compares with an estimated 60 percent of hunter-gatherers' children (Blurton Jones et al. 1992; Hill and Hurtado 1991; Howell 1979; Kaplan et al. 2000), approximately 60–76 percent of horticultural children (Early and Peters 2000:199; Hewlett 1991:8), and 98 percent of U.S. children surviving to age 16 (U.S. Bureau of Census 1992:9).[5] Four of those deaths were to children during their first year of life. Again, this sample is exceedingly small but yields an infant mortality rate of 14.0 deaths per 1,000 births, which compares with 24.6 deaths per 1,000 births in the state of Yucatan (INEGI 1991a) and 9.1 deaths per

1,000 births reported for the U.S. in 1990 (U.S. Bureau of Census 1992:64).[6] Although the death rate seems surprisingly low, with all children accounted for in the 2001 census who were alive in 1992–1993, only one child died in the intervening years.

Although infant and child mortality will always be biased in the direction of underreporting, there are reasons why it is currently (and may have been historically) low in the Yucatan. Contaminated water and the consequent risk of gastrointestinal disease is a primary vector affecting high rates of infant and child mortality. This risk is attenuated in this part of the Yucatan because of the absence of rivers or flowing surface water. Drinking water has been collected from closed wells for the last century, and prior to that, the only source of domestic water was rainwater collected from small surface pools. Furthermore, because of the lack of open, standing water, malaria may never have been as endemic as it is in other tropical climates. The community's remoteness—and the low population density in the Puuc region in general—further lessens the impact of contagious disease. Although child mortality may have been relatively low in the Yucatan interior for some time, immunization programs no doubt have made further gains in reducing child mortality.

Retrospective Demographic Trends

Appendix Table 4.4 shows characteristics of Xculoc mothers' reproductive careers—completed fertility, average birth interval, age at first and last births, and reproductive span—for past cohorts of mothers. A cohort groups all mothers who gave birth to their first child within that ten-year interval. Completed family size consistently varies between 7 and 8 children, except in the 1950 cohort, when family size drops to 6.5 children (median values). The reduction in family size for mothers in the 1950 cohort coincides with a delayed age at first birth and a shortened reproductive span. Although family size has fluctuated over the last seventy years, shifts are nondirectional over the last century.

Completed fertility estimates are "modified" because only women who became mothers, rather than all women, are included in the population of women at risk of conception. This is because the true population of women at risk in the past population is unknown. If a woman who lived in the earlier part of the century did not produce any descendants, she may not be accounted for in retrospective reproductive histories collected from villagers. If her siblings are still alive, she would be listed in their tally of siblings; otherwise, she would not be accounted for, thus underrepresenting the past sample of women. However, deceased mothers are known about through interviews with their children who live in Xculoc.

The age/sex pyramid compiled for the 316 individuals living in Xculoc at the time of the study not only gives a picture of the relative distribution of the population but also tracks general retrospective trends in fertility and mortality (Figure 4.3). Females represent 49 percent of the Xculoc population and males 51 percent. The broad base of the age/sex pyramid shows the relative greater representation of children under the age of 10 compared with older age groups of children. Although a broad-based age/sex pyramid is usually characteristic of high fertility, it can also, in effect, be created by high mortality in the previous ten to twenty years. If child mortality was high in the past, it would leave its mark in the underrepresentation of ten- to twenty-year-olds relative to younger ages.

To test this possibility, deceased children, who can be accounted for from retrospective reproductive histories, were reincorporated into the age/sex pyramid. When this was done, the broad base pattern was still evident. The high representation of children under the age of 10 is assumed, then, to be due to high fertility in the last ten years rather than the effect of high mortality ten to twenty years ago. The asymmetrical representation of males and females between the ages of 10 and 20 is probably due to the death of adolescent males with Duchenne muscular dystrophy (see endnote 4). From what is known historically about the village, migration and mortality rates have remained fairly constant, and the troughs and bumps in the midsection of the pyramid reflect surges and declines in general fertility rates. Other irregularities may certainly be due to the small sample size.

To put into perspective what the age structure reflects about fertility, the proportion of the Xculoc population represented in certain age classes is contrasted with the 1990 census data for the state of Yucatan, Mexico, and the United States.[7] Appendix Table 4.5 compares the proportion of very young children, children 15 and younger,

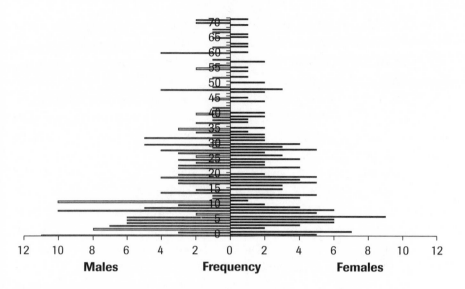

Figure 4.3   Xculoc age/sex pyramid (*n* = 316).

those 19 and younger, reproductive-age adults, and postreproductive-age adults in those populations. Xculoc has a somewhat higher representation of children in all age classes—those under the age of 5, under the age of 16, and under the age of 19—than does the general Yucatan population, which closely reflects the Mexican population at large.

It is evident from the proportion of children in the Xculoc population, the shape of the age distribution, and fertility trends that Xculoc is a high-fertility population and shows no indication of the fertility decline characteristic of the modern demographic transition. As well as having large families, several young dependents live at home through at least the twenty-fifth year of a typical Maya marriage. As families mature, not only does the number of children born into the family increase, but so does the number of children growing up and becoming economic participants.

Demographic Pressure across the Family Life Cycle

Chayanov's (1986 [1925]) innovative analysis of the economic-demographic life cycle of the rural agricultural family provides a useful framework in which to model demographic pressure as the family life cycle unfolds. Building on Chayanov's work and using the Maya reproductive history data, a picture of demographic changes over the life cycle of the typical Maya family can be constructed as children are born into and leave the family. The timing of these dynamics affects the economic pressure within the household to support dependents. In Chapter 8, consumption and production will be folded into this demographic profile of the family life cycle in order to look at the timing of children's economic contributions.

To build the family life cycle, I begin with a marriage union at the average age at first marriage for men and women. The first birth occurs after the median interval from marriage to first birth, and the second and subsequent births after their median intervals up to seven births, which is the average number of children born to mothers. An average life table is then used to calculate the age distribution of surviving family members at each successive year in a marriage duration. The best match to Xculoc's mortality profile is the Model West 11 life table (Coale and Demeny 1983), with a life expectancy at birth of 70 years, which corresponds to about 4.0 deaths per 1,000 per year, or

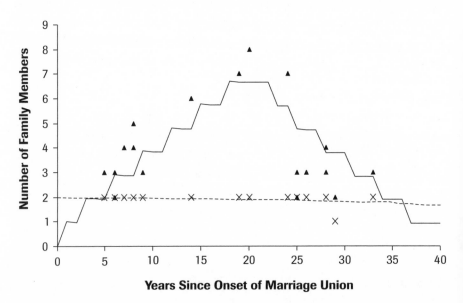

Figure 4.4 Demographic changes across the life cycle of the typical Maya family showing surviving children (solid line) and adults (dotted line). Plotting symbols show actual family composition of surviving parents (x's) and children (▲'s).

1.26 deaths per year given Xculoc's population. No one died during the study year, but when the census was re-collected in 2003, and everyone was accounted for from the 1992–1993 census, 12 deaths had occurred over the ten-year period, or 1.20 deaths per year.[8]

During the first twenty years of a marriage union, children are born into a family (Figure 4.4). The number of children peaks eighteen to twenty-three years into the marriage union, when all seven children are living at home. Thereafter, children begin to leave home and marry, and the number of children living at home declines over the next twenty years of marriage. The jaggedness in the line showing the number of household children across the marriage union reflects the discreteness of births and departures of children. The actual composition of the eighteen nuclear families included in the time-allocation study is also plotted on the figure and corresponds closely to the typical family.[9]

Maya parents have sustained high fertility, raising an average of seven children, and have done so through at least several generations of concomitantly very low child mortality. This is a remarkable demographic situation, and one that is not transparent from national aggregate data, which indicate that Mexico is well into the modern demographic transition. Nor are national data likely to reflect fertility trends in many small rural communities worldwide.

— 5 —

Sampling the Population

During the initial demographic survey, participants were asked a number of economic questions to get a sense of how people spent their time in order to design the time-allocation study. One of the questions they were asked was "How much time do you spend working in the fields?" Several weeks after starting the interviews, I noticed that the response on the women's forms was always the same: no time. Yet every morning I saw women leaving for the fields outside town. The time-allocation study would later find that women, though they spend less time working in the fields then men, allocate considerable time to field work. This discrepancy suggests that by cultural norm women did not think of themselves as field workers. If the analysis that follows in subsequent chapters had been based on interview data rather than direct observation, it would have revealed very different pictures of women's time budgets.

Many of the time-allocation studies concerning children are based on interviews in which participants, or their parents, are asked how they spent their time over the last month, week, or day. These recall interviews are contingent on participants accurately remembering their previous activities and on the interviewees answering the question that the interviewer thinks he or she is asking—a problem exacerbated when negotiating differences in language and cultural practice. For example, late one afternoon toward the end of my fieldwork, while I was recording scan samples, a mother turned to me—a nursing baby in one arm and tending the fire with the other—and said, "I've finished working for the day. You can go home if you want to." The water she was fanning the fire to heat was to bathe her three youngest children. She still had to prepare the evening meal of beans and tortillas and settle her six children for the night. Yet from her point of view the workday was over. When I asked her if she did not consider bathing and feeding her children to be work, she gave me a puzzled look—a stark contrast to a response that might come from a working American mother at the end of her day job.

This example illustrates that what is considered to be work may differ widely across cultures and among individuals. Recall methods—either through interviews or self-reported in dairies—can be problematic in having to account not only for memory error but also for individual variation in what participants report. If, for instance, you ask a child how much time he spent in school last week, will he include the time spent walking to school, the time spent doing homework, or the time spent at lunch or recess? More importantly, would all children answer the question in the same way? One method of bridging this gulf between what people do and what they think they do is direct observation (Betzig and Turke 1986; Draper 1976; Johnson 1978). Initially developed to record primate behavior (Altmann 1974), direct observation methods do not depend on having to reconstruct a participant's time use from recall. Rather, the observer documents the actions of the participant while in his or her company. This does not mean that the observer does not have his or her own set of perceptions in interpreting an individual's actions. Direct observation does not eliminate researcher bias, but it has the advantage of minimizing the number of participant filters for which a researcher has to account. Because the objective here is to compare time budgets across age, it was important to minimize introducing individual reporting differences as a source of variation.

In her thorough study on children's work among Zimbabwe agriculturalists, Reynolds (1991) tested the reliability of different time-allocation methods by comparing individual time-budget profiles that she had recorded using both recall and direct observation methods. Reynolds found a number of surprising and consistent differences. Compared with direct observation methods, children's self-reports of their activities tend to underestimate leisure and work activities, especially repetitive tasks, and overemphasize self-care activities. Borgerhoff Mulder and Caro (1985) caution that self-reported time budgets may be especially inaccurate for groups such as the Maya, who do not have timekeeping devices.

Although documenting individual activity budgets by direct observation has many positive aspects, it has the downside of being far more time consuming for the researcher than recall interview methods. Direct observation also requires that the anthropologist accompanies participants through their daily activities, which in some populations may not be feasible. Both recall and direct observation have their advantages and their disadvantages. Because my research question is about variability in how people spend time, I used direct observation methods for their accuracy and for their compatibility with a number of other extant time-allocation studies.

Of the fifty-five village households, nineteen were selected and agreed to participate in the time-allocation study. This sample includes 133 individuals and represents 42 percent of the village population. Participating households were chosen to satisfy two levels of stratification that reflect family maturation: (1) number of children and (2) age of children. Focal households include families with none up to eight children and households with only young children, only older children, and a range of children's ages. Data collection was designed to capture both how much time one spends performing a task and how efficient one is at that task by having the focal households participate in scan-sample and focal-follow observations.

Recording Scan-Sample Observations

Standard scan-sampling techniques were used to compile a database on the time Maya children and adults allocate to food production, domestic activities, child care, and leisure (Altmann 1974; Borgerhoff Mulder and Caro 1985; Gross 1984; Hames 1992; Hawkes et al. 1987; Johnson 1975; Johnson and Behrens 1989). During a scan sample, an individual is located at a specified time interval, and the observer instantaneously records what the participant was doing. This is an ideal method for collecting a large sample of behavioral data on multiple individuals. After repetitive observations, an accurate estimate can then be made about the proportion of time an individual spends in various activities (Dunbar 1976; Simpson and Simpson 1977). For example, if a mother's activity is recorded over one hundred scan observations, and during ten of those she is making tortillas, we can estimate that 10 percent of her time is spent making tortillas.

While many aspects of time-allocation procedures have been standardized, some flexibility is necessary to accommodate the ethnographic specifics of a study population. In some situations (in a classroom, for example), it is possible to randomly select a different individual from the pool of participants every ten or fifteen minutes throughout the day. It very quickly became clear that this was not possible in Xculoc for a number of reasons. The village is spread out, and people perform different daily activities in different village locations—inside their house, in their compound, at the *molino* or village *tienda*, in the plaza, as well as in the milpas, which are separated from the village by a half-hour walk. The search time to locate dozens of different individuals every day would have severely limited the number of scan samples I could have recorded and would have required disturbing the same family perhaps several times a day to inquire where the target individual was.

Although some activities take place outside in the *solar* yard, the Maya live in compounds that are surrounded by walls and in houses that are walled. To gain permission to enter a household compound, local etiquette dictates that you stand outside the compound wall and wait for a family member to invite you in. It is not possible to unobtrusively observe what someone is doing if he or she is inside the house, and the disruption of waiting to be let in would defeat the purpose of making an instantaneous observation of what the person is doing. To effectively collect an instantaneous observation, it is necessary that the recorder already be in the compound and that family members be going about their normal activities. In keeping with the village custom that women do not move about the village alone, it was more comfortable to be situated where a number of family members were present at any given time. This was of greater concern early in project, when I was establishing my field methods, than after I had lived in the village for some time. Given these considerations, the members of two or three households were sampled each day.

Households were sampled to ensure that a representative temporal cross-section was collected for each participant. Every attempt was made to equally sample all times of the day, days of the week, and seasons of the year in order to account for variation in how people spent their time across hours of the day, days of the week, and across the agricultural cycle. Further, for analytic purposes it is important to have a nearly equivalent number of observations per person, and every effort was made to ensure that individuals were sampled an equal number of times.

A household was sampled biweekly for an observation session of three to four hours. The observation day was limited to daylight hours, from seven in the morning to six at night. During an observation session, each family member's activity was recorded every fifteen minutes. Using this method, over 18,500 scan observations were collected for 133 individuals. Eight variables were coded for each observation. These include the person's identification number, the date, time (hour and minute), activity, object of the activity, activity weight, the location of the activity, and the presence or absence of the individual (Appendix Table 5.1). These variables are explained in Appendix C.

During an observation session, each of these variables was recorded onto coding sheets; each evening the data were entered into a database using a solar-powered computer. This was the best situational compromise between maintaining both consistency and flexibility. Coding sheets provide a format so that the recorder is prompted to systematically make an entry for each variable, yet the recorder can easily correct mistakes and jot down sundry narrative observations. Although I did have a handheld data recorder, I found that scrolling through the database and menus to make adjustments and corrections was cumbersome and would pull my focus away from the situation. Data recorders also distracted participants from what they were doing and drew unnecessary attention to the process of data recording. However, entering the day's data into a computer database each night was invaluable in catching coding problems and inconsistencies early on rather than discovering them sometime later, when the circumstances of the day had become blurred with other days.

Recording Focal-Follow Observations

Focal follows augment the scan samples by documenting a continuous sequence of an individual's activities. Scan observations are made at fifteen-minute intervals, but during a focal follow, an individual is continuously observed, and each change in activity is recorded with a start and stop time. One to several focal follows were recorded during a household scan session. The same variables and activity codes were used to record both scan observations and the focal follows (Appendix Table 5.2). Variables coded include the activity, the start and stop times, the activity's object, activity weight, location, and location identification (see Appendix C for description). If an activity was being monitored for a return rate, a measure of an individual's efficiency at a particular task—such as the number of meters planted or number of kilos ground per unit time—was recorded.

The duration of a focal-follow session varied, depending on the kind of activity in which the individual was involved. For example, young children's return rates can wildly fluctuate within a focal-follow observation session. A seven-year-old may intently harvest maize from a few plants, then stop to throw dirt clots at birds for a few minutes, then return to the task, and stop again a few minutes later. Adults, on the other hand, work more steadily and, reflecting this, have more consistent return rates. Especially when collecting return rates for young children, it is important that the duration of the focal follow is sufficiently long to encompass these fluctuations in productivity. A return rate estimated from a sample that includes only the few minutes during which a child exerts concerted effort would look very different from a half-hour sample that includes the time he or she also spent playing.

Focal follows can be used to retrieve a number of different kinds of information, including return rates, the duration and periodicity of activities, the exchange of resources, cooperation among individuals, and food consumption. Focal follows were collected for this study primarily to obtain return rates for task productivity. Consequently, selecting individuals to participate in a focal follow on any given day was guided by the opportunity to collect return rates. Individuals other than those who were part of the time-allocation sample were occasionally included in focal follows to record field work return rates.

Household Production and Individuals

Throughout this book, I refer to parents, families, households, and children as part of household production, which needs some clarification. Since natural selection operates on individuals, sharing, helping, and cooperation present a conundrum. The development of inclusive fitness theory (Alexander 1974; Hamilton 1964; Trivers 1974) has made considerable gains in explaining why the human and animal world is replete with examples of what appear to be cooperation. In human behavioral studies, much of this interest came out of the recognition that hunter-gatherers share food across groups composed of variously related and sometimes unrelated individuals, a behavior uncommon in nonhuman primates despite the fact that they live in social groups. This research has illuminated much about cooperation, conflict, and the nature of labor.

In subsistence economies, reallocations from net producers to net consumers generally take place within kin groups, which can vary, depending on family system, from large extended networks to the nuclear family. Social organization affects the distribution of the costs of reproduction through inheritance rules and interhousehold and intergenerational relationships (Davis 1955; overview in Das Gupta 1997). The role that extended kin take in distributing the cost of child-bearing and absorbing the cost to parents has been well documented among some groups of hunter-gatherers and horticulturalists (Draper 1989; Draper and Harpending 1987; Hames 1988; Hawkes et al. 1998; Turke 1988, 1989). In contrast to these extended kin systems are self-supporting nuclear families, where parents are the primary caretakers.

From one point of view, the nuclear family can be seen as the least costly social unit across which production and consumption exchanges are made and child-rearing costs are shared because it minimizes the maintenance of complex social obligations and of customs or institutions to monitor both sharing and cheating. On the other hand, small economic groups and male/female pair-bonds can be risky in the event of resource or labor shortfalls as well as other reasons. The costs and benefits of forming aggregate or disaggregate economic groups, extended or nuclear families, depend on, among other variables, subsistence ecology, land tenure, seasonal periodicity in labor demands, the social distribution of status and wealth accumulation, and relationship with the national economy.

Among the Xculoc Maya, the commensal group—usually the nuclear family—is the social unit across which production and consumption exchanges are made and the economic unit across which child-rearing costs are shared. The nuclear family is a successful economic and reproductive structure for today's Maya. But as economic conditions change, as they have in the past and are likely to in the near future, so do resource competition, how wealth is brokered, the role of fathers, of grandmothers, and household and labor organization. The formation of economic groups across which the cost of children is distributed might best be pictured not as culturally immutable or historically developing in a linear fashion but as transient and, perhaps, even frequently fluctuating in response to changing conditions.

How family labor gets organized is an interesting question. Inclusive fitness? Parents acting as managers? Because an individual has difficulty providing food and shelter for himself if he does not cooperate? As such, family labor is a classic collective-action problem because if resources and labor are pooled and shared an opportunity exists for some family members to not carry their weight, or to cheat (Hawkes 1992). In both the economic and the behavioral ecology literature, a long-standing debate considers whether a household represents a cooperative altruistic unit or one in which there is economic conflict, and whether the individual acts in self-interest or altruistically for the benefit of the household (Folbre 1986). The decisions of individual household members to contribute to work or not, and how individual variation in the reciprocation of benefits is construed in game theory or collective-action problems, are not addressed here. Although the household is analyzed as an economic unit, this does not mean that asymmetries in male and female reproductive agendas do not exist or that individual and household interests are isomorphic.

How Maya Children Spend Their Time

To pursue the question of whether helpers really help, the first analytic step addresses how Maya children spend their time—in what kinds of activities do Maya children participate, and what is the age and sex patterning of the time they allocate to productive tasks. This chapter serves as a descriptive introduction to the economic lives of Maya children and places them comparatively in the context of other time-allocation studies.

The Sample of Maya Children

Seventy-three children, defined here as unmarried offspring living in their parents' households, living in sixteen households, participated in the time-allocation observations. A subset of fifty-nine children was included in most of the following analyses. Babies, ages birth to 2 (there were eleven), were eliminated since children do not begin spending time in economic activities until they are 3 years old. A very few unmarried, nulliparous males (one) and females (two) over the age of 30 live in their parents' households. These older individuals work less than their younger siblings and appear to curtail their participation in household economics, neither investing in their siblings nor supporting children of their own. A number of unmarried males in their early twenties live in their parents' households and continue to work at levels comparable to their siblings and, where noted, are included in some analyses. No unmarried females 21 to 30 live in their natal household. Unless otherwise stated, time budgets are drawn from a sample of over nine thousand scan observations for fifty-nine individuals—twenty-six males ages 3 to 23 and thirty-three females ages 3 to 20.

Directional trends in the proportion of time that male and female children spend in field work, domestic work, child care, and total work are summarized in distributional graphs and compared using sample means. In analyses of variance, two mathematical adjustments are made to the proportional data to account for the potentially skewed distribution of variance and the unbalanced sample size of males and females. These adjustments are described in Appendix D. Unless otherwise indicated, the proportion of time spent in a task is tabulated as the sum of observations for that task divided by the total number of observations for an individual. When reading the values presented in the tables, it is important to keep in mind that the percentages, proportions, and hours represent the time spent in a task during an eleven-hour observation day, not over a twenty-four-hour period, and thus may be conservative estimates of the total time allocated to work. Assuming that people rest or sleep eight hours a day, this leaves five unaccounted-for evening hours, from six to eleven. The bulk of the workday occurs during daylight hours, for the same reasons that my observation day was restricted to the eleven daylight hours, although no doubt some of the unaccounted-for evening hours were spent in food preparation and in child care. The proportion of time allocated to a task can be converted into hours or minutes by multiplying the proportion by eleven observation hours, or 660 minutes.

Age and Sex Patterning in Maya Children's Time Allocation

Field Work

Field and garden work involve ground preparation, planting, crop maintenance, weeding, and harvesting. Related tasks include processing seed for planting, transporting goods between the village and milpas, checking on the condition of crops, hunting, and trapping vermin. (Agricultural tasks requirements were described in Chapter 2 and the agricultural cycle in Chapter 3.)

Since the introduction of fertilizers in the early-1990s and the shift to shorter fallow periods, new forest plots are less frequently prepared as the annual reuse of cultivated plots becomes more common. This recent shift in agricultural practices has precipitated a change in the extent to which children are involved in field work, especially during the spring, when plots are weeded and burned in preparation for planting. Children of all ages presently help in ground-preparation, and boys especially are eager to take part in field burning. Only fathers and adult sons plant, although younger children may assist by moving the string lines that are used to maintain straight rows. Weeding is often a household activity in which men, women, and children assist. Maize is stored on the stalk throughout the winter and is harvested several times a week as household needs require. Boys and girls often assist in harvesting maize and other crops. Maize is continuously transported from the fields to the village, and a child rarely returns empty-handed to the village.

Certain field tasks, such as planting, that have a scheduling constraint tend to occur at the exclusion of other subsistence tasks. Planting maize is closely regulated by rainfall patterns, and once the rains begin, crops must be planted over a short period of time. Other subsistence tasks are often delayed during planting because of its relative urgency. In contrast, the scheduling of field preparation, weeding, burning, and felling the forest is flexible, occurs over a several-month period, and is incorporated into the pursuit of other subsistence tasks.

Mothers' and children's schedules are less regulated by the agricultural cycle, since certain domestic tasks—such as chopping wood, hauling water, washing, and child care—occur daily, regardless of agricultural demands. I had anticipated that school-age children's participation in field activities, or at home, would be regulated to some extent by the school schedule. However, because classes were infrequently held, school rarely interfered with children's work activities.

A household spends an average of 6.9 person hours a day in field work, with the most time spent weeding and harvesting (Appendix Table 6.1). Field work is sex and age graded to some extent, such that boys spend more time in field work than do girls, children older than 11 work more than younger children, and males 15 and older spend the most time in the fields (Appendix Table 6.2). When children of all ages are considered, males allocate 13 percent of their time to field work, and girls 7 percent. The differences between male and female children's field-work effort are greatest for weeding and planting, whereas harvesting is not as strongly sex patterned.

The inflection in the time that male and female children allocate to field work occurs at about age 10, which is also the age at which male and female efforts diverge (Figure 6.1). Girls lag behind boys in the age at which they start to spend considerably more time in field work.

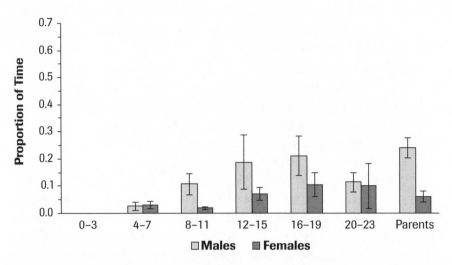

Figure 6.1   Proportion of time that Maya male and female children and parents allocate to field work over an eleven-hour observation day, showing mean values and standard errors.

Boys begin to increase their time spent in the fields after the ages of 8 to 11, which is when young girls devote much of their time to child care. Both boys and girls increase their field-work effort to about age 15, when work effort reaches a plateau. Individual variance is notable, as some children, regardless of their age, contribute little or nothing to field work. This probably is related to differences in age composition from household to household and whether a child has older brothers and sisters to help out.

Males spend more time in field work than females across all ages, though this difference is not significant when all ages are grouped (r^2 = .0365, p =.1489). The only significant difference between males and females is in the 16 to 19 age group (Appendix Table 6.3). Both males and females in this age group allocate more time to field work than does any other age group of children, but males spend almost twice as much time as females. The decrease in field work by unmarried males ages 20 to 23 likely reflects a reallocation of work effort to wage labor, which doubles in this age group.

Females 16 and older contribute as much time to field work as any age class of mothers, except for women over the age of 60, who allocate 20 percent of their time to field work. Note, though, that the sample of elderly women is very small. Mothers allocate between 0 percent (21- to 30-year-olds) and 11 percent (41- to 50-year-olds) of their time to field work. Mothers with no young children (0 to 6) living at home spend more than twice as much time in field work than do nursing mothers and mothers with young children. Males 16 to 23 contribute more time than fathers 20 to 40, who allocate between 8 percent and 18 percent of their time to field work, but much less than fathers over the age of 40, who spend 20 percent to 49 percent of their time in field work.

Domestic Work

Domestic activities include food processing, food preparation, collecting water and firewood, running errands, tending domesticated animals, sewing, washing, and cleaning. Except for cutting firewood, domestic tasks occur in the village, although not necessarily within the household *solar,* or compound, itself. Food processing and preparation, washing, cleaning, and sewing occur daily, while other tasks, such as water and wood collection, are scheduled intermittently throughout the week. A household spends a mean of 16.7 person hours a day in various domestic tasks (Appendix Table 6.4).

Young children assist in some aspects of maize processing, which is a lengthy and multitasked procedure, whereas other tasks are performed only by older children and adults. Shelling maize is often a social activity, and although teenagers and adults are principally responsible for this task, young children help out, doing what they can. After the maize is shelled, it is then heated, soaked overnight in lime water, and rinsed in various stages (Figure 6.2). The softened maize is then either ground by hand or carried to the *molino,* a gas-powered mill, to be ground. Households consume an average of 5.7 kilos of ground maize a day, most of which is for human consumption. Pigs, goats, ducks, chickens and turkeys, dogs, and cats are largely left to scavenge, although children occasionally feed fowl and pigs processed maize.

Although the bulk of their calories comes from maize, the Maya have a rich culinary tradition that includes many herbs, spices, fruits, vegetables, wild game, and domestic animals. Each of these foods is prepared in different ways, and a household spends more than two hours a day in a variety of food-preparation activities. Food may be cleaned, peeled,

Figure 6.2   Maya girl rinsing maize.

shucked, mashed, strained, pounded, crushed, chopped, cut, mixed, sorted (17 percent of all food-preparation observations), or butchered (5 percent). These tasks are accomplished with a machete, a low wood stool or table, gourds, and perhaps a wire mesh or an occasional plastic implement. Food may be cooked, roasted, seared, dried, or heated (24 percent of all food-preparation observations) and served to others (8 percent).

The process of making and cooking tortillas, the mainstay of the midday and evening meals, contributes to the majority of food-preparation observations (46 percent). Tortillas are cooked over a fire on a comal, traditionally made of ceramic, but now the Maya use the top of a 50 gallon oil drum. When the tortilla balloons, it is taken off the comal and slapped to deflate, a sound palpably synonymous with Xculoc at midday. Maize is also prepared in numerous other ways. *Posole*, a partially cooked and ground cornmeal, is prepared maize in its simplest form.[1] *Posole* is a portable snack that is often wrapped in a cloth and carried into the fields or forest, where the meal is mixed with water in a gourd and eaten by taking a lick of salt, a gulp, and an impressive bite of habanero chili. Atole is a cornmeal gruel, cooked either with salt or, occasionally, honey.

Young girls contribute very little time to food preparation but increase the time they spend helping their mothers from 12 years old throughout their teens (Appendix Table 6.5). Boys rarely help. Unlike in many other domestic tasks, mothers allocate much more time to food preparation than do daughters at any age.

Even though young children have a great deal of liberty to go where they please, much of their time is spent running errands. They deliver and receive messages, borrow and return things, and may go several times a day to the small *tiendas*, or stores, in town to purchase an egg, a candle, or a bag of cooking oil. Young children are the runners for the exchange of prepared food that occurs at midday. (As noted previously, mothers give children a small bowl of the family's midday meal to deliver to various relatives, who receive the food and refill the bowl with something from their own pot.)

A household consumes an average of 150 liters of water a day, which is used to cook, drink, bathe, wash clothes and dishes, and rinse the lime out of the brine in which raw maize is soaked. When the gas-powered water pump is working, women haul water from communal spigots to their *solars*. The water pump is usually run two to three times a week, and when water is available, women stop whatever else they are doing to haul water. Although they vary in size, all *solars* have a cistern of some kind, often a 50 gallon oil drum, in which the water is stored until the pump is run again a few days later. A household spends a mean of 1.0 person hours a day, or 2.0 to 3.0 hours several times a week, in water collection.

Figure 6.3 Maya girls preparing food.

All capable females usually help haul water, though if a mother has teenage daughters, the mother may not participate. This is one of the only occasions when young women move about the village unaccompanied, and young men and women have the opportunity to greet each other. Before they leave their *solar* to haul water, teenage girls often bathe, put on a clean dress and whatever gold jewelry they may have, and carefully plait their hair. This rare opportunity to interact with young men may contribute to the age patterning in water collection and that older girls spend considerably more time hauling water than most of their mothers (Appendix Table 6.5). Males very rarely help in this task.

The red dirt out of which Xculoc is built wreaks havoc on children's appearance. Children are bathed daily, and women can spend several hours a day washing clothes. Households allocate a mean of 2.9 person hours a day hand-washing clothes, an activity that females alone perform. Washing is a rigorous task that involves carrying and lifting buckets, scrubbing, wringing clothes in a hollowed log or cement trough, hanging clothes in trees or on lines, and discarding water (Figure 6.4). Women in a household often alternate days on which they are responsible for the household washing. Girls under the

Figure 6.4 Maya woman washing clothes.

age of 12 seldom help but, once they start, quickly reach adult levels of the time allocated to the task (Appendix Table 6.5).

Girls and mothers spend many late afternoon hours sewing and embroidering (Figure 6.5). A necessary and productive task, sewing is often a social activity as well, accompanied by conversation and good humor. Although young girls may wear ready-made clothing, all post-pubescent females wear traditional huipils—white dresses elaborately embroidered at the yoke and hem—and take great care and pride in their handiwork. In larger villages elsewhere in the Yucatan, although many women do wear traditional huipils, ready-made clothing is much more common. Xculoc males of all ages wear manufactured clothing. Women spend time mending men's clothing but do not make their shirts or trousers by hand.

A household spends a mean of 2.4 person hours daily in sewing activities. Girls under the age of 9 spend very little time sewing but begin learning soon thereafter (Appendix Table 6.5). The time that female children allocate to sewing increases after the age of 10. Mothers and teenage girls spend 7 percent to 11 percent of their time making clothes for themselves and their younger sisters. When asked, women say that weaving a hammock takes a hardworking week to

Figure 6.5   Maya girls embroidering huipils.

complete (men report that it takes much less time). Some villagers said that women still weave hammocks, although I never saw women engaged in this activity.

Every several days, groups of two or more women and teenage girls, often from related households, make a trip to the forest to cut fire-wood. Wood is plentiful around the village, although women will occasionally walk long distances into the forest to plots that have recently been felled for new fields, where they cut already-downed limbs into manageable pieces. Husbands rarely help, although boys may sometimes assist their sisters and mothers in cutting firewood.

The time that male and female children spend daily in these various domestic tasks is summarized in Appendix Table 6.6, and the time that girls under and over the age of 10 spend in these tasks in Appendix Table 6.7. Domestic work is markedly sex patterned (Figure 6.6). When children of all ages are pooled, girls spend 30 percent of their time in domestic activities, boys 6 percent. Females spend more time in domestic work than males in all age groups. Although young boys allocate some time to domestic work, a sex effect is established by the time children are 4 to 7 years old (Appendix Table 6.8).

By the age of 3, all girls spend some time in domestic chores. Girls'

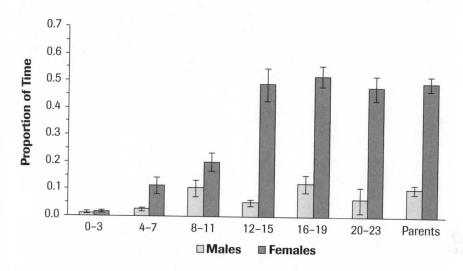

Figure 6.6 Proportion of time that Maya male and female children and parents allocate to domestic work over an eleven-hour observation day, showing mean values and standard errors.

work increases sharply between the ages of 4 and 15—doubling between ages 7 and 11 and again between ages 11 and 15. After the age of 15, girls reach a plateau at adult levels of domestic work effort (Appendix Table 6.9). Female children 12 and older spend between 49 percent and 52 percent of their time in domestic work, which is comparable to the time their mothers spend. Mothers between the ages of 20 and 60 spend between 44 percent and 60 percent, with a mean of 49 percent, of their time allocated to domestic tasks.

Boys' domestic work is much more variable with respect to age than girls'. Age and a quadratic term for age alone account for 82 percent (r^2 = .8253, p = .0001) of the variation in girls' domestic work, but only 23% (r^2 = .2312, p = .0555) in males' domestic work. Some males, regardless of age, contribute nothing or very little to domestic work, while an age effect is apparent for other males across the sample.

Child Care

Babies are in the perpetual care of someone until they can walk. When babies are not being carried or held, they are put in hammocks, which are ideal confinements, safe and cool, for young children. Parents and

Figure 6.7 Young girls with their siblings.

older siblings take great pleasure in young children, who when awake are constantly played with and shown affection. From a very young age, both male and female children are seen with their younger siblings in tow, carrying them, leading them by the hand, taking them on errands, and swinging them in hammocks (Figure 6.7).

A household spends a mean of 4.4 person hours per day in child-care activities (Appendix Table 6.10). *Direct care* includes nursing, feeding, bathing, dressing, delousing, grooming, and comforting a child. *Active indirect care* includes holding, carrying, playing, or walking with a baby. Both children and parents spend considerable time lying in hammocks entertaining or watching babies and young children, which is classified as *passive indirect care*. *Instruction* includes giving a directive or reprimand and explaining, reading to, teaching, or talking to a baby or young child. *Playing while in charge* refers to the common situation where a young child has been asked to watch his younger sibling, whom he takes outside and watches out of the corner of his eye while he continues to play. This is different from active indirect care in that

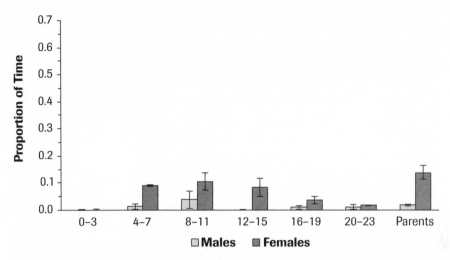

Figure 6.8   Proportion of time that Maya male and female children and parents allocate to child care over an eleven-hour observation day, showing mean values and standard errors.

the child being watched is not being played with. The percent of time that children and parents spend in these tasks is shown in Appendix Table 6.11. Of all child-care, children fund 49 percent and parents 51 percent.

Because child care is frequently embedded in other activities, its classification often can be ambiguous. A six-year-old may be taking care of his two-year-old sister, but he also may carry her next door to borrow something for his mother. Though child care has been traditionally underreported, it can also easily become a catch-all category. No unequivocal guidelines arbitrate what is child care, but consistently following some systematic criteria is important. In this case, child care was recorded as such only when it was a child's or parent's primary responsibility.

The time that children allocate to child care is nonmonotonically distributed across age. Quite young children regularly care for their younger siblings, increasing the time allocated between the ages of 4 and 11 and spending the most time between the ages of 8 and 11. After age 11, the time they spend in child care diminishes (Figure 6.8). The age patterning of child care differs from that of other types of work in that it is younger, not older, children who allocate the most time to caring for their siblings. This age pattern of caretaking has been both anecdotally noted and formally documented (Flinn 1988:220; Hames 1988:246; Nag et al. 1978:294–96; Weisner 1987; Weisner and Gallimore 1977; Whiting 1983; Whiting and Edwards 1988).[2]

Child care is strongly sex patterned, with females in all age groups allocating more time than males (Appendix Table 6.12). The sex effect is significant from a young age. Males in most age groups spend 1 percent or less of their time in child care, compared with females, who spend between 4 percent and 11 percent of their time caring for their younger siblings, with girls age 7 to about 14 spending the most time. Males contribute minimally to child care, with two exceptions. One boy has a crippled brother who is often in his charge. Another boy is the eldest in his family and is in the unusual situation of having three younger brothers all under the age of 6 and no sisters. Postadolescents spend very little time caring for children, and differences between males and females in older age groups are not significant.

Total Work

Total work subsumes the subgroups of domestic work and field work previously discussed, as well as the time spent in nonsubsistence labor, hunting, beekeeping, and wage labor. Nonsubsistence labor includes tasks such as mandatory community labor or minding the *tienda* or *molino*. Beekeeping is a primary source of cash income, and men divert attention to this task when honey becomes available. Hunting and wage labor are pursued during lax times in the agricultural cycle.

With the exception of one fifteen-year-old, boys do not engage in wage labor until they are at least 16 years old. Of all males 16 and older, 37 percent never engaged in wage labor, while the other 63 percent do so intermittently. Unmarried males 16 and older spend a mean of 28 percent (range 5 percent to 62 percent) engaged in wage labor. Including wage labor in total work is likely to overrepresent the proportion of time that males allocate to work. To some extent, if a male was away from the village during a scan sample, he was recorded as working for wages if other family members knew where he was and what he was doing on that particular day. But because males leave the village for wage labor, I did not directly observe what an absentee male was actually doing while he was gone. When an individual is not directly observed, intermittent nonworking activities (such as taking a break, eating, and resting) will be underrecorded. If a young man was working in the fields, the half hour he spent resting would be recorded as such. As a case in point, the two young men who spent the most time in wage labor also have a high proportion of time spent in total work relative to other men their age. Although recording activities that are not directly observed presents certain problems, to not include wage labor as total work would underrepresent male work effort.

Child care is not included in the tally of total work for several reasons. Although direct child care can be clearly observed, many indirect forms of child care (holding a child, talking to a child, playing with a child) are recorded depending on the observer's discretion and what suite of activities are classified as child care. Further, personal differences in child-care preferences may be substantial. For instance, infants in some households are put in a hammock, which is used similarly to a crib or playpen, much more often than in other households where infants are constantly held. By including child care as total work, these personal preferences would affect marked individual differences in overall work effort. Different ethnographers treat this situation differently and, depending on whether their classifications are liberal or conservative, could substantially inflate or deflate total work effort. Many time-allocation studies eliminate child care from work categories for these reasons, not because child care is considered a nonproductive activity, but because it is difficult to measure. My solution to these vagaries was to record child care in sufficient detail so that it could be reclassified as necessary from analysis to analysis. As presented below, total work does not include child care, but the proportion of time spent working is additive, and the reader can readily add or delete various work elements from the proportional values presented in the tables.

A household spends a mean of 30.0 person hours per day working (Appendix Table 6.13). By the age of 3, children begin to help out and then incrementally increase the time they allocate to work through early childhood. The time spent working sharply increases when children are 10 to about 15 years old. Children reach adult levels of work effort in their early teens and mid-teens for females and males, respectively. Female children 12 to 21 allocate 55 percent to 62 percent of their time to total work, and mothers 53 percent to 59 percent of their

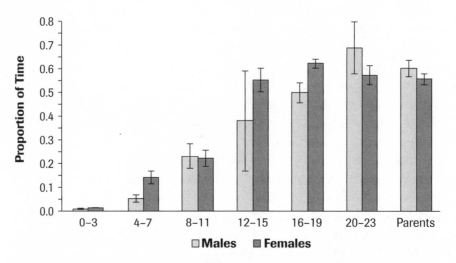

Figure 6.9 Proportion of time that Maya male and female children and parents allocate to total work over an eleven-hour observation day, showing mean values and standard errors.

time. Male children 12 to 23 allocate 38 percent to 69 percent of their time to work, and fathers 48 percent to 70 percent (Figure 6.9).

Age alone accounts for 90 percent and 85 percent of the variance in total work for females and males ages 3 to 23, respectively ($r^2 = .8972$, $p = .0001$; $r^2 = .8450$, $p = .0001$). Sex differences are much less pronounced for total work than any subgroups of work. When children of all ages are considered, females allocate 35 percent of their time to work, and males 33 percent (Appendix Table 6.14), but this difference is not significant ($r^2 = .0362$, $p = .1489$). Girls do, though, contribute more time to work at a younger age than do boys (Appendix Table 6.15). Girls between the ages 4 and 7 work more than twice as much as boys their age. Girls double their mean work effort across age groups until they are 15, when work effort plateaus. The sharp increase in female work effort between the ages of 8 and 15 is seen in the significant difference in time allocated to work between these age groups (Appendix Table 6.16). Males exhibit a similar pattern, although the rate of increase, or slope effect, is not as steep. Maya girls allocate 7 percent of their time to child care, compared to the 1 percent boys spend. If child care were included as total work, it would considerably boost the time girls spend working but have little effect on the boys' work effort.

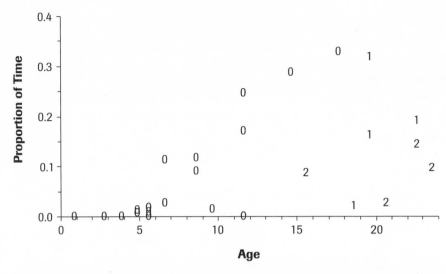

Figure 6.10 The proportion of time that Maya male children allocate to field work across age and wage labor status; plotting symbol indicates the ranked time that males allocate to wage labor: 0 = no participation in wage labor; 1 = 1–33% of an individual's total observations are spent in wage labor; 2 = 34–66% of an individual's observations are spent in wage labor.

Whether a family participates in wage labor has somewhat different effects on males and females. Unmarried males allocate less time to field work the more they participate in wage labor (Figure 6.10), but women who have a husband, son, or brother who participates in wage labor work about an hour more each day than women without a wage laborer living in their household. For families pursuing a mixed economic strategy of agriculture and some wage labor, unmarried males appear to substitute time spent in wage labor for time spent in field work, while females pick up the slack and increase their field-work effort.

Minge-Kalman (1978:189) noted in her time-allocation study among Swiss farmers that wives assume a greater portion of the agricultural work when husbands become wage laborers, and this appears to be the case among the Maya. Almost all of the food consumed in Xculoc is grown by villagers, and to maintain fields requires that someone continues to invest in field work regardless of whether men temporarily receive an influx of cash. Even if a husband or son works for wages for a week now and then and earns enough money to buy food for his family for a short period of time, agriculture requires an almost year-round labor investment to reap a harvest. Because the nature of agriculture is such that the payoff to work effort is considerably delayed, hour-for-hour field work and wage labor are not economic substitutes. Rather, wage labor appears to augment, not replace, field work.

This differs from the commonly noted situation where poor wage laborers maintain gardens because they cannot afford to buy all their food. Among the Xculoc Maya, all of the maize they consume is grown, as is the bulk of their other food. Wages are spent almost exclusively on nonfood items. The implication is that in the transition to a mixed economy, nonwage laborers, especially females and children, may work longer hours by spending time in tasks that absentee males would ordinarily do.

Maya children are never admonished for the two things that kids cannot help doing: making noise and getting dirty. Children are, though, asked to help out and are reminded or scolded for not doing what they are told. The Maya are exceptionally good humored and complain little about having to work, perhaps in part because repetitive daily tasks are often done in mixed-age groups and accompanied by storytelling and joking.

Children contribute to many aspects of work at a young age, helping earliest with child care and domestic chores. As they get older, children spend more time in the fields, contribute more to domestic work, and spend less time taking care of their siblings. Domestic work and child care are markedly sex patterned, with females allocating far more time to both chores. Females allocate somewhat more time to total work and less time to field work than males, although sex difference explains little of the variation for either field work or total work.

The extent to which age explains the variation in children's time allocation differs among various work activities. *Ordinary least squares* (OLS) is a useful statistical summary measure of the data's dispersion because coefficients of determination (r^2 values) are comparable across age and sex regression models for the different subclasses of work (Appendix Table 6.17). To complement the OLS, another estimate of dispersion appropriate to logistic regression models is summarized in Appendix Table 6.18 and compares the drop in deviance across a series of nested age and sex models. The method used to estimate the drop in deviance across models is explained in Appendix D. Results from both methods mark similar trends. While age explains a significant amount of the variation for all types of work, at any given age there is much less variation in the amount of time males and females allocate to total work than to domestic and field work. For example, a ten-year-old girl in one family may spend little time weeding because she has several older brothers who can work in the fields while she stays at home and helps her mother. Although she may spend less time in field work than other ten-year-old girls, her total work effort deviates little from that of other ten-year-old children. This scenario is played out differently depending on family composition, but it may aid in explaining why age accounts for much more of the variation when tasks are aggregated as total work.

Grouping all work also minimizes differences between males and females. Boys may spend more time in field work and girls more in domestic work, but little difference is seen in the overall proportion of time that they spend working. While the household sample would have to be very large, much larger than the village itself, to statistically include family composition as a source of variation in a formal model. Comparing work efforts across different classification levels suggests that family composition has an important effect on individual variation within age and sex groups.

– 7 –

Production and Consumption
across the Life Course

Human juvenility shares many characteristics with other primates—slow growth, long duration, high mortality. But human juveniles are anomalous in being fed by others through most, and quite often all, of their growth and development. Although subsidized by others, juveniles may also help out. For example, many economic and anthropological studies have found that agricultural children are hard workers (Cain 1977; Munroe et al. 1984; Minge-Kalman 1978; Nag et al. 1978; Odell 1986; Reynolds 1991; Sipas 1980; White 1973, 1975; Whiting and Whiting 1975). The Maya appear to be no exception. Maya children become economically active, participating in a variety of domestic and field activities, by the age of 6. After the age of 10, the time they spend working sharply increases, and by their mid to late teens, their work effort approaches that of their parents (Appendix Table 7.1).

But even though children may be hard workers, they do not necessarily produce more than they consume. As time-allocation studies among several groups of South American horticulturalists and foragers have found, although Piro, Machiguenga, and Ache children participate in food production, they do not become net producers—producing more than they consume—until their early twenties, remaining net consumers and depending on subsidies from others throughout their entire period of growth and development (Kaplan 1994, 1996, 1997). Thus, if hard-working children are not surplus producers, it raises the question at what age do children become independent of others as their main source of food and other necessities? To assess whether children's economic contributions actually offset constraints on parents' time, the time children allocate to work may be deceptive if not considered in tandem with their consumption.

Young children consume little and produce even less. As children mature, they consume more but also produce more. At some age, consumption plateaus, and production exceeds it. The timing of the transition from net consumption to net production shapes the age range of children dependent on others ends. Not only is the duration of children's dependence variable but so is the age at which children begin to reproduce and shift their economic effort into supporting their own children. If the span of time between when children become economically independent and when they are no longer available as keepers is variable across cultures, what conditions that variation is of interest because of its effect on the competing demands of parents having to support the disparate needs of both younger and older children and, ultimately, on the number of children parents can successfully raise.

In asking whether helpers really help, this second analytic step uses the time-allocation data to model the transition of Maya children from net consumers to net producers. The achievement of positive net production is then used as an empirical marker for the duration of juvenile dependence. The chapter concludes by comparing the Maya pattern of juvenile dependence to other food-production systems.

Measuring an Individual's Production and Consumption

Several concerns guide the choice of methods used to estimate an individual's production and consumption. First, I wanted to use a method that would add to the description of children's work presented in the previous chapter and that was comparable to work already done among several other groups of hunter-gatherers and horticulturalists. And second, to compare an individual's production relative to his or her consumption, both have to be expressed in a common currency. Although it is methodologically more straightforward to use money or calories to estimate an individual's production and consumption, neither is appropriate in the case of subsistence agriculturalists. The Maya participate only minimally in the cash economy and wage labor, and although wage labor does have monetary remittance, most men are employed only very intermittently, and women and children never engage in wage labor. Consequently, monetary earnings and expenditures would capture very little of either an individual's production or consumption. Also, few of the tasks that the Maya perform daily have a caloric output. Field activities such as planting, weeding, and maintaining crops have no readily measurable or standard caloric equivalency. Although harvesting has a clear caloric output, it is a seasonal activity. The many domestic activities—such as food processing, food preparation, hauling water, collecting firewood—that are necessary to get food from the field or forest onto the table and that women and children largely perform also have no measurable caloric output, or monetary equivalent, since their outputs—processed food, water, firewood—are not sold.

Although food may be one of the most important resources that an individual consumes, both children and adults consume much more than food in the way of resources and services. For example, some portion of the time that a mother spends washing clothes each day is consumed by her ten-year-old son. Likewise, he consumes some portion of the time that his sisters spend grinding maize, preparing food, hauling water, and mending clothes, the consumption of which is difficult to estimate in either caloric or monetary terms. Given these concerns, neither money nor calories adequately reflect work effort in the Maya case. Consequently, time was selected as the most suitable currency for measuring an individual's consumption and production.

That said, one of the methodological challenges of this research was developing how to accomplish this. A method had to be designed to convert the time-allocation data into a measure of production that is comparable across males and females of different ages and to convert consumption into time.

Two adjustments were made to the simple count of time so that work effort would be comparable across sex and age. The first adjustment accounts for the differential productivity, or efficiency, of females relative to males and of children relative to adults. If a mother and her thirteen-year-old daughter go into the forest to chop wood for an hour, they are likely to return having produced very different quantities of wood. For their work effort to be comparable, the discrepancy in their efficiency is accounted for by weighting the time spent in the task relative to the average productivity of a prime-age adult. The weights themselves are derived from return rates—amount produced per unit time, data collected during focal-follow observations. Seven domestic and field tasks (making tortillas, planting maize, harvesting maize, weeding, shelling maize, hauling water, and chopping wood) occurred frequently enough and by a wide enough age range of individuals to estimate the relative output of children and adults (Appendix Table 7.2). Productivity weights are calculated for age and sex groups and are expressed as the proportion of the adult mean. For example, the productivity weights for shelling maize are 0.4 for children under the age of 6, 0.64 for children 7 to 9, 0.75 for ten- to twelve-year-olds, and 1.0 for individuals over the age of 13.

Harvesting maize and chopping wood are the only activities with return-rate data for both males and females. On the basis of these measurements, the labor productivity of adult females is weighted at 84 percent that of adult males for tasks that require physical strength (Lee and Kramer 2002).[1] For tasks that do not require strength, such as food preparation, equal productivity weights are applied to males and females by age class. (These assumptions are reevaluated later in the chapter in a series of sensitivity tests.)

The second adjustment accounts for differences in the value of time (Becker 1981). If, for example, a child spends five hours a day rocking his baby brother in a hammock and his mother spends four hours a day chopping wood, a simple count of hours would lead to the conclusion that the child works more than the mother. Counting hour for hour that each spends in these very different tasks does not adequately reflect their relative work effort, and it is appropriate to weight an hour spent chopping wood differently than an hour spent in a hammock.

Work involves both a time and an energy investment. Some activities are more strenuous than others and require greater energetic or caloric expenditure. In economic terms, if two tasks take the same amount of time to perform but one task requires more energy, then its product is more highly valued at the margin than the product of another task. For this reason, tasks that are more calorically expensive are weighted more heavily than those that are less calorically expensive (Appendix Table 7.3). The scale of task-specific energetic expenditure (kcal/minute) is taken from experimental studies in which the rate of caloric expenditure was monitored while subjects performed a wide variety of domestic, agricultural, industrial, and recreational activities (Astrand 1971; Durnin and Passmore 1967; Montgomery and Johnson 1977; National Academy of Sciences 1989; Ulijaszek 1995). Based on these experiment data, the output of an hour of work is valued at (1 + .0019C) where C is the caloric cost of an hour of work spent in a particular activity, and .0019 is the price of a calorie relative to the value of an hour's work (Lee and Kramer 2002).

To convert consumption to time requires three sources of information: the social unit in which the output of production is shared, an individual's daily caloric requirements (data derived from an individual's weight, age, sex, and activity level), and the total production of the sharing unit (time spent working summed across the sharing unit). Among the Maya, the sharing unit is the household—in most cases, a nuclear family—whose members produce what they consume and consume the product of their labor. Exchanges of labor may occur across households from time to time, but no household is dependent on net transfers from nonhousehold members for support, nor are resources stored beyond subsistence needs or agricultural surpluses converted into individual monetary gains. The cash gained through wage labor is directed back to the family to purchase basic household necessities—cooking oil, candles, medicine. Consequently, it is assumed that household production and consumption balance over the long run.[2] The implications of this balancing assumption are that an individual household member may be a net producer or consumer and that the amount a household produces and consumes may change over the family life cycle, adjusting to demographic changes. But it assumes no long-term household saving, dissaving, or net interhousehold transfers. (See Chapter 3 for details on household composition and economics.)

Based on the observed time allocated to food-related activities, 80 percent of household production is related to food—the labor spent to cultivate food, process it, prepare and cook it, fetch wood and water, tend animals, maintain beehives, and hunt. The amount of that production that an individual household member consumes is estimated to be proportional to his or her daily caloric requirements.[3] If, for example, a household of five spends an average of 25.0 person hours a day working, 80 percent (20 hours) are estimated to be related to the production, processing, and preparation of food. If an eight-year-old girl's daily caloric requirement is 15 percent of the household's caloric requirements, she is estimated to consume 3.0 hours of household work that is related to food [$(25 \times .8) \times .15 = 3.0$]. The remaining 20 percent of household production (time spent washing, cleaning, sewing, building and maintaining structures, and the like) is allocated to its members on a per capita basis.[4] If the eight-year-old girl is one of five household members, she consumes an additional hour of work a day $[(25 \times .2) / 5 = 1.0]$ that is not related to food production. Her total consumption would then be 4.0 hours (Lee and Kramer 2002).

Although it cannot be known for certain how household production is allocated among its members, the method described above has the advantage of expanding the definition of consumption beyond food. By converting consumption to time, consumption could be defined more comprehensively to include the range of processing, preparation, and domestic production that an individual consumes. Including these activities as production, but excluding them as consumption, would underestimate an individual's consumption and, in doing so, bias net production to a younger age.[5]

Age at Net Production

Using the methods described above, a production and a consumption value is calculated for each individual in the sample. Production includes field work, domestic work, and wage labor—the same suite of tasks included as total work in Chapter 6.[6] The sample included 110 individuals, 47 males and 63 females, ages birth to 65. A spline smooth is fit to the individual data points to chart the average level of production and consumption by age and sex across the life course.[7] The age at which children achieve net production is given where the two functions intersect (Figure 7.1). The distance between the production and consumption curves gives the age-specific surplus production balance—either positive in the case of net producers or negative in the case of net consumers.

Consumption roughly quadruples between birth and age 12 and increases gradually thereafter. Girls spend more time working in their early adolescence than do boys and begin to produce more than they consume around age 15. This trend was seen in the time-allocation estimates in the previous chapter, where girls work about 15 percent more than boys during their teens. Boys begin to produce more than they consume somewhat later, about at age 16.5 (up to age 18.5, depending on smoothing procedure used; see endnote 7). After the age of net production, boys work about 5 hours a day and girls a little

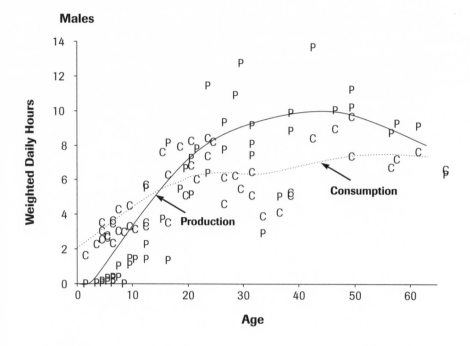

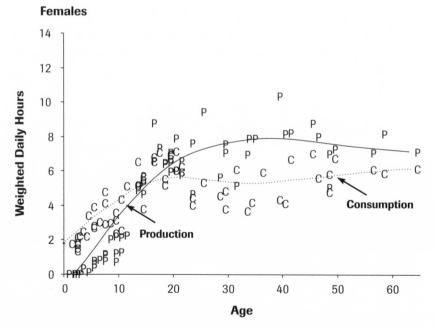

Figure 7.1 Production (dotted lines) and consumption (solid lines) across the life course of Maya males and females; hours weighted by productivity and energy expenditure.

more (unadjusted hours). Adults retain a positive production balance throughout their lives. Although males lag behind females in the time they spend working when they are younger, as adults both males and females work about 6.5 hours a day (unadjusted hours) in their 40s.

To evaluate how the relative efficiency and value of time assumptions discussed above affect the age at net production, the productivity and energy expenditure weights are added sequentially to the calculation of an individual's production and consumption in a series of sensitivity analyses (Appendix Table 7.4). When an individual's work effort is counted hour for hour with no adjustment made to age and sex differences in productivity or energy expenditure, (a), females become net producers at age 10, considerably younger than males, who achieve net production at age 19.

The hours that an individual spends working are then recalculated adding in the productivity weight, which is computed in several ways. In the first adjustment, (b), time is weighted for differences in adult and child productivity but only for those seven tasks for which empirical return rates were collected and weights calculable (weights are given in Appendix Table 7.2).[8] The time an individual spends in all other tasks is counted hour for hour. Since children are less efficient than adults, albeit variably from task to task, this adjustment raises the age at net production of girls to age 11 and of boys to age 18. In the next adjustment, (c), all time spent working is weighted by productivity, and males and females in each age class are weighted equally (1.0 for individuals over the age of 20, 0.8 for those 10 to 20, and 0.5 for children under the age of 10). Since the productivity weight is applied to all tasks, the age at net production further increases to age 13 for girls and decreases to age 17.5 for boys. Productivity is then weighted differentially for males and females for only those tasks that require physical strength, (d). All other tasks are age weighted as above. Under this assumption, the age at net production is 14 for girls and 17 for boys.

The energy expenditure weight is added to the productivity weight in the next two adjustments. When the productivity weight is applied only to those activities with observed return rates (as in b), and the time spent working is further weighted by individual differences in energy expenditure, (e), females reach net production in early adolescence, by the age of 12, and males a few years older, by age 17. These values have been reported in previous work (Kramer 2002; Kramer and Boone 2002). Here, I considered an additional adjustment. When the productivity weight is applied as described above for (d) and the energy expenditure weight folded in, (f), females reach net production at age 15 and males at age 16.5. This is considered the best estimate for children's age at net production because it minimizes unnecessarily undervaluing women's and children's economic activities by weighting only those tasks that are physically demanding.

Caveats and Directions for Future Research: Evaluating Wage Labor and Male and Female Work Effort

Each sequential adjustment in the sensitivity analyses narrows the gap between male and female age at net production. The difference between males and females diminishes because males spend more time in physically demanding tasks and are more efficient at those tasks. The decrease in male age at net production is greatest when the productivity weight is applied generally to work and less so when it is applied to only those tasks that are strength-dependent. Age differences in work effort are accounted for by the productivity weights, which are based on observed return rates. But the assumptions concerning the relative weighting of wage labor and of female work effort relative to male work effort deserve further examination.

There is no easy solution to assess the value of wage labor in a mixed-subsistence economy. The problem lies in determining whether an hour of wage labor is of greater, equal, or less value than an hour spent in some other kind of work. Assessing the value of wage labor relative to time spent in other tasks is relatively perfunctory in a market economy where crops are sold for profit and food is purchased. Because the Maya receive a salary for wage labor but not for field work, the actual benefit derived from an hour of field work compared with an hour spent in wage labor is ambiguous since they are not based on a common scale of remuneration.[9] In this analysis wage labor is not more highly valued than field work, as is often assumed, for a number of reasons.

Of the men in the sample age 16 and older, 63 percent engage in wage labor, but only on occasion, and the other 37 percent never did over the course of this study. Those men who spent some time as wage laborers tended to spend less time in field work the more time they spent working for wages (see Figure 6.10). But when the sample of men is disaggregated by wage-labor status, both groups—wage laborers and nonwage laborers—spend about the same amount of total time working. This is in keeping with what the Maya themselves have to say when asked to assess the value of wage labor compared with field work. In economic terms, the marginal value of participating in wage labor is more beneficial than spending an additional hour in field work at least some of the time or they would not engage in wage labor at all. In contrast, if the benefits afforded by wage labor outweighed those of field work, men would not engage in field work, and the community would have transitioned to a wage-labor economy and purchase, not grow, most of its food. While some men spend some time in wage labor, all adult males spend time growing food. All households in the village maintain a milpa, and the vast majority of the calories that a household consumes come from crop foods rather than from food purchased with wages. If, however, an hour spent in wage labor should be weighted more heavily, it might effect a decrease in the age of net production for males—albeit a slight one, since boys do not participate in wage labor prior to age 15.

Similarly, there is no easy solution or standard by which to weigh the relative value of male and female labor. Few tasks are performed by both Maya males and females, and many tasks are undertaken by only females. In contrast to the generally accepted use of wages in a market economy and foraging returns in hunter-gatherer economies, there is no conventional measure to weight the relative value of different agricultural and domestic tasks given our current understanding of the value of output. Since many tasks have no comparative measure of output, how do we weight the relative value of work that only men or women perform or only children or adults perform? How should an hour spent making tortillas compare to an hour spent planting maize? Both tasks are essential to food consumption and are performed exclusively by women and men, respectively. When energy expenditure is added, greater weight is given to strength-dependent tasks, to which males allocate more time. Thus, the amount of time men allocate to work will be somewhat inflated relative to women's allocation, all else being equal. While strength-based tasks are more energetically demanding, is this the only appropriate valuation?

I have argued that counting hour for hour does not adequately represent work effort and have used productivity and energy expenditure to adjust simple time values. Other, unidentified measurements may exist that crosscut male and female tasks. In a market labor economy, for example, investment in human capital (education, training) might be used to weight the relative value of different time allocations. But this is not applicable in the Maya case since children receive no formal training before they engage in subsistence activities. If new techniques are developed to assess the relative value of time, some adjustment in the methods presented here may be in order. As new research is carried out it may be fitting to incorporate more complex assumptions about the value of different tasks, but at this point, it would be spurious to adjust the data using more complex assumptions without supporting quantitative data and theoretic buttressing.

Several points are clear both from the analysis of net production and from the time spent working presented in Chapter 6. One, girls produce more and at a younger age than boys. If child care were included as work, this would further reinforce this difference. Two, females consume less than males. And three, when time is weighted by productivity and energy expenditure, it raises the value of male work relative to female work, narrowing the difference between male and female age at net production. The output of male and female labor could be valued slightly more, perhaps slightly less. There is a range of uncertainty. The sensitivity analyses, however, show that regardless of the weighting assumption, women become net producers at a younger age than males. And regardless of smoothing procedure, resolution, or the weighting assumptions made, both male children and female children become net producers several years prior to marrying and leaving their natal households.

Maya Children's Helping Behavior in Cross-Cultural Perspective

The corpus of the quantitative data on children's economic contributions among agriculturalists was collected in the 1970s as part of the research effort to resolve the debate about economic development, the demand for children as laborers, and the staggering population growth that was occurring in many agricultural-based economics. Although in many of these studies children's contributions are stated in terms of dollar amounts using aggregate national GNP data, out of this proliferation also came a number of important ethnographic case studies that presented the first time-allocation data on children's economic contributions among subsistence agriculturalists (Appendix Table 7.5).

Many of these studies find that children in subsistence agricultural economies contribute substantially to household production (Munroe et al. 1983, 1984; Nag et al. 1978; White 1975), although few report children's consumption. Those studies that do evaluate the net economic value of children tend to be for agriculturalists who, unlike the Maya, cash crop and are far more reliant on wage labor and the market economy. Results for these study populations are conflicting.

Cain (1977), in his seminal study in Bangladesh, combines both wage and nonwage labor as production but includes only food as consumption. This minimizes consumption relative to production, which overstates the economic value of boys (his analysis is restricted to males) and pushes the age at net production down. Cain did not have direct output measures of boys' productive activities and used age-specific wage rates as proxy weights. Other studies that include only wages earned as productive work find that children are a net cost to parents (Mueller 1976; Skoufias 1994; Stecklov 1999). Counting only the monetary earnings of children potentially underrepresents much of the domestic production in which children, and especially young children, participate in agricultural economies. It follows that these studies find a low relative value of children's economic contributions. Some studies use interview and census estimates for production and consumption or present only aggregate, not age-specific, estimates of children's production. A few studies are based on scan samples and time-allocation data (Johnson 1975; Minge-Kalman 1978; Reynolds 1991), but consumption data are not reported, or at least not in the same units of measure as production.

The wide range of estimates for children's economic value is not surprising given the social and economic diversity among the study populations. However, it remains unclear whether differences in subsistence ecology or data collection drive the reported differences in children's economic value across agriculturalists. The disparity in methods limits the possibilities for cross-cultural comparison on the issue of juvenile dependence. One exception is the production and consumption data for several groups of South American horticulturalists and foragers.

Kaplan (1994), who developed methods to calculate the relationship between production and consumption, found that among three South American groups (the Machiguenga, Piro, and Ache), children provide only 20 percent to 25 percent of their own caloric needs before the age of 18.[10] Children did not produce more than they consumed until early adulthood—ages 20, 21, and 21, respectively—after they already had children of their own.[11] This contrasts markedly with Maya children, who achieve net production during their teens and continue to reside in their natal households for a number of years after that before leaving home and beginning families of their own.

Subsequent analysis (Lee et al. 2002) makes it possible to more closely compare the Maya with two of the horticultural groups—the Piro and Machiguenga. Since the Maya data are in hours and the Piro and Machiguenga data in kilocalories, the production and consumption estimates of the three groups were standardized to glean comparable indices.[12] When males and females are disaggregated, the resulting male ages at net production are 21 for the Machiguenga, 20 for the Piro, and 16.5 for the Maya. For females, the age at net production is 25 to 35 for the Machiguenga, 19 for the Piro, and 15 for the Maya. Maya boys and girls stand out in terms of an earlier involvement in productive activities and their smaller negative production balance in childhood compared with the other groups. This is coupled with the relatively lower surplus production of Maya adults. The surplus production of older Piro and Machiguenga males is both notably higher than the surplus production of females in the same groups and much greater than the surplus production of Maya males. That is to say, the difference in surplus production between Maya male and female adults is much more modest. The low surplus production of Maya male adults is consistent with the higher net production of Maya women relative to other groups and with the relatively smaller deficits of Maya children.

The Maya production and consumption estimates include domestic work and the many food processing and preparation activities that women and children primarily perform, whereas the Piro and Machiguenga data do not. To look more closely at how this affects age at net production, the Maya production and consumption values are recalculated to include only those activities that are directly related to the production of food—field work, hunting, beekeeping, and tending animals.

When recalculated, Maya females never become net producers, and boys reach net production at age 13.5. At the adult maximum, when men and women are in their 40s and have the maximum number of dependents living at home, men spend about 4 hours a day, twice their consumption, in work directly related to food production. Women spend about 1.25 hours, just a little less than their consumption.

Several points can be made from these comparisons. In a subsistence economy that depends on foods that require processing and prepara-tion, and when it is women and children who largely perform these tasks (Ember 1983; Hawkes and O'Connell 1981), not including time spent in these tasks undervalues their economic contribution, and in the case of children, their potential role as helpers. For subsistence agricul-turalists, food processing and preparation, as well as many other domestic tasks, are not only critical to getting food to the table but also contribute to children's health and survival. To quote: "Labour is noto-riously difficult to measure. Women's labour, especially domestic, has been dubbed invisible because it is so hard to record. Children's labor is mercurial" (Reynolds 1991:41–42). The inclusion or omission of domestic production has its greatest implications when men's and women's or adult's and children's work are compared. If domestic work and food processing are taken seriously, Maya women and children make substantial contributions to total production. Children not only begin to pay for themselves in their teens but are producing surpluses that can be transferred to help parents meet the cost of younger chil-dren several years before they leave their natal home.

– 8 –

Children's Help from
a Parent's Perspective

Maya children spend a considerable portion of their time in productive activities and become net producers several years before they leave home. To assess the extent to which constraints on parents' time are actually offset by their children's help, this chapter addresses the question of whether helpers really help from the parents' perspective. While individual children may be hard workers, parents are in the position of managing all of their children's consumption demands and balancing time allocated to younger and older children. The question thus remains, how do parents economically experience their growing families and the competing demands on their time?

Much of the debate about the rationality of high fertility and whether children are an economic benefit or cost has been played out in the analytic framework of wealth flows and the net cost of childbearing (overview in Kaplan and Bock 2001). Wealth flows theory ties the demand for children to parental fertility in a specific way, from the point of view of a child's cumulative value, that is, the utility or economic return from an average child over some period of time—for example, up until they leave home or the age at which they repay their cumulative consumption. Wealth flows models, thus, assess the net cost of childbearing by measuring the transfer of resources, labor, or other utility across generations to evaluate whether parents invest more in their children than children pay back. This chapter first uses several methods to measure the net cost of childbearing and then considers whether this analytic framework adequately captures the cost of children from the parents' time budget perspective. I then suggest that children's production and consumption across the life cycle of the family is a more relevant assay for the utility that children provide in subsidizing their parents' continued fertility.

Wealth Flows and the Net Cost of Childbearing

Change in the demand for children has been key to much of the discussion about demographic transitions from high to low fertility (Becker 1960; Becker and Lewis 1973; Easterlin 1978; but see Boone and Kessler 1999; overview in Bongaarts 2002; Lee and Bulatao 1983; Szreter 1993). The net flow of wealth across generations has been linked theoretically to fertility rates such that if wealth increased as a function of the number of children, the demand for children should be high (Caldwell 1976, 1977). Although empirical tests question the often-made assumption that high fertility is economically beneficial to the family, Caldwell's wealth flows theory was important in bringing the family and household as a unit of analysis into the fore and in shifting the focus from children as consumers of wealth to children as producers of wealth.[1]

Cain's (1977) classic study of Bangladesh children is often cited as lending support to Caldwell's hypothesis that, in traditional societies, the net flow of wealth is upward from younger to older generations.[2] Yet subsequent empirical tests among high fertility, preindustrial populations found that, to the contrary, children are costly, and wealth flows downward from parents to children throughout childhood and often well into adulthood (Kaplan 1994; Lee 1994c, 2000; Lee and Kramer 2002; Mueller 1976; Stecklov 1999; Turke 1988, 1989). Using age-specific production and consumption, Kaplan (1994) tested Caldwell's hypothesis among three groups of high-fertility South American horticulturalists and foragers and found that, contrary to Caldwell's prediction, in all three groups the net direction of wealth flows was downward, from parents to children. In another assessment of the net economic asset of children, Lee (2000) reanalyzed Kaplan's data and Mueller's (1976) data for several groups of agriculturalists. Similar to Kaplan's results, Lee found a downward trending transfer of resources among all preindustrial populations.

Kaplan's and Lee's results provide a provocative comparison with the Maya on the question of wealth flows, since Maya children become net producers in their teens, at a much younger age than Kaplan's three study groups (see Chapter 7), and remain in their natal households for a number of years before they leave home and marry. Although the common-sense view that agriculturalists have many children because they are an economic benefit is deeply embedded in ideas about high fertility, children's economic contributions may look quite different from the perspective of a parent's compared with the child's. How, then, does the early age at net production play out in terms of Maya children's net cost?

Average Age of Consumption and Production

One vantage point to measure the net cost of childbearing is the average age of net production and consumption, which estimates the average age at which an hour of work is consumed relative to the average age at which an hour of work was produced (Lee 1994a, b, c, 2000; Willis 1988). When the average age of consuming is less than the average age of producing, the net direction of wealth transfers in a population is inferred to be from older to younger members.

The average age of producing is calculated for Maya males by multiplying an individual's observed production by his corresponding age, summing over all individuals, and dividing by the total production of the sample. The same calculation can be made for females and for the average age of consuming. The observed (not the smoothed) weighted production and consumption values used are those presented for total work, as seen in Figure 7.1. For Maya males, the difference between the average age of producing and the average age of consuming is 3.9 years; for females, 3.8 years (Appendix Table 8.1).[3] These results show that for both sexes the net direction of Maya transfers is downward from older to younger individuals, which is consistent with the general pattern of downward transfers in the agricultural and horticultural and forager populations as reported by Lee (2000:44). Lee found that the gap between the average age of producing and consuming was eleven years for Kaplan's South American data and six years for Mueller's (1976) data for agriculturalists from Egypt and India.[4] Variation in the magnitude of the downward transfers across the three groups and the relatively narrower margin between the average age of producing and consuming are not surprising given the young age at net production for Maya children (Lee and Kramer 2002).

Cumulative Net Production: The Payback Age for Maya Children

Cain (1977) was one of the first to calculate the net economic value of children to their parents using time-use data. Cain asked at what age a child had produced enough to pay back all of his consumption up to that age. Or, in other words, at what age does the cumulative value of a child's production minus his or her cumulative consumption equal zero? Using Cain's method (1977:222), I ask the same question: At what age do Maya children pay back their cumulative consumption? This payback age gives a comparative measure by which to assess the net cost of childbearing.

The age at which a child's cumulative production exceeds his cumulative consumption denotes the age at which Maya children pay back their lifetime consumption or dependence on others. Figure 8.1 plots the cumulative net production, or the sum of production minus the sum of consumption, up to each age for Maya males and females. For males the cumulative balance is still negative at age 22, which is the average age that males leave home and marry. Males do not fully offset their cumulative consumption until age 30, shown where the curve crosses 0. Females also have a negative balance at age 19, which is the average age at which they leave home and marry. They reach the payback point at age 31—a year later than males.[5]

The payback age for Maya children departs considerably from Cain's original finding that males had produced enough by the age of 15 to pay back their own consumption and their own as well as a sister's by

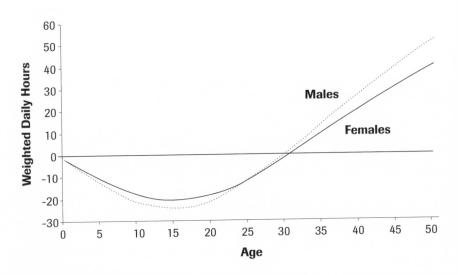

Figure 8.1 **Cumulative net production from birth for an individual Maya male and female.**

the age of 22 (assuming that his sister marries and leaves home by the age of 15).[6] Much of the difference between the Maya and the Bangladesh results is likely due to important modifications in what is included here as production and consumption and what Cain included as production and consumption.[7] For example, if a Bangladesh boy breaks even by the age of 15, it means that he has repaid the cost of his cumulative food consumption. But repayment of any other kind of consumption, such as clothing or medicine, would add to that age. Furthermore, food consumption in Cain's study includes only the cost of the field labor used to produce the food, not the time costs to process and prepare food, as does the Maya calculation; nor does Cain's calculation include the consumption of domestic production. The omission of processing and domestic costs from Cain's calculation of male children's consumption is likely to significantly underestimate the age at which a Bangladesh boy repays his cumulative consumption costs relative to the Maya estimate.

The widely held view that agriculturalists have many children because they are needed to work on the family farm is deeply entrenched in assumptions about high fertility. Wealth-flows models appeal to this common-sense view that agriculturalists have many children because they are economic assets. However, empirical tests repeatedly demonstrate that the net flow of wealth is downward from parents to children and the net cost of childbearing is negative. The Maya data confirm this. Both estimates of wealth flows—average age of consumption and production and cumulative net production—show that, even though Maya children are net producers in their teens, they are a net cost throughout the duration of time that they spend living in their natal household. Although children may be a net cost, it is worthwhile reconsidering what the net cost of childbearing actually measures.

The Net Cost of Childbearing: Relevance of a Concept?
One of the important implications of Chayanov's (1986 [1925]) insight that consumer demands and labor supply shift across the life cycle of the family is its relationship to parity-specific reproductive decisions. Comprehensive explanation of fertility variation is enigmatic, in part, because family size is the outcome not of a single event but of a long series of tradeoffs and decisions that parents negotiate

over the duration of their union. This is especially the case in noncontracepting, high-fertility populations, such as the Maya. While natural fertility populations cannot consistently achieve the low fertility of two or three children in contracepting populations, cross-cultural studies show considerable variation in the age at first birth, birth intervals, and family size (Bentley et al. 1993a, 1993b; Campbell and Wood 1988; Hewlett 1991; Sellen and Mace 1997; Wood 1994).

Across natural fertility populations, for example, birth intervals range between 20 months (Hutterites, a North American Anabaptist sect) and 36.5 months (!Kung). Total fertility rates (TFR) range between 4.3 children (Gainj, Highland New Guinea horticulturists) and 9.8 children (Hutterites), and as low as 3.7 in eighteenth-century European populations (Bentley et al. 1993b; Campbell and Wood 1988; Sellen and Mace 1997; Wood 1994).[8] When child survival is at stake because of competing demands on parents' time or because of the health risks of living in a dangerous environment, parents appear to adjust the timing of births to some extent (Blurton Jones 1986, 1987, 1989; Blurton Jones and Sibley 1978; for theoretic discussion, Low et al. 1992). The range of variation across noncontracepting populations presumably does not occur as the random outcome of biological determinants but reflects some flexibility in the timing of sequential births.

A net-cost approach makes the tacit assumption that parents make a one-time tradeoff about family size relative to their children's cumulative cost. However, if the process of fertility is dynamic, it is perhaps more appropriate to likewise view children's helping behavior not through a static model but through the dynamic process of family maturation and continuously shifting availability of helpers and consumer demands.

The Timing of Children's Economic Contributions

Maya parents have large families, and throughout much of their marriage duration, parents have multiple dependents living at home. To emphasize the presence of young children and the demographic pressure of dependents, Figure 8.2 shows the number of children under the age of 10 that Maya mothers 40 and younger have living their household. All mothers have at least two children younger than age 10, 50 percent

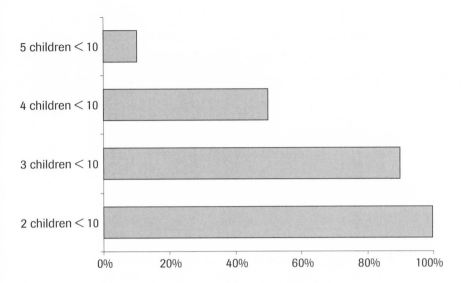

Figure 8.2   Percentage of Maya mothers with number of children under the age of 10.

have four or more children under the age of 10, and 10 percent have five or more children younger than age 10.[9] Large families with multiple dependents are costly in terms of the amount of work that is required to support them. The average daily person hours of work to support the household generally increase with household size (Figure 8.3).[10] An average household, for example, of four members consumes about 20 person hours of work per day, and a family of eight about 40 person hours of work per day.[11] In either case, this is more time than parents have hours in a day.

When parents reach limits in their availability of time or resources, they have a couple of options. As the number of dependents grows with the family, parents can meet their family's increasing consumption demands by absorbing the increase out of consumption—they and their children can consume less.[12] The Maya live close to subsistence level, and a reduction in consumption would mean a decrease in essential investments (food, hygiene), which parents would opt for under only very grim circumstances.[13] Since child mortality is markedly low and has been for several generations, it seems unlikely that Maya parents have routinely depended on this option in their family planning.

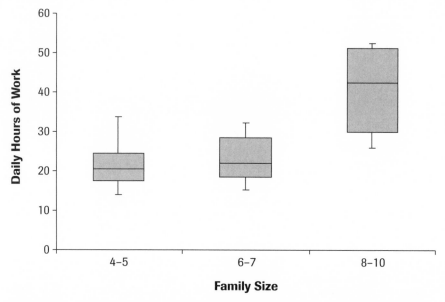

Figure 8.3   Average person hours of work that a family spends daily in productive activities (total work), showing first-quartile, median, third-quartile, minimum, and maximum values.

Parents could also absorb the increase in consumption out of leisure—they could work harder.[14] In fact, Maya parents do work harder as their family's consumption demands increase. Both fathers and mothers spend an average of 60 percent of their day working (excluding child care) in their 40s, when they have the maximum number of children living at home. Whether this represents an upward limit to work effort (or if parents could actually work harder and have their children work less as they have more children) is an interesting question. Nonetheless their production surplus is not sufficient to meet their children's consumption (Figure 8.4). Regardless of family size, in each case, parents' work effort alone does not meet their family's consumption needs.[15]

The results from Chapter 7 suggest a correlation between Maya parents not having enough time in the day to support their large families and the relatively young age at which children become net producers. The implication that follows is that the surplus labor of older children is transferred to help support their younger, dependent siblings. But the previous analysis also showed that Maya children are a net cost throughout the duration of time that they spend living in their natal

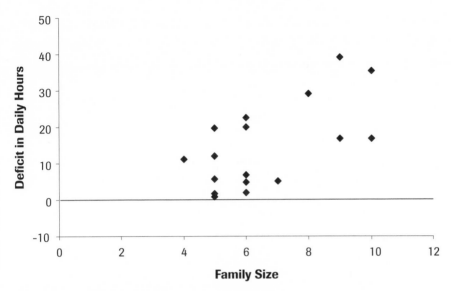

Figure 8.4 Daily family labor deficit, estimated as total household consumption minus parental production.

households. Thus the implication that the production surplus of children is transferred to subsidize younger siblings cannot be made by assumption but deserves further consideration.

The Demographic and Economic Life Cycle of the Maya Family

Using the Maya reproductive history and time-allocation data, I first consider the extent to which demographic changes across the typical family life cycle generate economic pressure on the household and then affect parents' and children's economic activity. Starting with the family life cycle (see Figure 3.4), the average age and sex production and consumption schedules from Chapter 7 (see Figure 7.1) are used to derive a model that expresses changes in consumption demand and labor supply across the life cycle of the family.[16] The ratio of consumers to producers over the family life cycle, known as the Chayanov dependency ratio, indicates whether the family's demographic composition places it in a state of relatively high or low consumption needs

Figure 8.5   Ratio of consumers to producers across the Maya family life cycle.

relative to family labor (Figure 8.5). The consumer-to-producer ratio peaks between the ninth and fifteenth years of a marriage union, when the ratio has more than doubled since the onset of the marriage. (Note that the ratio has been normalized to unity at year 0 of the marriage.) This is the most difficult time for parents economically. After the fifteenth year of marriage, early born children contribute more and more to production, and the ratio begins a sustained, slow decline, reaching a trough after the thirtieth year of marriage (Lee and Kramer 2002).

When parents' share of total family production is plotted across the family life cycle, parents are responsible for virtually all of their family's production during the first five years of the marriage union, when children are too young to work (Figure 8.6). As the earlier-born children mature and increasingly help out, parental share of total family production declines to below 40 percent between the twentieth and thirtieth year of the family life cycle. It then starts to rise again as older children marry and leave home.

The inverse of this graph indicates the level to which parents would have to increase their production if children hypothetically made no economic contribution. If children hypothetically produced nothing,

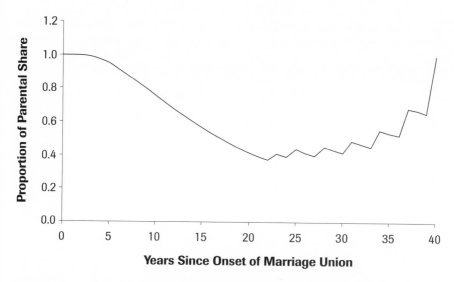

Figure 8.6   Parental share of total family production across the Maya family life cycle.

parents would have to work 2.5 times as hard as they do to maintain their children's consumption needs between the twentieth and thirty-third year of the family life cycle, as firstborn children are leaving home. Without the economic contributions of children, parents would have to increase their work effort by 150 percent in their 40s and 50s, with each parent working more than 16.5 hours a day.[17] Parents clearly could not possibly sustain this level of production.

What share, then, of children's consumption is met by Maya children themselves? In a typical family, children as a group produce more than half of what they consume after the thirteenth year of the family life cycle, when the mother is still in her prime reproductive years (Figure 8.7). By the twentieth year of the family life cycle, children as a group produce 80 percent of what they consume. And, starting around the twenty-eighth year of the family life cycle, children, as a group, produce virtually all of what they consume. The economic contributions of Maya children clearly offset a substantial portion of their consumption costs and, importantly, do so during the peak economic squeeze in the family life cycle (Lee and Kramer 2002).

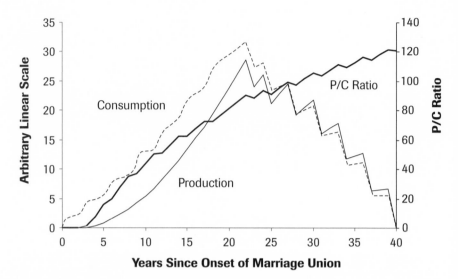

Figure 8.7 The production and consumption of children as a group in a typical Maya household across the family life cycle.

Helpers Do Help

While it may be true that children do not pay back their net consumption while they live in their natal households, the net cost of childbearing may tell us little about how fertility decisions are actually made. What appears to be relevant to the economics of reproduction is not the net cost of childbearing but the timing of consumption demands and children's help across the life cycle of the family. While an individual child is a net cost to a Maya parent, it is the timing of all of their children's help as it shifts across the demographic life cycle of the family that enables Maya parents to continue childbearing and raise more children than they might otherwise. The Maya experience a significant life-cycle squeeze when the ratio of consumers to producers more than doubles between the tenth and twentieth years of a marriage union. This squeeze is countered by an increase in labor effort by household members, as is predicted by Chayanov's law.

Despite their negative net asset value, Maya children play a vital economic and reproductive role in the family in several ways. Any contribution that children make reduces the amount of subsidy needed from someone else and helps to underwrite their cost. Not only do younger children help to defray their costs, but Maya mothers are still of reproductive age when their eldest children reach adolescence and become net producers. Without the contributions that children make as a group, Maya parents would have to double or triple their work effort beyond observed values. Through labor transfers, children enable their parents to continue childbearing during family life-cycle stages when parents themselves do not have sufficient time and resources to support their family.

— 9 —

How Long to Stay and Help?

The time that older children spend working could be directed toward two very different ends. They could spend their time helping to support their younger siblings, enabling parents to maintain short birth intervals and raise more children than they might otherwise be able to support—the scenario that the Maya results so far support. Alternatively, their time could be directed toward establishing their own families. Why Maya teenagers stay in their natal families as net producers and continue to direct their work effort toward helping their siblings rather than leaving home once they are economically "independent" may have several explanations. First, since Maya parents benefit from their children's help by raising more children than they might be able to otherwise, parents may be reluctant to forgo the work of their older children. If teenagers also benefit by staying, the opportunity cost of their helping may be relatively low, as Clutton-Brock (2002) has suggested for non-human cooperative breeders.

Second, children's labor is embedded in household production. If more people working together lowers the per unit cost of production, the young age at net production may reflect to some extent the effects of an economy of scale and working as part of a larger production unit. Teenagers may be too young and inefficient to support a household on their own. Although teenagers are net producers when total work is considered, they have not yet achieved adult proficiency at certain tasks, such as maize processing and planting, that are critical to establishing a household and supporting a family on their own. And third, girls at age 15 (the age at net production for females) are not yet fully grown and no doubt have much to gain by staying at home a few more years. But as children reach their later teens and sexual maturity, the cost of their staying and helping increases.

The age at which girls reach sexual maturity, leave home, and marry affects age at first birth, a robust predictor of family size in natural fertility populations (Campbell and Wood 1988). While sexual maturity is a constraint on the age at first birth, it does not determine its timing, which is quite variable even across natural fertility populations (Alvarez 2000:450; Howell 1979; Hill and Hurtado 1996; Low 2000:130–35; Wilson and Woods 1991). When first birth is postponed beyond sexual maturity, it presents an explanatory challenge since delayed reproduction carries a fitness cost, a topic that has been an emphasis of research in both animal and human studies (Emlen 1982, 1991; Pagel and Harvey 1993). Evidence generally supports the suggestion that, among nonhuman cooperative breeders, sexually mature offspring delay their own reproduction when constraints arise either on mating opportunities or on the availability of the resources or territory necessary to compete for mates and successfully reproduce (Brown 1987; Clutton-Brock 1991; Koenig et al. 1992; Stacey and Koenig 1990; Woolfenden and Fitzpatrick 1984). Likewise among humans the postponement of marriage, low marriage rates, and high rates of celibacy are associated with ecological constraints on the accessibility of land or wealth necessary for reproduction (Clarke 1993; Clarke and Low 1992; Strassman and Clarke 1998; Voland et al. 1991). But how does the age of leaving home and initiating reproduction shift when life is made easier—when constraints are eased on producing resources necessary for reproduction?

The Maya data provide a natural experiment to follow how the tradeoff to stay and help or go and reproduce is played out when a situation emerges for a potential increase in labor effeciency. One empirical test of this tradeoff is to observe how older Maya girls alter their time expenditures when modernization comes to their village and introduces a change in the efficiency with which two key resources are procured and processed.

Laborsaving Technology and Its Effect on Female Age at First Birth

In the mid-1970s a gas-powered mill and a water pump were built in Xculoc. This mechanized technology markedly increased the efficiency with which maize could be ground and water collected (see Figure 9.1). The well was broken for several continuous months during the 1992–1993 field season, during which time women resumed drawing

Figure 9.1   Maya women and girls retrieving water from the mechanized pump.

water with ropes and buckets by hand from the 50 meter deep well, a time-consuming and energetically demanding task (see Figure 9.2). The situation presents a window onto how older girls reallocate their time when laborsaving technology is and is not available and how that affects constraints on their leaving home and initiating reproduction.[1]

Water and ground maize are crucial to Maya subsistence and are produced exclusively by women. Women not only resumed hand drawing water for three months while the well was broken, but women also frequently ground corn with a hand grinder rather than take it to the *molino,* either because of not having enough cash on hand or because the *molino* was broken. Consequently, return rates could be collected while the pump was broken and when women ground maize by hand (Appendix Table 9.1). As estimated from the return rates, women save on the order of two and half hours a day when using the laborsaving technology to grind maize and collect water (Kramer and McMillan 1998).

Although the laborsaving technology increases the efficiency with which certain resources are produced, what girls do with the saved time depends on the value of alternate time expenditures. If the goods produced with the technology are valuable relative to other ways that time

Figure 9.2   Maya women and girls hand drawing water from the well.

and energy can be invested, they may spend more time hauling water or grinding maize. Alternatively, the time saved while performing one task may be reallocated to other activities. Thus, if the technology increases the rate at which maize is produced, reproductive-age girls have a number of alternate options in reallocating the time saved.

Given the increase in efficiency, more water or maize can be produced in the same amount of time, or the same amount of water and maize can be produced in less time. Whether these girls choose to collect more water and process more maize depends on the economic value of water and maize and the value of other goods and services produced with that time. Since neither stored water nor ground maize is a marketable commodity, young women are not expected to reallocate the time saved into producing more water or ground maize. A second option is reapportioning the saved time by spending more time in other productive activities—producing goods for sale or consumption—or in child care.[2] A third option would be to spend the saved time in leisure.

To evaluate how reproductive-age, nulliparous girls ages 16 to 20 reallocate their time, the time-allocation data for these young women was modeled as a function of age and the presence of the laborsaving

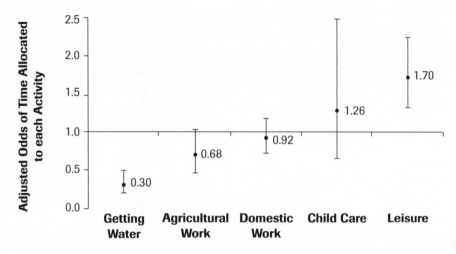

Figure 9.3 The probability that young unmarried Maya women will engage in a particular activity when they have access to laborsaving technology; the Y-axis gives the adjusted odds ratios and confidence intervals from the fitted model.

technology in a mixed random and fixed effects model using a logistic-link function (Kramer and McMillan 1998).[3] Figure 9.3 shows the confidence intervals and adjusted odds ratios of engaging in an activity during any particular scan observation when the gas-powered pump was working. Where the confidence interval spans 1, evidence is insufficient to conclude that there is a significant change in the time allocated to that activity when the gas-powered pump is working.

When the laborsaving technology is available, older female children (1) allocate less time to collecting water; (2) do not change the time they allocate to field work, domestic work, or child care; and (3) allocate more time to leisure (resting, sleeping, socializing, eating, religious activity, and personal maintenance). When laborsaving technology is available and older girls have a choice of how to spend the time saved, they do not reallocate the time toward income-producing activities or child care. Instead, they are 1.7 times as likely to spend time in leisure activities. But they also do something else—they leave home and marry at a younger age.

Reproductive histories (Chapter 4) were used to construct a multi-variate logistic regression model to estimate the change in the age at first birth before and after the introduction of the modern technology.

Since the probability of a woman giving birth to her first child spans the year that the modern technology was introduced, person-years-at-risk rather than number of women is used to compose the sample groups. Each woman, thus, contributes the number of person years during which she is at risk of giving birth to her first child, before and after the introduction of modern technology. To improve accuracy a person year was included starting at age fifteen if it occurred after 1960. No other exclusion criteria were used. Fifty women who eventually became mothers were included in the sample. Variables added to the model include mother's age-at-risk, a quadratic term for age, interaction effects, the presence or absence of technology, and year-at-risk, which measures for a general historical effect. From this set of predictor variables, the best-fitting model to predict the probability of a mother's age at first birth included age, age squared, and the presence/absence of technology (deviance = 191.12; df = 214).

The presence of technology has a positive and significant effect (p = .0220; Appendix Table 9.2). Note that the term for the general historical effect drops out of the model as insignificant, suggesting that there has not been an incremental decrease in women's age at first birth over the last century due to general secular trends (Kramer and McMillan 1999). After the introduction of mechanized technology in the mid 1970s, a significant drop occurs in age at first birth, from 21.2 to 19.5 years old.[4]

The reallocation of the time saved from productive activities to leisure after the introduction of laborsaving technology can be linked to the age at which women give birth to their first child because it affects the two conditions necessary to initiate child bearing—fecundity and exposure to conception. Not only is time saved, but the reallocation of time spent in calorically expensive activities to time spent in leisure activities (resting and socializing represent more than 60 percent of leisure observations) may incur a substantial calorie savings. When using the technology, women save on the order of 300 calories a day (Kramer and McMillan 1999:505). This is sufficient, for example, to satisfy the increase in energy expenditure required during the luteal phase of the menstrual cycle (Strassman 1996).

Puberty, the process leading to sexual maturation, takes a number of years and a sequence of events—skeletal and pelvic maturation, fat deposition, development of reproductive physiology, and stable ovarian function—to accomplish (overviews in Bogin 1999a; Ellison 2001; Wood 1994). The onset of puberty is triggered by hormonal changes but the timing and duration of subsequent events can be mediated through changes in energy balance (determined by caloric intake relative to energy expenditure). While the relationship between hormones and energy balance is complex and not fully understood, there is an apparent relationship between a positive energy balance and completion of sexual maturation and stable ovarian function (Ellison 1990; Rosetta 1990; Strassmann 1996; Ulijasek 1995). A recent comparison of the maturation trajectories of urban and rural Zambian girls suggests that the duration of time to complete sexual maturity can be affected by nutritional condition, in this case by the preferential feeding of pubescent girls (Gillett-Netting et al. n.d.). Likewise, if an increase in labor efficiency means that young women spend less time in calorically demanding activities, the positive tip in energy balance may truncate the duration of reproductive maturation.[5]

But sexual maturation and fecundity are only one condition necessary to initiate reproduction. The other is exposure to conception, which in the Maya case is initiated by leaving home and marrying. Not only is the time savings afforded by mechanized technology substantial, but a greater age range of family members can assist in maize processing and water collection since the technology reduces the skill and strength requirements for performing these tasks. Drawing water by hand from a well 50 meters deep requires considerable strength, but girls of all ages can carry buckets of water from the centralized spigots to their homes. Likewise, while only older teenagers and women have the upper-arm strength to grind maize by hand, younger girls are able to carry a bucket of maize to and from the *molino*.

If household work can be accomplished more expediently, with less energetic cost, and by a greater age range of family members, then the marginal value—the additional value of a person's labor when added to the work already provided by other family members—of the help that young unmarried girls provide to the family may diminish with the increase in labor efficiency. In other words, if the surplus labor of young women who are still living at home is less vital to help support younger dependents, then they should be less constrained from leaving home and starting a family of their own should the opportunity arise.[6] The introduction of laborsaving technology appears to have had a positive effect on both of these conditions necessary to initiate reproduction by relaxing physiological constraints on female sexual maturation and constraints on leaving home, since they are less needed as helpers in their family.

Parent/offspring conflict is alleviated from both points of view. Parents should be more willing to let their daughters marry at a younger age if their leaving home does not compromise the help mothers need to support their children. The increase in efficiency attenuates the labor cost to support a family, and younger children can more easily make up for the loss of an older sister. From the older girls' point of view, they may leave home and initiate reproduction at a younger age when conditions become more favorable through a decrease in the cost of independent breeding introduced by the laborsaving technology. Young women may be better able to manage supporting children at a younger age because they can reallocate the time saved at these two time-consuming female tasks toward childrearing activities.

Changes in Young Men's Futures?

The extent to which young, sexually mature teenagers are willing to help is expected to vary with the opportunity costs of alternate economic opportunities. Under what economic conditions might the costs and benefits tip in favor of not helping? In a nonmonetary economy, little opportunity exists for net producers to save their production surplus or turn it into future resources. But the situation is quite different in a wage-labor economy where, by contrast, wages can be banked for the future or converted into resources necessary for marriage and reproduction. Under these conditions, teenagers might be more reluctant to work for their families. As young men approach reproductive age and have more opportunities to earn wages, they may be less willing to transfer their production balance to help their younger siblings. The Maya economy is within this continuum, largely based in subsistence farming, with some men working for wages some of the time, and females never engaged in wage labor.

Currently, Maya males marry and have their first child two years older on average than females, but it will be interesting to observe what happens to male age at marriage as future economic options change. Although competition for—or lack of—land on which to build a home or grow crops to support a family disenfranchises sexually mature males in some land-tenure and inheritance systems and is associated with some males delaying or even forgoing reproduction, young Xculoc males do not face these constraints. The point was made in Chapter 3 that arable land is still plentiful for young couples to establish plots of their own because of low population density, which is just now returning to what it was before European contact. Further, by law, ejido lands are communally insoluble and can be neither owned nor inherited; nor are there other forms of partible inherited wealth. Although there is currently no competition for land, given current rates of population growth, this is likely to change. As villagers become more enmeshed in the national economy and economic options become more diverse, greater variance is likely to occur among individuals in regard to their access to resources, wealth accumulation, and the age at which teenagers leave home and invest in their own families.

– 10 –

Do Helpers Really Help?

Short birth intervals, the prolonged duration of time that children depend on someone's care, and the fact that children of different ages benefit from different time and resource investments all contribute to competing demands on a mother's time. Although humans extend resource provisioning to juveniles, juveniles also provide a source of assistance. Helpers, so defined because they redistribute the cost of childbearing, alleviate constraints on the time and resources mothers spend supporting offspring, allowing her to reinvest her effort in reproduction. But do they?

Because children have the analytically confounding attribute of being both producers and consumers, whether their economic contributions actually underwrite fertility has never been fully resolved. In part this is because the value of children's labor has been defined several ways. My methodological goals were severalfold. The first was to observe how in one population different measures of children's economic contributions affect our picture of their value; and second, to evaluate which measure best reflects the utility of that help in underwriting parents' reproductive success. Because the Maya are beginning to undergo changes in their subsistence options (see Postscript), my other interest was to develop a framework that could continue to be used to evaluate the relationship between helpers and fertility as Xculoc transitions economically and demographically.

A life course of work emerges as Maya children develop from net consumers to net producers. Children contribute more to household labor as they mature, and although their consumption also rises, their work effort increases more rapidly. Teenagers allocate as much time to productive activities as do their parents. When their net value (the balance of how much children produce and consume) is considered, Maya children become net producers in their teens. Thereafter, they continue to live in their natal households, maintaining a positive production balance, for a number of years before leaving home and marrying. Even so, children are a net cost; the net transfer of wealth is downward from parents to children throughout the duration of time that they spend living in their parents' households.

Yet despite their negative cumulative cost, Maya children play a critical economic and reproductive role in two important ways. Children's production offsets a substantial portion of their cumulative costs (girls pay back 94 percent of their cumulative consumption before leaving home, and boys pay back 80 percent), and also of the day-to-day costs to support a family. Without the contributions of their children, Maya parents would have to double or triple their work levels beyond observed values. When dependency ratios rise, and parents reach bottlenecks in their ability to support dependents, the timing of their children's economic contributions plays a key role in underwriting the cost of large Maya families and enabling parents to continue childbearing during life-cycle stages when they themselves may not have sufficient time and resources to support their family. When a shift in labor efficiency occurs through the introduction of laborsaving technology, help from younger children appears to compensate for the loss of older sisters, who leave home at a younger age to initiate their own reproductive careers. Importantly, if children's economic contributions are viewed from the perspective of the family life cycle, it is the collective help from younger children, not just net producers, that makes the difference in Maya parents being able to support large families. In the Maya situation, both parts of the question appear to be true: children do help, and their help has a positive effect on fertility.

The demographic transition is well under way in most countries and is considered complete in many industrialized nations. Yet a very different picture is revealed when we look at disaggregated data from small-scale societies in unindustrialized parts of the world. Contemporary Maya farmers have large families within the human family size continuum and as such represent a challenge for parents to meet their children's consumption needs. Getting help from older, coresident children appears to be a successful strategy of compensating for increasing consumer demands on parents without their having to lengthen or compromise the future of older children, who go on to raise large families themselves.

One of the important implications of Chayanov's (1986 [1925]) insight that consumer demands and labor supply shift across the life cycle of the family is its relationship to parity-specific reproductive decisions. Comprehensive explanation for the variation in completed family size, both through time and across populations, is illusive in part because family size is the outcome not of a single event but of a long series of tradeoffs and decisions that parents negotiate over the duration of their union. Given the observed variation in family size in noncontracepting populations, from as few as four children to as many as eight children (Campbell and Wood 1988; Hewlett 1991; Wood 1994), Maya parents presumably have some play in lengthening birth intervals, delaying age at first birth, and downwardly adjusting family size to some extent. The fact that they do not and, meanwhile, sustain low infant-mortality rates indicates that Maya parents have resolved labor and resource constraints to support these families.

Other Options: The Role of Older Adults

Because both consumption and the capacity for work diverge over the life course, predominantly when young and in some cases also late in life, children in all societies are subsidized by others for some period of time. Often, though certainly not always, fathers help provide for dependent children. Yet even among the Maya, where mothers and fathers contribute equal time to household production, parents together have enough hours in the day to care for only about four children, far fewer than their median family size of seven children (see Figure 8.4). Mothers need, and get, assistance to support their children. The roles that spouses, children, grandmothers, extended kin, and governments play in subsidizing dependents have been well documented across a diversity of disciplines. These studies have in common the appreciation that mothers are in a bind to support multiple dependents on their own.

In a cooperative breeding reproductive strategy, individuals predicted most likely to help mothers raise their young are those for whom the cost to forfeit or delay their own reproduction is low (Emlen 1984). For humans this includes not only prereproductive individuals, who have been the focus of this book, but also postreproductive individuals. Besides the long duration of human juvenility, the other conspicuous human life history feature is the duration of time that females spend in a postreproductive stage. Among some groups of foragers, grandmothers help their daughters by providing competent child care and food for older children by being reliable food collectors (Hawkes et al. 1989, 1997; Hurtado et al. 1992). In other foraging contexts, grandmothers care for young children, allowing their daughters to spend time away from camp foraging. The surplus production of grandmothers in these cases helps to alleviate their daughters' competing demands of feeding older children and providing child care to younger children.

The production and consumption age profiles for older Maya adults (see Figure 7.1) show that six of the seven adults ages 55 to 65 are net producers. Older adults not only continue to support themselves, but as net producers, their surplus production is also being transferred to help support others. Because of the effects of large family size and short generational time, grandmothers, however, are also mothers through much of their postreproductive lives. Most Maya mothers still have several dependents living at home when they are well into their postreproductive years and are already grandmothers themselves. In these families it was the teenage daughter rather than the mother who was sent to help their older married sisters with young children, while the mother cared for her own dependent children. Maya parents are often in their early 60s when their last child leaves home and marries. By this age, parents have well over twenty grandchildren. These older parents may have several children living in their household, including an older son with his spouse and children. Labor is pooled across these commensal groups, and these grandchildren no doubt benefit from the help of older, coresident adults. Grandparents are the caregivers in 4 percent of all child-care observations. In most cases, grandparent child care occurs in the situation described above: in extended families where a married son, his wife, and children live with his parents.

Maya mothers live, on average, not many years after their last child leaves home. Maternal life span, generational time, child mortality, birth interval, and fertility affect how long women are economically unencumbered by their own children. Across the family life cycle, as Maya mothers age and their older children leave, their production surplus stays more or less constant. The potential competing interests of grandmothers who are also mothers raises the question of who the recipients of their production surplus are. If their production surplus does not decline in step with the number of children living at home, is it because older women have older dependent children who consume more than younger children or because they are supporting grandchildren? These questions remain unanswered and provide valuable direction for future research.

Old-Age Security?

Both the forager and the Maya data give little support to the idea that parents in preindustrial populations are motivated to have large families so that their children will provide for them in old age. In the tradition of wealth flows theory, the demand for children in pretransitional populations is high because children are both producers of wealth and providers of security to parents in their old age, when their productivity declines. Theoretic models and empirical tests, however, are as divided on the issue of the generational direction of wealth flows (see Chapter 8) as they are on high fertility as a form of old-age security. In an overview of empirical evidence, it appears that while adults are likely to report care by their children in old age as a reason to have children, empirical evidence is lacking to support that high fertility actually increases the likelihood of old-age security (Kaplan and Bock 2001). Studies among hunter-gatherers and horticulturalists show that older adults are often net producers whose work supports members of younger generations (Hawkes and Jones 1997). In a comparative study of the Maya, Piro, and Machiguenga, older Maya adults were found to generate a smaller surplus than the two groups of South American horticulturalists (Lee et al. 2002). But Maya children also require comparatively smaller net transfers from parents, since they are hard workers themselves. These studies together underscore the point that, under the conditions of high fertility, mothers rally help from whomever they can—their mothers, their sisters, spouses, and children.

Humans' Demographic Edge

One potentially interesting implication of prolonged human juvenility is that it may lend to giving humans their demographic edge.
Humans for millennia have successfully made a living in the vast
range of habitats from the tropics to the Arctic. This propensity for
widespread geographic proliferation appears to have its antecedents
deep in hominid evolution. While hominid evolution is traditionally
explained as long-term directional selection to constant environmental trends and stable pressure, Potts (1998) points out that the
idea of an environment of evolutionary adaptiveness is inconsistent
with what is now known about local and global dynamics in the
environmental past.[1] Rather than digging in adaptively to fill a particular niche, increased versatility is an alternate means of coping
with variable environmental conditions. Potts argues that hominid
locomotor, cognitive, and social traits are mechanisms that broaden
adaptability to a range of environmental conditions. Concomitant
with those traits is the evolution of a human life history pattern
favorable to reproductive success and survival in variable environments. Prolonged juvenility may, ironically, have been key to the
demographic success of humans. On the one hand, the extended provisioning of juveniles allowed humans to move into habitats they
could not otherwise occupy (Hawkes et al. 1998; O'Connell et al.
1999). On the other hand, the complexity of the human feeding
niche provided many tasks at which children are productive and even
can produce surpluses, relieving competing demands on mothers'
time (see Chapter 1).

Population growth in long-lived, large mammals is generally limited
by long generational time. The great ape life history of long birth intervals, extended infancy, and high juvenile mortality places further constraints on lifetime reproductive success. Although the population
growth potential of the great apes is near demographic equilibrium
(Bogin 1998; Galdikas and Wood 1990; Nishida et al. 1990), humans,
by contrast, are capable of staggering population growth.

The combination of the relatively long period of human juvenile
dependence, the younger age at weaning, and shorter birth intervals
has several potentially positive effects on maternal reproductive success, both through fertility and mortality. The lengthening of child-

hood as a developmental stage shifts the period of dependency from breastfeeding to food provisioning, allowing mothers to produce children in relatively rapid succession. Yet the potential gain in lifetime fertility through shorter birth intervals could be countered by elevated mortality risk because maternal time and resources are spread too thin. Comparative mortality rates, however, show that juveniles in traditional hunter-gatherer populations have a greater probability of surviving to reproductive age than do nonhuman primates (Kaplan et al. 2000:157; Appendix Table 1.2).

The traditional view of past population growth is that gains in fertility were kept in check by high child mortality. Recent models, however, suggest that past population growth occurred in fits and starts, with periods of sustained growth interspersed with episodic crashes in mortality (Boone 2001; Keckler 1997), rendering a net effect of low population growth until the onset of the modern demographic transition. Nonetheless, population growth prior to the modern demographic transition was sufficient to produce an estimated world population of one billion in 1800. This magnitude of growth, though diminutive relative to what it would be during the modern transition, is demographically remarkable compared with the great ape population growth dilemma. The difference in mortality patterns and population-growth potential suggests that the particular mix of human life history traits has had the net effect of resolving maternal constraints on raising multiple dependents.

The distribution of the costs of reproduction is key to holding in balance the combination of a fast reproductive rate and long period of dependence. Human juveniles, presumably self-feeders early in hominid history, began to depend on others for their survival. The varied roles that older adults, fathers, and other related and nonrelated adults play in subsidizing dependents punctuates the finding that flexibility in alternative allomaternal strategies has been crucial to mothers supporting multiple dependents under variable demographic and ecological conditions. From the mother's perspective, although multiple dependents increase the demand for care, they are also a potential source of help. From the juvenile's point of view, the human feeding niche has an important characteristic. It incorporates a broad diversity of resources that require variable capture and processing costs. In many ecological conditions children are able to produce some of what they need at the level of their own consumption and some of what they need in excess of their own consumption. Juveniles, because they have this unusual feature of being both dependents and helpers, increase the range of options for mothers to redistribute their dependent children's consumption needs and, in many ways, may underlie the human demographic edge.

The Unfolding World of the Maya

The Maya of Xculoc are poised on the edge of a rapidly transitioning world. Change was initiated in the late-1970s, when a mechanized water pump and maize mill were installed in Xculoc that affected women's workloads and a shift to younger age at first birth. During the next twenty years, little else changed in the village. Because of the long distances to commercial centers and lack of motorized transportation, villagers continued to be removed from much involvement in the wage labor or the market economy. Some men occasionally participated in wage labor—as they probably had for the decades prior to my research—when clothing, medicine, or building materials were needed. Fertility remained high, and the Maya maize subsistence economy and buying power remained more or less the same. Then, in the late-1990s, a spate of developments began. Economic options are expanding as contact with the labor market and the national economy accelerates. With that will come a diversification in how people will spend their time and in future fertility tradeoffs.

In 1998, electric lines were built, connecting the village to a source of power. At first this brought a lightbulb into every house, and villagers talked about the savings of electric light compared to the cost of buying candles. As elsewhere, the oddities of Yankees ball caps and "Got Milk?" T-shirts have been present in Xculoc for some time, but electricity has brought its own, sometimes novel, juxtapositions of the outside world and village life—children avidly watching the snowy curtain of a TV with no reception or a seventy-year-old man explaining in rapturous detail how the earth revolves around the sun to a background of children playing Ms. Pac-Man. Shortly after the arrival of electricity, water lines were extended from the centralized pump into each *solar*, further diminishing the time women spend hauling water. But the water pump frequently breaks, as it did during the 2003 field season, and women resume hauling water bucket by bucket from the well. Because development projects usually occur during election years, villagers were confident that a new pump would be installed before the 2003 election.

The ability to purchase market goods is being funded, not as expected through increased participation in wage labor, but through intensified maize production. The average land under cultivation per household doubled in 2003 compared with a decade earlier. The old men talk about the long hours they spent clearing land on the hill slopes before new hybrid maize varieties and fertilizers were introduced through bank loans and government subsidies in the early-1990s. Yet an edge of skepticism is apparent in what they perceive to be an increase in morbidity among older people due to exposure to fertilizers and pesticides. Men are mixed in their perception of future land constraints and whether sufficient arable land is available in their ejido for their sons to farm.

In 1995 a new elementary school and a junior high school were built in the village. As mandated by the government, to attend school girls must wear a voluminous pleated-skirt uniform; meanwhile, they are now instructed in after-school programs in their traditional Maya handicrafts. Groups of girls cluster around their teachers to learn how to embroider traditional huipils, when just a few years before, they had spent long afternoon hours making them in the company of their mothers and sisters.

A rudimentary health clinic was built in the late-1990s. The age/sex pyramid on the wall illustrates the expanding population of young children in Xculoc. A doctor now visits the village bimonthly, but the clinic lacks even basic equipment, medicine, or bandages.

Prior to 2000, female productive activities centered in their homes and fields. Several years ago, groups of women began to organize a number of cooperatives—a *tortilleria* (automated tortilla production), a *molino,* and several cattle collectives—through bank and government loans. The *tortillerias* and *molinos* have been successful investments, and the cooperatives expect to pay back their loans within the next several years. The cattle collectives are less successful due to the lack of forage and standing water around Xculoc.

In 2002, following the devastation of hurricane Isidora, the almost complete loss of crops, and no relief assistance, young women began working in wage labor for the first time. A clothing maquiladora (foreign-owned factory) in a large town several hours away sends a bus to the village before dawn to pick up workers and returns them at seven or eight at night. Most workers are young, unmarried women, although a few young men also participate. Young women and their parents complain about the long hours, the low pay, and the danger to the young women of being unchaperoned in town. When asked, many villagers said that their daughters would quit once the crops are harvested this fall and they no longer need the wages to buy food.

Three collectives of men have purchased tractors, also from bank loans, but are behind on their repayment schedule because of the loss of crops last year and the lack of cash flow to maintain the tractors and purchase replacement parts. The men are concerned that the tractors will be repossessed because they are unable to produce sufficient maize surpluses to repay the loans.

The village's traditional communal ejido lands were recently resurveyed by the Mexican government. The dispute over some 2,000 hectares that villagers in Xculoc think should be theirs can be resolved only by paying legal fees and attending meetings in the regional capital. In the calm and patient way characteristic of villagers, the ejido *comisario* aptly expresses what it means to have one foot firmly embedded in subsistence agriculture and the other now connected to the outside. He explains that he does not have the money for the bus fare to travel to the city to attend the meetings, and the village does not have the funds to process the dispute claim.

Young people now have more options in how they spend their time—going to school, working for wages, working in agricultural or commercial production. In the past, villagers' relatively equal and adequate access to land resources and the means of subsistence meant that women had similar background constraints to fertility. However, greater variation in reproductive strategies among villagers is certainly to ensue with changing venues for the accumulation of wealth, differential access to the means of production, competition for land, and the payoff to investing in children's education and forgoing their help in household production.

While the lives of villagers are in many ways becoming easier, villagers are also increasingly aware of their relative economic status and inability to compete in the national economy. In 2003 I heard villagers refer to themselves as poor for the first time. Although many of these changes leave the anthropologist cold to the goals of development, many villagers are proud of the steps they are taking toward modernization and look forward to the opportunities that the road now being built connecting their village to a paved road will bring. Still they walk the rows of their freshly tilled fields dropping yellow seeds in the ground, anticipating the coming rainy season with the hope of a successful harvest. The unfolding story will illuminate much about how people transition through changing economic options and the effect such change has on children's lives and families.

While yet unknown, it is likely that in coming decades land constraints and greater inclusion in the national and global economy will reshape the economic contribution of children. These changes offer an opportunity to look outside the traditional view that children's economic value is explained by subsistence classification or cultural norm, and toward the effects that changing economic options have on the distribution of the cost of childbearing and the role of children as helpers in transitional subsistence economies.

– APPENDIX A –

Tables

Table 1.1 Comparative life history variables.

	Age at weaning	Age at menarche	Age at first breeding	Birth interval length (years)	Daughters per year	Lifetime surviving fertility	Probability of surviving to sexual maturity
Orangutans	6.0[a]		14.7 (9–18)[h]	9.2 (6.1–10.4)[h]	0.063[k]	—	—
Chimpanzees	5.0[b]	11[e]	13.7[i]	5.8[i]	0.087[k]	2[j]	.35[j]
Gorillas	3–4[c]	7–8[f]	10–11[f]	3.9[f]	0.126[k]	3[j]	—
Humans	2.37[d]	12–18[g]	19.7[i]	3.1[d]	0.142[k]	6.1[l]	.6[j]

a. Galdikas and Wood (1990).
b. Pusey (1983).
c. Fossey (1979).
d. Alvarez (2000:450) (mean for the Ache, Amele, !Kung and Turkana).
e. Pusey (1990).
f. Watts (1991).
g. Eveleth and Tanner (1990:162–165).
h. Wich et al. (in press).
i. Boesch and Boesch-Achermann (2001).
j. Kaplan et al. (2000:158) (human mean for the Ache, Hadza, Hiwi and !Kung).
k. Hawkes et al. (1998:1337).
l. Bentley et al. (1993b:779) (mean for fifty-seven groups of foragers, horticulturalists and agriculturalists).

Table 1.2 Why helpers help for various classes of helpers.

Helper's status	Types of explanation (benefit to helper)	Select sources
Sexually mature, nonbreeding related sibling	Benefits of delayed dispersal	Koenig et al. (1992)
	Indirect fitness benefits (kin selection)	Brown (1987); Dugatkin (1997); Emlen (1991)
Unspecified kin	Direct benefits to helper by raising survival, mating, or learning (may include reciprocity or mutualism)	Cockburn (1998); Clutton-Brock (2002); Clutton-Brock et al. (1999, 2001); Grinnell et al. (1995)
Nonrelated adults	Reciprocal altruism	Davies (1991); Ivey (2000)
Postreproductive females	Kin selection	Hawkes et al. (1989, 1997, 1998); Hill and Hurtado (1991); O'Connell et al. (1999)
Fathers	Resource provisioning/paternity confidence	Irons (1983); Lamb et al. (1987); Lancaster and Lancaster (1983); Kaplan et al. (2000)
	Male competition over sexual access	Blurton Jones et al. (2000)
Juveniles	Benefits of learning and maternal experience	Hrdy (1977, 1981); Ivey (2000); Lancaster (1971); Fairbanks (1990); Tardif et al. (1984); Weisner (1987)

Table 4.1 Birth interval length by parity for living Xculoc mothers, in years; missing values indicate small sample sizes. The 50 percent quartile is equal to the median.

Parity	*n*	Maximum	Minimum	25%	Quartiles 50%	75%
1–2	51	7.2	1.0	1.6	2.0	3.0
2–3	46	7.1	1.0	1.8	2.2	3.0
3–4	40	7.1	0.9	1.7	2.0	2.9
4–5	27	7.1	1.1	1.8	2.1	2.8
5–6	22	6.3	1.0	1.6	2.1	3.0
6–7	17	5.8	1.3	1.9	2.1	3.0
7–8	12	5.9	1.4	1.8	2.4	3.0
8–9	4	—	—	—	3.2	—
9–10	2	—	—	—	—	—

Table 4.2 Age-specific fertility for the number of children ever born to Xculoc mothers. The 50 percent quartile is equal to the median.

			Children ever had			
Age group	*n*	Maximum	Minimum	25%	Quartiles 50%	75%
16–25	12	4	1	1.0	2.5	4.0
26–35	19	8	3	3.0	4.0	5.0
36–45	5	8	5	6.0	7.0	8.0
46+	19	11	3	5.5	7.0	8.0

Table 4.3 Age-specific fertility for the number of surviving children of Xculoc mothers. The 50 percent quartile is equal to the median.

			Surviving children			
Age group	*n*	Maximum	Minimum	25%	Quartiles 50%	70%
16–25	12	4	1	1.0	2.5	4.0
26–35	19	8	2	3.0	4.0	5.0
36–45	5	8	5	6.0	7.0	8.0
46+	19	9	3	5.0	6.0	7.0

Table 4.4 Retrospective fertility characteristics for Xculoc mothers.

Cohort	Completed fertility			Age at first birth	IBI	Age at last birth	Reproductive span (years)
	Median	Mean	SD				
Pre–1930	7.0	7.6	2.88	20.0	2.6	37.0	17
1930–39	8.0	7.2	2.05	20.0	3.0	42.0	24
1940–49	8.0	7.8	1.30	19.0	2.0	42.0	23
1950–59	6.5	6.5	2.56	22.6	2.3	36.7	14
1960–69	8.0	7.0	1.9	22.4	2.1	39.1	17
1970–79	8.0	7.3	1.1	20.2	2.1	36.0	16
1980–89	—	—	—	19.2	2.0	—	—

Note: A cohort groups mothers who gave birth to their first child within the ten-year interval. Cohort median values were determined for completed fertility, age at first birth, birth interval between the first and second child (IBI), age at last birth, and reproductive span (*n* = 66 mothers). Missing values indicate cohorts still in their childbearing years.

Table 4.5 Percentage of the population represented by children, reproductive-age adults, and postreproductive-age adults for the study population, the state of Yucatan, Mexico, and the United States.

Age group	Xculoc	Yucatan	Mexico	United States
0–4	18%	13%	13%	8%
0–15	47	40	41	23
0–19	56	49	50	29
20–44	30	33	30	40
45 and older	14	17	15	31

Sources: Census data for the Yucatan from INEGI (1991a:cuadro 2), for Mexico from INEGI (1991b:cuadro 2), and for the United States from the U.S. Bureau of Census (1992:15).

Table 5.1 Example of a scan-sample recording sheet.

Case	ID	Date	Time	Individual's presence	Activity	Activity ID	Weight	Object	Object ID	Location	Location ID	Notes
232	189	1/20	10:00	2	Harvests	2601	1	Maize	501	Milpa	9	Milpa S of town
232	190	"	"	1	Washes	101	1	Clothes	601	Yard	283	Returns with 30 kg
232	191	"	"	2	Chops	540	1	Firewood	629	Forest	7	
232	192	"	"	1	Rinses	304	1	Maize	501	Yard	283	
232	193	"	"	1	Carries	612	1	Sister	196	Yard	283	
232	194	"	"	1	Plays with	662	1	Brother	195	Year	283	
232	195	"	"	1	Plays with	662	1	Brother	194	Yard	283	
232	196	"	"	1	Being carried	642	1	By sister	193	Yard	283	
232	189	"	10:15	1	Unloads maize	2103	1	Maize	501	Yard	283	Returns with 35 kg sack
232	190	"	"	1	Places on fire	321	1	Beans	502	Kitchen	280	For husband, who has just arrived
232	191	"	"	1	Swings with sister in hammock	613	1	Sister	198	House	281	
232	192	"	"	1	Rinses	304	1	Maize	501	Yard	283	
232	193	"	"	2	Gets ground	303	1	Maize	501	Molino	13	
232	194	"	"	1	Feeds	411	1	Chickens	801	Yard	283	
232	195	"	"	1	Eats	701	1	Tortilla	512	Yard	283	
232	196	"	"	1	Being swung in hammock	643	1	By older sister	191	House	281	

Table 5.2 Example of a focal-follow recording sheet.

Case	ID	Date	Begin time	End time	Activity	Activity ID	Weight	Object	Object ID	Location	Location ID	Amount/notes
278	48	1/19	5:03	5:48	Shells	306	1	Maize	501	Yard	283	4.0 kg (uses a curved machete to start each ear)
279	109	1/21	9:06	9:19	Harvests	2601	1	Maize	501	Milpa	9	9.0 kg
"	"	"	9:19	9:31	Harvests	2601	1	Maize	501	Milpa	9	9.5 kg
"	"	"	9:31	9:35	Loads sack	2603	1	Maize	501	Milpa	9	
"	"	"	9:35	9:56	Harvests	2601	1	Maize	501	Milpa	9	16.5 kg
"	"	"	9:56	10:05	Fixes	2682	1	Machete	610	Milpa	9	
"	"	"	10:05	10:22	Harvests	2601	1	Maize	610	Milpa	9	12.0 kg
			10:22	10:36	Eats			Posole	512	Milpa	9	
"	"	"	10:36	10:41	Harvests	2601		Maize	501	Milpa	9	5.0 kg
"	"	"	10:41	10:53	Talks	2697		To cousin	231	Milpa	9	

NOTE: In all Chapter 6 tables, unless otherwise indicated, the proportion and percentage of time is tabulated from the sum of observations for a task divided by the total number of observations for an individual. Proportions, percentages and hours represent time spent in a task during an eleven-hour observation day. Adjustments made to proportional data are described in Appendix D.

Table 6.1 The mean number of hours that a Maya household spends daily in field-work tasks.

Field-work activity	Daily hours
Weeding	2.1
Planting	0.7
Harvesting	1.9
Garden work	0.5
Related tasks	1.7
Total	6.9

Table 6.2 The mean proportion of time that Maya male and female children ages 4–23 allocate to field-work tasks. Proportions are given both as the proportion of total time (subtask observations/total observations) and as the proportion of field work (subtask observations/field-work observations). Total time proportions are listed first and in boldface.

Field activity	Proportion of time	
	Males	Females
Weeding	.05	.02
	.20	.09
Planting	.02	.01
	.07	.05
Harvesting	.04	.02
	.38	.19
Related tasks	.02	.02
	.10	.24
Totals		
Percentage	13%	7.0%
Mean daily hours	1.4	0.8

Table 6.3 The mean proportion of time that Maya male and female children ages 0–23 allocate to field work. *p* values are for sex comparisons within age groups.

	Age group					
	0–3	4–7	8–11	12–15	16–19	20–23
Males	.00	.03	.11	.19	.21	.11
	(1.000)	(.9786)	(.0783)	(.1334)	(.0675)	(.7797)
Females	.00	.03	.02	.07	.11	.10

Table 6.4 The mean number of hours that a Maya household spends daily in domestic tasks.

Domestic activity	Daily hours
Washing	2.9
Sewing	2.4
Food preparation	2.1
Food processing	1.9
Errands	1.8
Hauling water	1.0
Collecting firewood	1.0
Other	3.7
Total	16.7

Table 6.5 The mean percentage of time that Maya female children and mothers allocate to domestic tasks by age group.

Domestic activity	Age group					
	4–7	8–11	12–15	16–19	20–23	Mothers
Food preparation	0.4%	1.0%	4.0%	5.0%	5.0%	10.0%
Washing	0.4	0.4	8.0	10.0	12.0	12.0
Sewing	0.3	1.0	11.0	11.0	9.0	7.0
Hauling water	1.0	1.0	5.0	4.0	9.0	2.0

Table 6.6 The mean number of minutes that Maya male and female children ages 3–23 spend daily in domestic tasks.

Domestic activity	Daily minutes	
	Males	Females
Food processing	1	22
Food preparation	1	18
Errands	9	26
Washing, cleaning, general maintenance	1	22
Sewing	—	33
Hauling water	—	23
Collecting firewood	7	8
Tending animals	—	5
Construction and maintenance of structures	13	—
Nonconsumable resource procurement and processing	1	1
Total	33	176
% Total time spent in domestic work	(6%)	(30%)

Table 6.7 The mean proportion of time and number of minutes that Maya female children ages 3–10 and 11–20 allocate daily to domestic tasks. Minutes are listed second and are in boldface.

Domestic activity	Daily time	
	Ages 3–10	Ages 11–20
Food processing	.02	.06
	13	40
Food preparation	.01	.05
	7	33
Errands	.05	.04
	33	26
Washing, cleaning, general maintenance	.02	.16
	13	106
Sewing	.01	.11
	7	73
Hauling water	.01	.05
	7	33
Collecting firewood	.01	.02
	7	13
Tending animals	.01	.01
	7	7
Total	.14	.50
	92	330

Table 6.8 The mean proportion of time that Maya male and female children ages 0–23 allocate to domestic work. *p* values given for sex comparisons within age groups.

	Age group					
	0–3	4–7	8–11	12–15	16–19	20–23
Males	.01	.02	.10	.05	.12	.06
	(.8510)	(.0049)	(.0398)	(.0001)	(.0001)	(.0001)
Females	.02	.11	.20	.48	.52	.47

Table 6.9 The mean proportion of time and number of hours that Maya female children ages 0–23 allocate to domestic work. *p* values given for age-group comparisons.

	Age group					
	0–3	4–7	8–11	12–15	16–19	20–23
Proportion	.02	.11	.20	.52	.55	.49
	(.0492)	(.0633)	(.0001)	(.6480)	(.6699)	
Hours	.2	1.2	2.2	5.3	5.7	5.2

Table 6.10 The mean number of hours that a Maya household spends daily in child-care tasks. Values are calculated for households that have at least one child under the age of 7.

Child care activity	Daily hours
Nursing[a]	.6
Direct care	.6
Active indirect care	1.5
Passive indirect care	1.0
Instruction	.6
Playing while in charge	.2
Total	4.4

a. Includes only those households that have a nursing mother.

Table 6.11 The mean percentage of time that parents and Maya male and female children ages 3–21 and older spend in child-care tasks.

| Child care task | Parents | Children | |
		Male	Female
Nursing	1.0%	—	—
Direct care	2.0	0.0%	0.0%
Active indirect care	1.0	1.0	4.0
Passive indirect care	2.0	0.4	2.0
Instruction	2.0	0.1	0.1
Playing while in charge	—	0.1	0.6
Totals	8.0	1.0	7.0

Table 6.12 The mean proportion of time that Maya male and female children ages 0–23 allocate to child care. *p* values given for sex comparisons within age groups.

| | Age group | | | | | |
	0–3	4–7	8–11	12–15	16–19	20–23
Males	.000	.01	.04	.005	.01	.01
	(.7369)	(.0147)	(.0553)	(.0496)	(.3326)	(.5029)
Females	.004	.09	.11	.08	.04	.02

Table 6.13 The mean number of hours that a Maya household spends daily in total work.

Activity	Daily hours
Domestic work	16.7
Field work	6.9
Wage labor	3.6
Hunting and beekeeping	1.5
Nonsubsistence tasks	1.3
Total	30.0

Table 6.14 Mean percentage of time that Maya male and female children ages 3–23 allocate to total work.

	Time allocated	
Activity	Males	Females
Domestic work	6%	30%
Field work	11	5
Wage labor	14	—
Hunting and beekeeping	1	—
Nonsubsistence tasks	1	—
Total work	33	35

Table 6.15 The mean proportion of time that Maya male and female children ages 0–23 allocate to total work. *p* values given for sex comparisons within age groups.

	Age group					
	0–3	4–7	8–11	12–15	16–19	20–23
Males	.01	.05	.23	.38	.50	.69
	(.8611)	(.0089)	(.9180)	(.0414)	(.1398)	(.2448)
Females	.02	.14	.22	.55	.62	.58

Table 6.16 The mean proportion of time and number of daily hours that Maya female and male children allocate to total work across age groups. *p* values given for age group comparisons within sex.

	Age group					
	0–3	4–7	8–11	12–15	16–19	20–23
Proportion	.01	.05	.23	.38	.50	.69
Males	(.3341)	(.0001)	(.1170)	(.1785)	(.0311)	
Hours	0.1	0.5	2.5	4.2	5.5	7.6
Proportion	.02	.14	.22	.55	.62	.58
Females	(.0226)	(.0001)	(.1368)	(.3231)	(.6425)	
Hours	0.2	1.5	2.4	6.1	6.8	6.4

Table 6.17 Ordinary least squares regression results for the time Maya children ages 3–23 allocate to work after adjusting for age and sex. r^2 values are in boldface and p values are listed below.

	Domestic work	Field work	Total work	Child care
Age Age^2	**.3879**	**.3008**	**.8509**	**.1613**
	.0001	.0001	.0001	.0160
Sex	**.4175**	**.0365**	**.0362**	**.2724**
	.0001	.1489	.1489	.0001
Age Age^2 Sex	**.7019**	**.3612**	**.8701**	**.3642**
	.0001	.0001	.0001	.0001

Table 6.18 Logistic regression results for the time Maya children ages 3–23 allocate to work after adjusting for age and sex. The value given is the percentage change in the drop in deviance when an intercept and the adjusted effect of age or sex are added to the model.

	Domestic work	Field work	Total work	Child care
Age Age^2	.12	.07	.21	.05
Sex	.12	.01	.01	.05
Age Age^2 Sex	.21	.09	.21	.07

Table 7.1 Percentage of time Maya male and female children and parents allocate to various activities.

	Males aged				Females aged			
	3–8	9–14	15–20	Parents	3–8	9–14	15–20	Parents
Domestic work	3%	10%	9%	10%	10%	34%	53%	49%
Field work	3	14	16	24	2	5	10	6
Wage labor	—	—	24	13	—	—	—	—
Hunting, beekeeping	<1	<1	<1	10	—	—	—	—
Nonsubsistence labor[a]	—	—	8	4	—	—	—	—
Child care	<1	5	<1	2	7	12	3	14
Total work[b]	6	25	54	60	12	39	63	56
	.6 hr	2.6 hr	6.3 hr	6.6 hr	1.3 hr	4.3 hr	6.9 hr	6.3 hr

Note: Dash indicates no observed time spent in the activity.
a. Obligatory community labor, travel to a job, or minding a business (the *molino* or *tienda*).
b. Does not include child care.

Table 7.2 Productivity weights based on observed return rates. Weight represents
the proportion of the adult mean.

Task	Sex	Age	Weight
Making tortillas	Female	≤13	0.62
		14–17	0.82
		≥18	1.00
Planting maize	Male	≤11	0.26
		12–13	0.413
		14–18	0.98
		≥19	1.00
Harvesting maize	Male	≤11	0.47
		12–18	0.95
		≥19	1.0
	Female	12–14	0.75
		15–18	0.77
		≥19	1.00
Weeding	Male and female	<8	0.5
		8–10	0.75
		≥10	1.00
Shelling maize	Male and female	≤6	0.40
		7–9	0.64
		10–12	0.75
		≥13	1.00
Hauling water	Female	≤5	0.45
		6–11	0.75
		≥12	1.00
Cutting firewood	Female	<11	0.45
		11–15	0.65
		16–17	0.85
		18–19	0.90
		≥20	1.00

Table 7.3 Activity levels and energy expenditures (kcal per minute) for various Maya tasks.

Activity level	Caloric expenditure	Activity
Resting	1.0	Sleep
Very light	1.5	Child care Personal maintenance Social activities Religious activities Political activities
Play	1.9	Children's play and leisure Babies when awake
Light	2.5	Domestic maintenance Food processing Food preparation Tending animals Sewing Errands Hunting Beekeeping Wage labor Resource processing Construction Community labor
Moderate[a]	5.0	Field work Sports Firewood collection Water collection

Note: Activity levels are reported in Durnin and Passmore (1967) and National Academy of Sciences (1989). Caloric expenditures assigned to each activity level are taken from Durnin and Passmore (1967:47); Montgomery and Johnson (1977:100–102); National Academy of Sciences (1989:27). Ulijaszek (1995:35–39).

a. Heavy (7.5–9.9 kcal/min) is the activity level assigned to activities such as running, heavy manual digging, playing basketball (National Academy of Sciences 1989:27). No commonly performed Maya task sustains this level of caloric expenditure.

Table 7.4 Estimated age at net production for total work calculated under different assumptions.

Weight assumption	Age at net production	
	Males	Females
a. Hours spent working (no adjustment)	19	10
b. Hours spent working adjusted by productivity (weight applied only to tasks with observed return rates)	18	11
c. Hours spent in total work adjusted by productivity (weight applied to all tasks, and equally to males and females by age class; >20 = 1.0, 10–20 = .8 and <10 = .5)	17.5	13
d. Hours spent working adjusted by productivity (weight applied equally to males and females by age class, as above, for non-strength-dependent tasks; sex graded for strength-dependent tasks only	17	14
e. Hours spent working adjusted by productivity (weight applied only to tasks with observed return rates) and energy expenditure	17	12
f. Hours spent working adjusted by productivity (weight applied as in d) and energy expenditure	16.5	15

Note: See Table 7.2 for task-specific productivity weights.

Table 7.5 Select case studies of children's participation in household production. Groups included limited to those with an agricultural/horticultural subsistence base. Child care separated out where possible.

Study population location	Subsistence	Type of work[a]	Estimate of work effort		Consumption	Method	Source
			Male	Female			
Java	Agriculture	FW, DW, TA, WL CC	*16- to 18-year-olds*[b] 7.8 hrs/day 0.3 hrs/day	10.5 hrs/day 0.1 hrs/day	Not reported	Interview	White (1975:141)
Java	Agriculture	FW, DW, WL CC	*15- to 19-year-olds*[b] 7.9 hrs/day 0 hrs/day	9.4 hrs/day 0.8 hrs/day	Household expenditure on food	Interview	Nag et al. (1978:294–5)
Nepal	Agriculture	FW, DW, TA, WL CC	*15- to 19-year-olds*[b] 9.4 hrs/day 0.1 hrs/day	11.1 hrs/day 0.02 hrs/day	Household expenditure on food	Interview	Nag et al. (1978:295–6)
Bangladesh	Agriculture, wage labor	FW, DW, WL CC	*16- to 21-year-olds*[b] 9.5 hrs/day	9.4 hrs/day	Calorie consumption from standardized tables	Interview	Cain (1977:216)
Rural India	Agriculture, wage labor	FW, DW, WL	*14- to 17-year-olds*[b] 5.8 hrs/day	5.6 hrs/day	Not reported	Interview	Skoufias (1994:340)
India	Agriculture	FW	*13- to 18-year-olds* 2.6 hrs/day (other measures reported)	—	Not reported	Interview	Vlassoff (1979:420)

Table 7.5 (continued)

Study population location	Subsistence	Type of work[a]	Estimate of work effort		Consumption	Method	Source
			Male	Female			
Egypt	Commercial agriculture	WL	*12- to 15-year-olds* 5.2 hrs/day (other measures reported)	4.13 hrs/day	Food consumption as proportion of mean adult from national data	Interview	Mueller (1976:107,112)
Botswana	Agriculture, herding, foraging, wage labor	DW, FW, F, TA	*15- to 19-year-olds*[b] 40.9%	45.15%	Interview		Mueller (1984:332–333)
		DW, FW, F, TA CC	41.8%	48.5%			
Rural Switzerland	Agriculture, wage labor	FW, DW CC	*Children* 0.9 hrs/day			Time-allocation diaries	Minge-Kalman (1978:190)
Machiguenga	Horticulture, foraging	FW, DW, F CC	*6- to 13-year-olds*[b] 2.7 hrs/day 0.1 hrs/day	1.9 hrs/day 0.5 hrs/day	Not reported	Scan samples	Johnson (1975:305–306)
Canchinos, Peru	Agriculture, herding	FW, DW, TA CC	*6- to 10-year-olds*[b] 42.1%[c] 4.8[c]		Not reported	Scan samples	Munroe et al. (1983:360)

Table 7.5 (continued)

Study population location	Subsistence	Type of work[a]	Estimate of work effort		Consumption	Method	Source
			Male	Female			
Kikuyu, Kenya	Horticulture, herding	FW, DW, TA CC	*6- to 10-year-olds[b]* 52.6%[c] 4.1%[c]	52.6%[c] 4.1%[c]	Not reported	Scan samples	Munroe et al. (1983:360)
Logoli, Kenya	Horticulture, herding	FW, DW, TA CC	*6- to 10-year-olds[b]* 27.4%[c] 9.1%[c]	27.4%[c] 9.1%[c]	Not reported	Scan samples	Munroe et al. (1983:360)
Zimbabwe	Agriculture	FW, DW, TA CC	*10- to 18-year-olds[b]* 23% 1%	60% 5%	Not reported	Scan samples	Reynolds (1991:63)
Botswana	Agriculture, foraging, herding	FW, DW, TA, F CC	*7- to 15-year-olds[b]* 27% <1%	20% 1.6%		Scan samples	Bock (1995:101)

Note: Reported values for time spent working were converted into hours per day wherever possible and for juveniles wherever possible so that values are comparable across groups. Time was *not* converted to hours if the length of observation day was unclear or unreported.

a. Type of work included in estimate. Child care separated out where possible. FW = field work; DW = domestic work; TA = tending animals (includes herding); WL = wage labor; F = Foraging; CP = craft production; CC = child care.

b. Other age groups are reported by the author.

c. Male and female values reported as combined by the author.

d. Time spent working reported by the author as a proportion, but converted to hours per day.

Table 8.1 Average age of production and consumption for Maya males and females.

	Average age of production	Average age of consumption
Males	32.0	28.1
Females	26.4	22.6

Table 9.1 Return rates and time savings for Maya women to collect water and grind maize when laborsaving technology is not and is available.

Task	Amount[a]	Time
Collecting water		
Hand drawn with ropes	150 liters	170 minutes
Hauled from pump	150 liters	67 minutes

A woman can save approximately 1.7 hours per day when water is hauled from the powered pump.

Grinding maize		
With a hand grinder	8 kilos	61 minutes
At the *molino*	8 kilos	20 minutes

A woman can save an additional 40 minutes per day with mechanized maize processing.

a. Average daily household use.

Table 9.2 Results of the best-fit model for the probability of a mother giving birth to her first child.

Variable	Parameter estimate	Adjusted change in deviance	*p* value	Adjusted odds ratio
Intercept	−3.9446			
Age effect	0.6911	14.8993	.0001	1.996
Age^2 effect	−0.0301	5.8857	.0153	0.970
Presence/absence technology	0.8905	5.2436	.0220	2.436

Source: Kramer and McMillan (1999:510).

Food List

The following food list includes domesticated animals, animals that are hunted, foods that are cultivated in milpas and kitchen gardens, and foods that are foraged. Purchased foods are not included. The names given are what Xculoc villagers responded when asked for the Maya and Spanish names of the foods that they regularly consume. Some of these food items are not found in Spanish dictionaries. Where possible, Maya spellings are taken from Heath de Zapata (1980) and Bevington (1995).

Spanish	Maya	English
Fruits and nuts		
ciruela	abal	plum
marañón	marañón	cashew
mamey	mamey	sapote
plátano	ha'as	banana
ziricote[a]	kopte	
ramon[b]	óox	breadfruit
limón	limón su'uts	lime
limón dulce	limón chuhuk	sweet lime
mango	maango	mango
naranja dulce	xchiina	orange
naranja agria	su'uts' pak'áal	sour orange
piñuela	choon	
piña	piña	pineapple
coco	coco	coconut
papaya	put	papaya
tamarindo	tamarindo	tamarind
almendra	almendráas	almond
sandía	sandía	watermelon
guayaba	pichi'	guava
guayaba	chachac	guava
guayaba de monte	huayunn	guava
nopal	paak'am	prickly pear

Spanish	Maya	English
saramullo	tzarmuy	
granada	granada	pomegranate
nance	chi'	
pitalla	pitalla	
mandarina	mandarina	mandarin

Starches and vegetables

maíz	nal (elote), xi'im' (shelled)	maize
chile jabanero	ik	habanero
chile simple	xcat' ik	chili
cebolla	cebooya	onion
tomate	p'aak	tomato
cebollina	cebollina	chives
camote	is	yam
calabaza	xcat k'úum	squash (large seed)
calabaza	xtoop k'uum	squash
calabaza	xmeejen k'uum	squash
calabaza	tzol	squash
cacahuate	cacahuate	peanuts
frijol blanco	eeb	white beans
frijol negro	bu'ul	black beans
aguacate	on	avocado
chaya	chay	(leafy green)
pepino	pepino	cucumber
jicama	chiikam	jicama

Hunted game

puerco del monte	kitan	boar
cabritto	yuuk	bocket deer (*Mazama americana*)
venado	keeh	white tail deer (*Odocoilius virginianus*)
armadillo	weech	armadillo
iguana	huh	iguana
tusa	bah	mole
conejo	t'u'ul	rabbit
pavo del monte	kutz	wild turkey
pisote, tejon	chi'ik	coati
tepezcuintle	haale	paca
agutí	tsuu	agouti
ardilla	ku'uk	squirrel
tortuga	aak	tortoise
chachalaca	bach	chachalaca
paloma	tsu tsuy	dove
paloma	tsak bakal	dove
tortolita	mucuy	turtledove

Spanish	Maya	English
paloma	uukum	dove
loro	t'uut'	parrot
Domesticated animals		
cochino	k'eek'en	pig
gallina	kaax	chicken
pato	kuuts ja'	duck
pavo	uulum	turkey
cabra	taman	goat
Herbs and spices		
achiote	ko'xu	annato
yerba buena	yerba buena	peppermint
cilantro	cilantro	coriander
Other		
	leec	gourd (*Crescentia* sp.)
	chuuh	gourd
sabila	sabila	(soap)
henequén	ki	sisal hemp
jícara	luch	gourd (*Lageneria* sp.)
miel	ka	honey

a. Also used to wash dishes.
b. Also used as fodder for domesticated animals.

– APPENDIX C –

Explanation of Scan and Focal-Follow Variables

An individual's *activity* at the instant of the scan was classified from a list of more than three hundred possible activity codes. Activity codes are hierarchically organized to contain several levels of information. For example, if a woman is kneading maize dough with water, the activity code is recorded as 341. The 300 signifies that it is a food-processing or preparation task, the 40 that it is a tortilla-making task, and the 1 that it is the specific task of kneading maize dough. Coding activities in a nested hierarchy preserves detail for future research yet facilitates flexibility of lumping together activities for analysis. Suites of activities can be readily regrouped for specific analysis or to make groupings compatible with other studies, as needed.

The *object of the activity* was recorded when applicable. If the activity was cooking, for example, the food being cooked was recorded. The object of an activity may also be a person, as in the case of child care. If a girl is carrying a baby, the object records the relationship of the baby to her; whether the baby is her brother, sister, or cousin; and the baby's identification number.

The *activity weight* records whether someone is doing more than one task simultaneously. If a mother is nursing a child and stirring a pot, both activities are recorded and given a weight of 0.5. Most observations (94 percent) had a weight of 1.

The *location* where the activity occurred was recorded in two ways. First, the general location where the activity took place—such as in a kitchen, in a *solar* yard, in the plaza—was identified. Second, during the mapping, each structure, yard, garden, and communal place (the church, well, plaza, *molino*) was given a unique identification number, which was also recorded for each scan observation.

The presence or absence of the individual who was being observed was coded. Since the members of a household were sampled as a unit, it was not always possible to locate each household member at each fifteen-minute-interval scan. During an observation session, a son or father might be away doing wage labor or be in the forest hunting or tending bees. In these cases, if a family member was absent for most or all of an observation session, I would ask other family members where the individual was. Or, if the person returned, I would ask the individual directly. If a family member had gone out only briefly and returned, I would ask the participant what he or she had been doing, although many times a reliable deduction could be made. (If a girl left the *solar* with a bucket of whole maize and returned twenty minutes later with it ground, I was fairly confident that she had been at the *molino* getting maize ground. Or, if a mother gave a young boy a directive, and he left the house and returned with a handful of salt, he most likely was running an errand for his mother.) To account for these differences, each observation was ranked by one of four levels of observation reliability. The highest rank was assigned when the behavior was directly observed. A lower rank was given if the behavior was not directly observed but I had reliable information either by asking or deducing what the individual was doing, as in the above examples. Eighty-five percent of observations came under these two categories. The third-ranked code was given when the behavior was not directly observed because the person was some distance from the village, such as away hunting, doing wage labor, visiting a relative in another village, or in the fields. A fourth code was used if I temporarily could not find someone or could not find out what he or she was doing for a particular observation. In these cases, no activity was recorded.

— APPENDIX D —

Adjusting an Analysis of Variance for Proportional Data

Two adjustments have been made in the calculation of the analyses of variance in Chapter 6. First, because the variance is not independent of the mean in proportional data, when calculating the p values for differences between age and sex groups the proportions are transformed using the *arcsine of the square root of the proportion*. Because the value range of proportional data is constrained by 0 and 1, the distribution of the variance is not constant. The potential range of variance at the extreme values of 0 and 1, where the distribution is bound, necessarily differs from the variance at central values. The *arcsine transformation* stabilizes the nonconstant variance and renders it independent of the mean. However, since the mean proportions are transformed, the values are expressed in a unit of measure that is not readily interpretable. Thus, the means themselves are reported as the untransformed proportions, while the p values for the differences between groups are reported using the arcsine transformation of proportion.

In the second adjustment, the means for male/female comparisons are calculated using a least squares (LS) mean procedure, which adjusts for unbalanced data and diminishes the possible effects of skewed sample size differences between classes of data. The age distribution in this Maya community is such that there are more older girls than boys. Since the time spent working tends to increase with age, the clustering of data points around older girls will tend to inflate mean values for girls and deflate values for boys. LS means, in a sense, adjust for this bias and are used when reporting differences between sexes when the proportions are pooled across age groups.

Where an ordinary least squares model (OLS) is used, the proportions are transformed to the arcsine for the same reasons described above. The *arcsine transformation* tends to improve the fit of the model slightly, but coefficients and r^2 values are not appreciably different from models using the untransformed proportion as the response variable.

Deviance as an Estimate of Dispersion

Ordinary least squares regression models are used to summarize the age and sex patterning across different classes of work because results are easily interpreted and are familiar to most readers and because coefficients of determination (r^2 values) can be compared across models. However, logistic regression is a more appropriate model for proportional data. The response variable—work—is expressed as a proportion, or the sum of specific task observations divided by the sum of the total number of observations. By definition, proportions are bound by the values of 0 and 1. Ordinary least squares regression theory assumes that the mean of the response variable is a linear function of the predictor variables. However, since the shape of the distribution is dictated by the constraints of 0 and 1, the distribution of proportional data is not continuously linear. Rather, observed proportions tend to distribute in a sigmoidal shape, since the unit increase in y per unit increase in x is necessarily smaller as the proportion nears 0 or 1 and greatest as it nears .5. It follows that predictions made from logistic and linear models will tend to become increasingly different as probabilities approach 0 or 1. Thus an OLS model that has a non-0 slope would eventually predict values that are greater than 1 or less than 0. An obvious solution is to transform the data so that it assumes a more linear shape. Response proportions are commonly transformed to a logit, or log odds, scale and maximum likelihood estimates used for estimating parameters. The resulting logistic regression model expresses the proportion of successes, where a success in this case is the activity observed, such as domestic work, as a function of (in this case) age.

   Deviances in logistic regression are analogous to the residual sum of squares (RSS) used to compute coefficient of determination in regular regression theory. However, deviances can be compared only across nested, or hierarchical, models. Although there is no direct estimate of dispersion or r^2 correlate in logistic regression, deviances (-2 log likelihood) can be compared across nonnested models in the following way.

$$r^2 = 1 - (\text{RSS}_{\text{intercept + effect}} / \text{RSS}_{\text{intercept}})$$

comparably

$$= 1 - (\text{Deviance}_{\text{intercept + effect}} / \text{Deviance}_{\text{intercept}})$$

This gives an r^2-like measure for the difference in the amount of variation explained by the model. Specifically, it gives the percentage difference in the drop in deviance when age and sex are added to a logistic model. Appendix Table 6.18 shows the results using this method for the same age and sex models summarized in Appendix Table 6.17.

– NOTES –

1. Children as Helpers at the Nest

1. The mean completed family size of 7.3 is for women who were 45–55 in 2000. Note that a standard total fertility rate (TFR) is not reported, given village size and the small sample of mothers who give birth each year in an age group, but it would be a lower number since a TFR includes all women in a population, not just mothers. See Appendix Table 4.4 for completed fertility over time.

2. *Young children* is defined using Bogin's (1999a) definition of childhood as the period between weaning and the eruption of permanent teeth, usually complete by age 7.

   Nonhuman primate juveniles also have more restrictive diets and higher protein and digestibility requirements than do adults (Janson and van Schaik 1993).

3. *Older children* here refers to children who eat adult food but who are not yet fully grown or have not yet reached sexual maturity. The term *juvenile* is variously defined for humans and is addressed later in this chapter.

4. The mean age at first birth averaged across four natural fertility populations (Ache, Hadza, Hiwi, and !Kung) is given as 19.7 (Kaplan et al. 2000:158).

5. Fitness is defined as "the number of reproductively successful offspring it contributes to the next generation" (Fleagle 1999:63), and can be thought of as equivalent to an individual's reproductive success.

6. Male investment in offspring is common in a number of cooperative breeding species (Asa 1997; Woolfenden and Fitzpatrick 1984), including callitricids (Goldizen 1987; McKenna 1987). Among humans, paternal assistance varies widely, but it can be vital to raising young (Hurtado et al. 1992; Iron 1983; Kaplan 1996; Kaplan et al. 2000; Lancaster and Lancaster 1983, 1987). Where to place the help of fathers varies in the cooperative breeding literature. In avian studies, where ideas about cooperative breeding were developed, the help of fathers was traditionally considered male parental investment. But when genetic testing made it possible to ascertain paternity, it became clear that many male helpers were not the fathers after all. In recent studies, to avoid making assumptions about paternity, male assistance in raising young has been considered an extension of allomothering (Hrdy 2001).

7. These are the figures most often cited. However, more recent overviews on cooperative breeding suggest some definitional problems in the earlier research and give higher estimates for cooperative breeding in birds, as high as 8–17 percent (Cockburn 1998; Heinsohn and Double 2004).

8. *Helpers-at-the-nest* was first introduced into ethology by Skutch (1935) and reintroduced into behavioral ecology by Emlen (1978). The term *helper* is variously defined in the behavioral ecology literature, sometimes as a sexually mature, nonbreeding adult and sometimes more generally as an individual who provides allo-maternal care. I use the term *helper* in its more general application, as a

nonparental individual who provides allocare. Although a distinction is sometimes made in their usage, the terms *helper* and *allomother* (alloparent) are used
interchangeably. See Solomon and French 1997:3–6 for an overview of the usage
of *cooperative breeding, communal breeding,* and *helper* terminology.

9. Rapid growth may increase infant survival for several reasons, one of which is
that a larger body size attenuates the risk of predation and is perhaps why cooperative breeding and male parental investment are associated with small primates
(Mitani and Watts 1997).

10. Jamieson and Craig (1987) present an alternative to the inclusive fitness explanation for helping behavior: "The act of feeding young by auxiliary nonbreeders
was virtually indistinguishable from the act of feeding offspring by parents. This
led to the suggestion that the provisioning of nestlings by auxiliaries (i.e.,
helpers) might be maintained in communal breeding populations as a byproduct
of the evolution of the stimulus-response provisioning mechanism found in birds
in general" (Jamieson 1991:271). This nonadaptive point of view that helping is
the unselected consequence of parental care of altricial young has been rigor-
ously challenged (Emlen et al. 1991; but see Tardif 1997).

11. Emlen (1991) outlines four general direct and indirect ways that helpers may
benefit from helping. Helping may enhance (a) their probability of survival, (b)
their likelihood for future mating opportunities, or (c) future fecundity.
Alternatively, helpers may benefit indirectly, by (d) increasing the reproductive
success of other breeders (augmenting the survival of siblings or increasing their
rate of reproduction).

12. The difficulty of measuring the opportunity cost to a helper for spending his or
her time in other activities and measuring the effect of helping on a helper's
inclusive fitness has been remarked on by other authors, who have reported
mixed results in empirical studies (Tardif 1997).

13. Among fork-marked lemurs, "low female fertility was best predicted by large
family size associated with delayed dispersal by previous offspring. Although
there is no obvious benefit from full-grown offspring in their territory, adults tolerate delayed natal dispersal, probably because dispersal poses extraordinary
costs for the offspring. These costs are likely to accrue from decreased foraging
efficiency in unfamiliar habitats because exudate feeding requires very rigid
feeding itineraries" (Schülke 2003:11).

14. The view that children are "a poor man's capital" (Vlassoff 1979:428) appears
earlier (Boserup 1965; Clark and Haswell 1967), but not as the focus of theoretic development. (Note that Vlassoff himself advocated the opposite—that children are not a means to wealth.)

15. "The demand for children must still remain at the heart of most explanations of
fertility change" (Lee and Bulatao 1983:233). An overview of the intellectual history of fertility change written a decade later reiterates this same point of view.
"To understand changing fertility requires historic reconstruction in specific contexts of the varying ways in which changes have occurred in the perceived relative cost of childbearing. This is the central complex variable involved in fertility
change" (Szreter 1993:692–93).

16. In its broadest definition, to describe the general life stage shared by all mammals, juvenility is defined as the duration between weaning and sexual maturity. In humans, the period of growth following weaning has been further subdivided into three developmental stages—childhood, juvenility, and adolescence. Each is defined based on a distinct pattern of growth velocity and developmental trajectories (Bogin 1991, 1997, 1999b). Unless otherwise indicated, I use *juvenile* here and throughout this book to refer to the more general mammalian life stage from weaning to sexual maturity.

17. Juveniles have been characterized by biologists as "animals that would be likely to survive death of their caretaker or loss of parental provisions, but have not yet matured sexually" (Pereira 1993:19). Human juveniles (using either the definition as beginning at weaning or after childhood), however, are not likely to survive the loss of their caretakers, since they are not self-feeders or economically independent.

18. Smith (1991) estimates that the first molar erupted at about age 3–3.5 in australopithecines, several years earlier than in modern humans, when it occurs at about 5.5–6.5 years.

19. Net cost can be calculated as a child's economic contribution (production) minus his or her economic cost (consumption).

20. Here and throughout, labor-market population refers to an economy based largely on wage labor, cash exchange, and the national or global market.

2. Sources of Variation in Children's Time Allocation

1. Skill and strength are used here as criteria to distinguish task requirements. For a complete discussion of skill and strength as forms of investment in embodied capital, see Bock 1995; Bock and Johnson 2002; Kaplan and Bock 2001.

3. Situating the Maya

1. *Aguadas* are clay-sealed, shallow depressions often associated with fracture lines in the underlying bedrock. Water seeps in from shallow aquifers and collects in these sealed depressions, creating seasonal or permanent springs. Water also collects in *chultuns (sartenejas)*, which are hollows or pools in the limestone outcrops. *Chaltuns* fill with rainwater during the wet season and may be up to several meters in diameter.

2. Cook and Borahs (1974) meticulous study estimates the Maya population of the Yucatan Peninsula at 2.3 million in 1500 and 240,000 in 1549. Note that they included the modern-day states of Yucatan, Campeche, and Quintana Roo as part of the Yucatan Peninsula.

3. In this part of Mexico the term *rancho*, which refers to a small ranch or farm, is often used instead of *hacienda*, which refers to a large estate.

4. Seventy-nine percent of the community listed "Catholic" as their religious affiliation during the household survey. This compares with 86 percent for the state of Yucatan and 90 percent for Mexico. Nine percent of the state of Yucatan declares *Protestante* or *Evangelica* as their religious affiliation (INEGI 1991b: *cuadro* 10, pp. 96–97).

5. Aréchiga 1978; Aréchiga and Serrano 1981; Benedict and Steggerda 1937; Cook

1919; Emerson and Kempton 1935; Gann 1918; Godas et al. 1988; Higbee 1948; Kintz 1990; Landa 1982 [1566]; Lewis 1951; Linton 1940; Lundell 1933; Matheny 1978; Press 1975; Redfield 1941, 1950; Redfield and Villa Rojas 1934; Reina and Hill 1980; Restall 1997; Roys 1943, 1957; Ryder 1977; Steggerda 1932, 1941; Stephens 1996 [1843]; Thompson 1930; Villa Rojas 1945.

6. Each person consumes on average 0.8 kilos of ground maize daily or about 1.75 pounds. Cowgill (1962) made a very similar estimate of 1.7 pounds (range 1.3–2.0 pounds).

7. Current value in 1993.

8. *Conosupo*, the Mexican government's agricultural collective, bought bulk corn for 15 to 20 cents per kilo (current value in 1993).

9. Killer bees have recently outcompeted the nonstinging honeybees traditionally used in honey production. Hives are now maintained away from the village to be at a safe distance from young children.

10. The guns are Remington .22 rifles, that have been passed down from father to son, probably since the 1920s.

11. September is the wettest month, with a mean monthly rainfall of 200 millimeters (8 inches). March is the driest month, with 20 millimeters (<1 inch) (Dunning 1992; Wilson 1980). The precipitation data that we recorded during the 1992–93 field season generally reflect these statewide patterns (Dore 1996).

12. The temperature data that we collected in the village yielded a mean high of 33.2° C (92° F) and a mean low of 19.6° C (61° F) with a range of 9° C to 26° C.

13. Because humidity was measured at midday, when temperatures are at their highest, humidity values may be lower than at other times of day.

14. Farmers interviewed in 2003 had a mixed response to the question of whether land was sufficient for their sons to cultivate milpas in the future. A few men responded that they were concerned, while others did not perceive near-future constraints on land availability.

15. Maya word for conical karstic hills.

16. The mean weight per ear of fresh maize is 168 grams with the cob and 125 grams without the cob ($n = 40$).

17. Cowgill (1962) made a similar estimate for the Peten lowlands.

18. This is changing very rapidly. During the 2001 and 2003 field seasons, economic interviews showed that villagers are financing the purchase of cash-economy goods through the intensification of maize cultivation and are doing less wage labor now than they were at the time of the initial study.

4. Maya Families

1. The state of Campeche census reported 314 residents in Xculoc in 1990 (INEGI 1991c), and we recorded 316 in 1992.

2. Children, for the most part, are born in the village, though some mothers may go to a relative's or midwife's house in a larger town to give birth. To register a birth, parents must travel to the regional center, and birth certificates were not routinely applied for in the past. To vote in the 2000 presidential election, villagers for the first time were issued voting cards, which could not be obtained

without birth documentation. What we found during our 2001 census was that these birth documents were often issued many years after birth, especially the older the person was. In some cases, people readily pulled out these cards and whatever other birth documentation they had. In other cases, an unspoken avoidance to do so was apparent. To maintain the confidence of villagers, we respected any reluctance to show us these legal documents.

3. The number of births included in this sample differs from that included in the birth-interval sample because the birth-interval sample included only those births in parities one through seven.

4. A number of boys—both living in the village and tracked through reproductive histories—suffer from an inherited disease that begins to afflict them in their early childhood and causes their muscles to atrophy. By adolescence they are unable to walk and are confined to handmade carts. They seldom survive adolescence and typically die around the age of 15, depending on the disease's severity. The disease is passed through females, although only males manifest the symptoms. The disease currently afflicts only the sons of one group of sisters. These boys are cared for as well as possible. When asked, parents said that health-care providers have told them that nothing can be done to help. Although not diagnosed by a doctor who has seen these children, the physical symptoms described match that of Duchenne muscular dystrophy (Carol Clericuzio, MD, dysmorphologist, University of New Mexico Hospital).

5. The Early and Peters estimate is for Yanomani children's survival to age 10 (76 percent). Hewlett's estimate is for thirteen groups of horticulturalists, with 60 percent of children surviving to age 15.

6. When reproductive histories were re-collected in 2001, of the ninety-seven births reported since 1993, one infant and no children were reported to have died in the same interval. This gives an infant mortality of 10.3 per 1,000.

7. Xculoc is located 1 kilometer south of the Yucatan/Campeche state boundary in the state of Campeche. However, only summary data, not age-specific census data, are available for the state of Campeche. Thus, 1990 census data for the state of Yucatan were used instead.

8. Experiments with different life tables showed that the timing of demographic pressure across the family life cycle is not very sensitive to the level of life expectancy within a plausible range, for which seventy years would be the upper limit. Note that the age distribution implied by the Model West 11 life table (with a TFR of 7.2) closely fits Xculoc's age distribution (Lee and Kramer 2002).

9. Only those families who participated in the time-allocation study were included, since the individual production and consumption data that were the result of that study will be folded into this figure in Chapter 8.

6. How Maya Children Spend Their Time

1. *Posole* is the term the Maya use to refer to maize gruel, different from the hominy stew of the American Southwest.

2. In addition, Bove et al. (2000:462) and Ivey (2000:861) report time allocated to

child care, but the age-group classes are not comparable to the Maya data on this point.

7. Production and Consumption across the Life Course

1. In labor market economies, because males commonly receive a higher wage than females, male work is often weighted more heavily than female labor. For example, Mueller (1976) gives women a productivity weight of .75 compared with that of men based on agricultural wage data for India and Egypt. This weight was applied to all labor. However, there is no reason to expect that males in a nonlabor market economy would be more efficient than females at tasks, such as making tortillas, that do not require strength, are not physically demanding, and that males never perform.

   Tasks requiring physical strength include field work, hauling water, chopping firewood, grinding maize, shelling maize, pounding maize, rinsing maize, and washing clothes.

2. This balancing assumption has been used in other economic analyses of intergenerational wealth flows (e.g., Stecklov 1999).

3. An individual's *resting energy expenditure* (REE), or the daily caloric requirement for a resting individual, is a function of multiplying an individual's weight by standard coefficients for age and sex (National Academy of Sciences 1989; World Health Organization 1985; for other applications, see Kaplan 1994). REE is then multiplied by an individual's average daily activity level, since each individual expends an additional amount of energy based on his or her activity load. An individual's average daily activity level is derived by summing the time he or she spends in each activity level after multiplying it by the coefficient for that activity level as shown in Table 7.3.

4. Theoretically, an infinite number of patterns of interage net-transfers is possible (consistent with the observed differences between production and consumption at each age), since, for example, A could make a net-transfer to B, who could net-transfer to C, which would be indistinguishable from a net-transfer directly from A to C, unless the actual transfers were observed. Thus, following Stecklov (1999), I make the canonical assumption of the "common pot," that is, every family member is assumed to put his/her production into a common family pot. The pot is then shared out—in this case, 80 percent to family members according to their energy-based consumption needs and 20 percent based on family size.

5. As was done, for example, in Cain's (1977) work.

6. Consumption does not include the consumption of primary care by infants and babies, and production does not include the time spent in child care. The reasons for not including child care as a part of total work are discussed in Chapter 6.

7. Since the shape and location of the production and consumption curves can potentially vary with smoothing procedures, experiments were made with different smoothing procedures and resolutions in S+ and SAS with a variety of settings. Although no standard statistical method is routinely used to evaluate which smoothing procedure bests represents the underlying behavior of the population, if the crossover point of the production and consumption curves remains stable across

methods, this suggests that the curves reflect the underlying data and not the choice of smoothing method, per se. Across methods, the curves and crossover point remain very stable for females, changing little with smoothing procedure, span width, or resolution. The crossover point for males varied by a year or so, plus or minus, depending on span width and resolution. The broader range in the crossover point for males compared with that for females reflects the greater variability in age-specific male production. But in none of the experiments with smoothing procedure was there a wild fluctuation in male crossover point. The smoothing method selected and used in these analyses is a SAS spline routine with an interpolation value of 65. It is conservative in the sense that it is a moderate span width with a low resolution to avoid the risk of overfitting the data (Lee and Kramer 2002).

8. Children 20 and younger spend 29 percent of their work time and 8 percent of all time over an eleven-hour observation day in these seven tasks.

9. The energy cost of wage labor is weighted less than it is for field work to compensate for the fact that I did not observe men engaged in wage labor firsthand and could not exclude the time spent resting and eating, as I did for field work (see Chapter 6).

10. All three groups live in forested areas of South America. The Machiguenga are horticulturalists who also hunt and gather and live in a riverine environment in southeastern Peru. The Piro live at the base of the Andes, in southern Peru, and practice a mixed economy of horticulture, hunting, gathering, and wage labor. The Ache live in the subtropics of eastern Paraguay and currently have a mixed economy of horticulture and foraging.

11. Males and females were aggregated to obtain these ages for net productivity.

12. The age profiles have been standardized by dividing all the production and consumption schedules for a group by the average daily consumption of males and females from ages 0 to 49 (calculated as the sums of the male and female consumption profiles from ages 0 to 49 divided by 100). The units of consumption and production cancel out, leaving comparable indices (Lee et al. 2002).

8. Children's Help from a Parent's Perspective

1. Although these empirical tests have shown that net flows from children are negative, it is important to keep in mind that these studies are based on measurable production—time, calories, or money. As originally conceived, Caldwell (1976) included other aspects of children's value—such as political power, old age security, and risk sharing—in his consideration of net flows.

2. In later work, Cain critiqued Caldwell's perspective (Fricke 1990:108).

3. The younger average ages for females probably reflect sex differences in the village's age distribution. For example, male children ($n = 21$) under the age of 4 have a greater representation than female children ($n = 14$). Since younger children are less productive than older children, this discrepancy in n values pushes the average ages up for males compared with females.

4. Mueller's (1976) data are drawn from previously published surveys of nine agricultural societies that include Western, Indian, and Egyptian communities. The socioeconomic situation of these populations is unclear. However, I suspect that

the narrower margin of resource flow for the Maya as compared with Mueller's data is because Mueller's agricultural groups are much more embedded in the wage-labor and market economy, and unlike the Maya, parents buy food, finance educational costs, and forfeit children's labor by sending them to school. This may, in part, explain why Mueller concludes that agricultural children have a negative economic value. Her production and consumption calculations also differ substantially from the methods used here. Mueller's consumption indices are translated into a dollar amount, and production includes only those tasks that have a GNP value. Differences between her results and the Maya results are likely to reflect these different measures of children's economic value.

5. Experiments with life-table mortality assumptions had little effect on the cumulative payback age.

6. Note that while this earlier study is the one most frequently cited, Cain (1982) later revised his position, pointing out that discounting the rate of return on the value of children over the duration of time that a child lives in his parents' household would substantially affect the break-even point. "Any positive rate of time discount would push the break-even point to a higher age . . . it is no longer clear that the labour of children in rural Bangladesh compensates for their consumption over the period that children typically remain members of their parents' household" (Cain 1982:164).

7. The Maya time-allocation data (a) were collected using direct observation rather than interview methods and (b) were weighted for efficiency and energy expenditure, as explained in Chapter 7. (c) Estimates of Maya individual caloric needs were based on energy expenditure derived from age, sex, body weight, and activity load rather than standard age-sex charts for caloric requirements. (d) Importantly, Cain's production estimate included a variety of tasks, but consumption included only calorie consumption, which overstates cumulative production and lowers the estimate of the payback age. (e) The Maya values are adjusted for survival probabilities, whereas Cain's calculations assume that everyone survives to age twenty. (f) Both males and females are included in the Maya calculation, whereas Cain's analysis was limited to males. Other factors could be taken into account to estimate the cumulative payback age, such as the opportunity costs that parents pay to forgo alternate investment opportunities that may also yield a return and to which children may be compared as investments. Such discounting is not calculated for either the Maya or Bangladesh sample.

8. TFR estimates the total number of children (total live births) that a woman would have in her lifetime if she survived to the end of her childbearing years. A TFR is calculated by summing observed age-specific fertility rates and is usually expressed per 1,000 women. A TFR is commonly used in demographic studies as a reasonable estimate of average completed family size within a population.

9. It is a stochastic effect of a small population that at the time of the census no mother had only one child.

10. These are unadjusted daily hours of total work as described in Chapter 7.

11. Although work effort generally increases with household size, it does not monot-

onically increase because of the effect of an economy of scale on household production and because of differences in age composition among families of the same size. Smaller families have either young children or older, teenage children, while larger families, which show a stepped increase in median cost, are composed of both younger and older children.

12. In Chayanov's study (1986 [1925]), among his Russian peasant study population, when the average family was under demographic pressure, workers increased their labor in proportion to demand rather than decreasing consumption. But in a German factory worker study, Chayanov notes that consumption did vary. Whether a family responds to changes in demographic pressure by adjusting consumption or production depends on a number of factors, including how rapidly the marginal utility of consumption and leisure changes and whether the quantity of consumption or the quality of labor varies. The Maya are most likely similar to the Russian peasant scenario, since they live close to subsistence levels and would probably downwardly adjust consumption only under dire circumstances (Lee and Kramer 2001).

13. Parents in labor-market economies have the option of purchasing not only goods but also child care beyond the hours in the day that they have time to care for their children. In these economies, parents can save for the future, go to the bank and borrow, depend on government institutions, or modify their income and luxury expenditures. Parents in contracepting populations also have the option of adjusting their number of dependents by delaying first birth or extending birth intervals. Maya parents do not use contraception or participate in financial markets to save and dissave as an option to compensate for changes in consumption across the family life cycle.

14. Mothers and fathers increase their work effort at different points in the family life cycle, reflecting sex differences in the kind of care that each provides their children (see Figure 7.1). Maternal work effort increases markedly during early parities and reaches a maximum early in the family life cycle, whereas paternal work effort increases and plateaus later in the family life cycle. Demands on a woman's time are greatest when they are young mothers and have multiple young children who require primary care. Time spent in domestic work, which women fund and which is a large component of their total work effort, increases sharply during early parities, when mothers have no helpers old enough to assist them. From about marriage years five to twenty, a Maya mother will have more or less the same number of young dependents living in her household—one child being born as another reaches productive age. In contrast, the demand on a father's time is greatest as families mature and the number of weaned children that need to be fed increases. Reflecting this, fathers spend almost twice as much time in field work when all of their children are over the age of 6. Fathers allocate 19 percent of their time to field work when they have children under the age of 6 living at home and 37 percent when they have no children under the age of 6.

15. Because the average age and sex values for production and consumption reflect the very economic pressures that I wish to measure, this effect first has to be removed. For example, a forty-year-old woman is likely to have seven children

living at home, and her level of production and consumption is in response to her economic circumstances of having to support many dependents. Because household economic pressure is already built into an individual level of production and consumption, to use these values would underestimate the extent of these pressures. To ameliorate the problem, the production and consumption for each age and sex are modeled as the product of an age- and sex-specific standardized profile and a household-specific fixed effect. It is these estimates, then, that are used in the following analysis of consumer demand and labor supply (Lee and Kramer 2002).

16. Hames (1988:247) found that, among the Ye'kwana, if a mother were the sole caretaker of her children, she would have to work 14.5 hours a day in labor and child care.

9. How Long to Stay and Help?

1. Little theoretic or empirical research has focused on the lag time in behavioral adjustments when environmental conditions change and, specifically, with respect to technological conditions. In addition, although it has been fifteen years since the introduction of mechanized water collection, other changes in labor conditions have been minimal (see Postscript for more recent changes). Thus, the time-allocation data is assumed to reasonably represent time-allocation budgets before and after the introduction of the gas-powered technology in the mid 1970s.

2. At the time of this study, no woman in the community worked for wages.

3. There are no girls over the age of twenty in the sample living in their parents' household.

4. The fitted probabilities from this model are graphed in a distribution function. The median age at first birth for women in the two groups (before and after the introduction of laborsaving technology) is given at the 0.5 level of probability.

5. A mean age at menarche of 13.3 has been reported for Yucatan Maya women (Yewoubdar 1989) from a village of 2,500 near an urban area and market center. More appropriate estimates for the Xculoc Maya are the ages of 14.5 (Sabharwal et al. 1966) and 15.1 (Eveleth and Tanner 1990) reported for rural Guatemalan Maya women. Eveleth and Tanner's estimate is from the recalculated probits using Sabharwal et al.'s data. At the time of this study, young Xculoc women reached their maximum body size (weight and skinfold) at age twenty.

6. Whether mothers compensate for their daughters' reallocation to time spent in leisure by working harder or whether they enjoy the same reduction in time spent in calorically expensive activities is yet to be determined.

10. Do Helpers Really Help?

1. This idea was developed and modeled by Symons (1979) and Foley (1996).

— REFERENCES —

Alexander, R. D. 1974. The evolution of social behavior. *Annual Review of Ecological Systems* 5:325–83.

Altmann, Jeanne. 1974. Observational study of behavior: Sampling methods. *Behaviour* 49:227–67.

———. 1980. *Baboon Mothers and Infants.* Cambridge, MA: Harvard University Press.

Alvarez, Helen Perich. 2000. Grandmother hypothesis and primate life histories. *American Journal of Physical Anthropology* 113:435–50.

Aréchiga, Julieta. 1978. Anthropometria nutricional en la poplación infantil de Chan Kom, Yucatan. *Etudios de Cultura Maya,* vol. 11, pp. 31–55. México DF: Universidad Nacional Autonoma de México.

Aréchiga, Julieta, and Carlos Serrano. 1981. Parámetros anthropométricos de creciemiento en un grupo indígena Mayance (Tojolabal). In *Estudios de Cultura Maya,* vol. 13, pp. 307–37. México DF: Universidad Nacional Autonoma de México.

Asa, Cheryl. 1997. Hormonal and experiential factors in the expression of social and parental behavior in canids. In *Cooperative Breeding in Mammals,* ed. by Nancy Solomon and Jeffrey French, pp. 129–49. Cambridge: Cambridge University Press.

Astrand, Irma. 1971. Estimating the energy expenditure of housekeeping activities. *American Journal of Clinical Nutrition* 24:1471–75.

Bales, K., J. Dietz, A. Baker, K. Miller, and S. Tardif. 2000. Effects of allocare-givers on fitness in infants and parents of callitrichid primates. *Folia Primatology* 71:27–38.

Barlow, K. R. 1997. Foragers That Farm: A Behavioral Ecology Approach to the Economics of Corn Farming for the Fremont Case. PhD dissertation. Salt Lake City: University of Utah.

Becker, G. S. 1960. An economic analysis of fertility. In *Demographic and Economic Change in Developed Countries.* National Bureau Committee for Economic Research, Conference Series 11, pp. 209–31. Princeton, NJ: Princeton University Press.

———. 1975. *Human Capital,* 2nd ed. New York: Columbia University Press.

———. 1981. *A Treatise on the Family.* Cambridge, MA: Harvard University Press.

———. 1993. *Human Capital,* 3rd ed. Chicago: University of Chicago Press.

Becker, Gary S., and H. Gregg Lewis. 1973. On the interaction between the quantity and quality of children. *Journal of Political Economy* 81(2, pt. 2):s279–s288.

Benedict, F. G., and Morris Steggerda. 1937. *The Food of the Present Day Maya Indians of Yucatan.* Carnegie Institute of Washington, Publication 456, Contribution 18. Washington, DC.

Bentley, Gillian, T. Goldberg, and G. Jasienska. 1993a. The fertility of agricultural and non-agricultural societies. *Population Studies* 47:269–81.

Bentley, Gillian, G. Jasienska, and T. Goldberg. 1993b. Is the fertility of agricultural-ists higher than that of nonagriculturalists? *Current Anthropology* 34:778–85.

Bereczkei, Tamas. 1998. Kinship network, direct childcare, and fertilty among Hungarians and Gypsies. *Evolution and Human Behavior* 19(5):283–98.

Betzig, Laura, and Paul Turke. 1986. Parental investment by sex on Ifaluk. *Ethology and Sociobiology* 7:29–37.

Bevington, Gary. 1995. *Maya for Travelers and Students: A Guide to Language and Culture in Yucatan.* Austin: University of Texas Press.

Bird, Douglas W., and Rebecca L. Bliege Bird. 2002. Children on the reef: Slow learning or strategic foraging? *Human Nature* 13(2):269–97.

Bledsoe, Caroline. 1995. Marginal members: Children of previous unions in Mende households in Sierra Leone. In *Births and Power: Social Change and the Politics of Reproduction,* ed. by W. P. Handwerker, pp. 81–100. Boulder, CO: Westview.

Bliege Bird, Rebecca, and Douglas Bird. 2002. Constraints of knowing or constraints of growing? Fishing and collecting by the children of Mer. *Human Nature* 13(2):239–67.

Blurton Jones, Nicholas. 1986. Bushman birth spacing: A test for optimal interbirth intervals. *Ethology and Sociobiology* 7:91–105.

Blurton Jones, Nicholas, Kristen Hawkes, and Patrica Draper. 1987. Bushman birth spacing: Direct test of some simple predictions. *Ethology and Sociobiology* 8:183–203.

———. 1989. The cost of children and the adaptive scheduling of births: Towards a sociobiological perspective on demography. In *Sociobiology of Sexual and Reproductive Strategies,* ed. by A. E. Rasa, C. Vogel, and E. Voland, pp. 265–82. London: Chapman and Hall.

———. 1993. The lives of hunter-gatherer children: Effects of parental behavior and parental reproductive strategy. In *Juvenile Primates,* ed. by Michael E. Pereira and Lynn A. Fairbanks, pp. 309–26. New York: Oxford University Press.

———. 1994a. Foraging returns of !Kung adults and children: Why didn't !Kung children forage? *Journal of Anthropological Research* 50(3):217–48. 1994b. Differences between Hadza and !Kung children's work: Affluence or practical reason. In *Key Issues in Hunter-Gatherer Research,* ed. by E. S. Burch Jr. (and L. J. Ellana), pp. 189–215. Oxford: Berg.

Blurton Jones, Nicholas, Kristen Hawkes, and James O'Connell. 1989. Measuring and modeling costs of children in two foraging societies: Implications for schedule of reproduction. In *Comparative Socioecology: The Behavioural Ecology of*

Humans and Other Mammals, ed. by V. Standen and Robert Foley, pp. 367–90. Oxford: Blackwell Scientific.

———. 1997. Why do Hadza children forage? In *Uniting Psychology and Biology: Integrative Perspectives on Human Development,* ed. by N. Segal, G. E. Weisfeld, and C. C. Weisfeld, pp. 164–83. Washington, DC: American Psychological Association.

———. 1999. Some current ideas about the evolution of human life history. In *Comparative Primate Socioecology,* ed. by P. C. Lee, pp. 140–66. Cambridge: Cambridge University Press.

Blurton Jones, Nicholas, and Frank W. Marlowe. 2002. Selection for delayed maturity: Does it take twenty years to learn to hunt and gather? *Human Nature* 13(2):199–238.

Blurton Jones, Nicholas, and R. M. Sibly. 1978. Testing adaptiveness of culturally determined behavior: Do Bushman women maximize their reproductive success by spacing births widely and foraging seldom? In *Human Behaviour and Adaptation,* ed. by N. G. Blurton Jones and V. Reynolds. pp. 135–57. London: Taylor and Francis.

Blurton Jones, N., L. Smith, J. O'Connell, K. Hawkes, and C. L. Samuzora. 1992. Demography of the Hadza, an increasing and high density population of savanna foragers. *American Journal of Physical Anthropology* 89:159–81.

Bock, John. 1995. The Determinants of Variation in Children's Activities in a Southern African Community. PhD dissertation, Department of Anthropology. Albuquerque: University of New Mexico.

———. 1999. Evolutionary approaches to population: Implications for research and policy. *Population and Environment* 21:193–222.

———. 2002a. Learning, life history, and productivity: Children's lives in the Okavango Delta, Botswana. *Human Nature* 13(2):161–97.

———. 2002b. Evolutionary demography and intrahousehold time allocation: Schooling and children's labor among the Okavango Delta peoples of Botswana. *American Journal of Human Biology* 14(2):206–21.

Bock, J., and S. E. Johnson. 2002. Male migration, remittances, and child outcome among the Okavango Delta peoples of Botswana. In *Handbook of Father Involvement: Multidisciplinary Perspectives,* ed. by C. S. Tamis-LeMonda and N. Cabrera, pp. 308–35. Mahwah, NJ: Lawrence Earlbaum.

Boesch, C., and H. Boesch-Achermann. 2000. *The Chimpanzees of the Taï Forest: Behavioural Ecology and Evolution.* Oxford: Oxford University Press.

Bogin, Barry. 1991. The evolution of human childhood. *BioScience* 40:16–25.

———. 1997. Evolutionary hypotheses for human childhood. *Yearbook of Physical Anthropology* 40:63–89.

———. 1998. Evolutionary and biological aspects of childhood. In *Biosocial Perspectives on Children,* ed. by Catherine Panter-Brick, pp. 10–44. Cambridge: Cambridge University Press.

————. 1999a. *Patterns of Human Growth*. Cambridge: Cambridge University Press.

————. 1999b. Evolutionary perspectives on human growth. *Annual Review of Anthropology* 28:109–53.

Bogin, Barry. 2002. The evolution of human growth. In *Human Growth and Development*, edited by Noël Cameron, pp. 295–320. Amsterdam: Elsevier Science.

Bongaarts, John. 2002. The end of the fertility transition in the developed world. *Population and Development Review* 28(3):419–43.

Bongaarts, John, and R. G. Potter. 1982. *Fertility, Biology, and Behavior: An Analysis of the Proximate Determinants*. New York: Academic Press.

Boone, James L. 1988. In *Human Reproductive Behavior: A Darwinian Perspective*, ed. by Laura Betzig, Monique Borgerhoff Mulder, and Paul Turke, pp. 201–19. Cambridge: Cambridge University Press.

————. 2002. Subsistence strategies and early human population history: An evolutionary perspective. *World Archaeology* 34(1):6–25.

Boone, James L., and Karen L. Kessler. 1999. More status or more children? Social status, fertility reduction and long-term fitness. *Evolution and Human Behavior* 20:257–77.

Borgerhoff Mulder, Monique. 1988. Reproductive success in three Kipsigis cohorts. In *Reproductive Success*, ed. by T. H. Clutton-Brock, pp. 419–35. Chicago: University of Chicago Press.

Borgerhoff Mulder, Monique, and T. M. Caro. 1985. The use of quantitative observational techniques in anthropology. *Current Anthropology* 26:323–35.

Boserup, Ester. 1965. *The Conditions for Agricultural Growth: The Economics of Agrarian Change under Population Pressure*. Chicago: Aldine.

Bove, Riley B., Claudia R Valeggia, and Peter T. Ellison. 2002. Girl helpers and time allocation of nursing women among the Toba of Argentina. *Human Nature* 13(4):457–72.

Bronson, F. H. 1989. *Mammalian Reproductive Biology*. Chicago: University of Chicago Press.

Brooke, Thomas. 1975. The ecology of work. In *Physiological Anthropology*, ed. by D. Damon, pp. 59–79. London: Oxford University Press.

Brookefield, H. C. 1972. Intensification and disintensification in Pacific agriculture. *Pacific Viewpoint* 13:30–48.

Brown, J. L. 1974. Alternate routes to sociality in jays—with a theory for the evolution of altruism and communal breeding. *American Zoology* 14:63–80.

————. 1975. *The Evolution of Behavior*. New York: Norton.

————. 1987. *Helping and Communal Breeding in Birds*. Princeton, NJ: Princeton University Press.

Cain, Mead. 1977. The economic activities of children in a village in Bangladesh. *Population and Development Review* 3:201–27.

——. 1982. Perspectives on family and fertility in developing countries. *Population Studies* 36(2):159–75.

Caldwell, J. C. 1976. Toward a restatement of demographic transition theory. *Population and Development Review* 2:321–66.

——. 1977. The economic rationality of high fertility: An investigation illustrated with Nigerian survey data. *Population Studies* 31:5–27.

——. 1978. A theory of fertility: From high plateau to destabilization. *Population and Development Review* 4(4):553–77.

——. 1982. *Theory of Fertility Decline.* New York: Academic Press.

——. 1983. Direct economic costs and benefits of children. In *Determinants of Fertility in Developing Countries,* ed. by R. A. Bulatoa and R. D. Lee, pp. 458–93. New York: Academic Press.

Campbell, Kenneth L. and James W. Wood. 1988. Fertility in traditional societies. In *Natural Human Fertility: Social and Biological Determinants,* ed. by Peter Diggory, Malcolm Potts, and Sue Teper, pp. 39–61. London: Macmillan.

Charnov, E. L. 1991. Evolution of life history variation among female mammals. *Proceedings of the National Academy of Sciences* 88:1134–37.

——. 1993. *Life History Invariants: Some Explorations of Symmetry in Evolutionary Ecology.* New York: Oxford University Press.

Chayanov, A. V. 1986 [1925]. *The Theory of Peasant Economy,* ed. by Daniel Thorner, Basile Kerblay, and R. E. F. Smith. Madison: University of Wisconsin Press.

Clark, Colin, and Margaret Haswell. 1967. *The Economics of Subsistence Agriculture,* 3rd ed. London: Macmillan.

Clarke, Alice L. 1993. Women, resources, and dispersal in nineteenth-century Sweden. *Human Nature* 4(2):109–35.

Clarke, Alice L., and B. Low. 1992. Ecological correlates of human dispersal in 19th century Sweden. *Animal Behaviour* 44:677–93.

Clutton-Brock, T. H. 1991. *The Evolution of Parental Care.* Princeton, NJ: Princeton University Press.

——. 2002. Breeding together: Kin selection and mutualism in cooperative vertebrates. *Science* 296:69–72.

Clutton-Brock, T. H., P. N. M. Brotherton, M. J. O'Riain, A. S. Griffin, D. Gaynor, R. Kansky, L. Sharpe, and G. M. McIlrath. 2001. Contributions to cooperative rearing in meerkats. *Animal Behaviour* 61:705–10.

Clutton-Brock, T. H., D. Gaynor, G. M. McIlrath, A. D. C. Maccoll, R. Kansky, P. Chadwick, M. Manser, J. D. Skinner, and P. N. M. Brotherton. 1999. Predation, group size and mortality in a cooperative mongoose, *Suricata suricatta. Journal of Animal Ecology* 68(4):672–83.

Clutton-Brock, T. H., and G. A. Parker. 1995. Punishment in animal societies. *Nature* 373:209–16.

Coale, Ansley, and Paul Demeny. 1983. *Regional Model Life Tables and Stable Populations.* New York: Academic Press.

Cockburn, A. 1998. Evolution of helping behavior in cooperatively breeding birds. *Annual Review of Ecology and Systematics* 29:141–77.

Cook, O. F. 1919. Milpa agriculture, a primitive tropical system. *Annual Report 1919,* pp. 307–26. Washington, DC: Smithsonian Institution.

Cook, Sherburne F., and Woodrow Borah. 1974. *Essays in Population History: Mexico and the Caribbean,* vol 2. Berkeley: University of California Press.

Cowgill, Ursula. 1962. An agricultural study of the Southern Maya Lowlands. *American Anthropologist* 64(2):273–86.

Crognier, Emile, A. Baali, and M. K. Hilali. 2001. Do "helpers at the nest" increase their parents' reproductive success? *American Journal of Human Biology* 13:365–73.

Crognier, Emile, M. Villena, and E. Vargas. 2002. Helping patterns and reproductive success in Aymara communities. *American Journal of Human Biology* 14:372–79.

Cumming, D. C. 1990. Physical activity and control of the hypothalamic-pituitary-gonadal axis. *Seminars in Reproductive Endocrinology* 8:810–12.

Cumming, D. C., G. D. Wheeler, and J. T. Harber. 1994. Physical activity, nutrition and reproduction. *Annals of the New York Academy of Sciences* 709:55–76.

Das Gupta, Monica. 1997. Kinship systems and demographic regimes. In *Anthropological Demography,* ed. by David L. Kertzer and Tom Fricke, pp. 36–52. Chicago: University of Chicago Press.

Davies, N. B. 1991. Mating systems. In *Behavioural Ecology: An Evolutionary Approach,* 3rd ed., ed. by J. R. Krebs and N. B. Davies, pp. 263–94. Oxford: Blackwell Scientific.

Davis, Kingsley. 1955. Institutional patterns favouring high fertility in underdeveloped areas. *Eugenics Quarterly* 2:33–39.

Denevan, William, ed. 1976. *The Native Population of the Americas in 1492.* Madison: University of Wisconsin Press.

Denham, Woodrow W. 1974. Infant transport among the Alyawara tribe, Central Australia. *Oceania* 64(4):253–77.

Dore, Christopher. 1996. Built Environment Variability and Community Organization: Theory Building through Ethnography in Xculoc, Campeche, Mexico. PhD dissertation, Department of Anthropology. Albuquerque: University of New Mexico.

Draper, Patricia. 1976. Social and economic constraints on child life among the !Kung. In *Kalahari Hunters and Gatherers,* ed. by R. B. Lee and I. Devore, pp. 199–217. Cambridge, MA: Harvard University Press.

———. 1989. African marriage systems: Perspectives from evolutionary ecology. *Ethology and Sociobiology* 10:145–69.

Draper, Patricia, and Elizabeth Cashdan. 1988. Technological change and child behavior among the !Kung. *Ethnology* 27:339–65.

Draper, Patricia, and Henry Harpending. 1987. Parental investment and the child's environment. In *Parenting across the Life Span: Biosocial Dimensions,* ed. by J. Lancaster, J. Altmann, A. Rossi, and L. Sherrod, pp. 207–35. New York: Aldine de Gruyter.

Dugatkin, L. A. 1997. *Cooperation among Animals.* Oxford: Oxford University Press.

Dunbar, R. I. M. 1976. Some aspects of research design and their implications in the observational study of behaviour. *Behaviour* 58(1–2):58–78.

———. 1987. Demography and reproduction. In *Primate Societies,* ed. by B. B. Smuts, D. L. Cheney, R. M. Seyfarth, R. W. Wrangham, and T. T. Struhsaker, pp. 240–49. Chicago: University of Chicago Press.

———. 1998. The social brain hypothesis. *Evolutionary Anthropology* 6(5):178–90.

———. 2003. Why are apes so smart? In *Primate Life Histories and Socioecology,* ed. by Peter M. Kappeler and Michael E. Pereira, pp. 285–98. Chicago: University of Chicago Press.

Dunning, Nicholas P. 1992. *Lords of the Hills: Ancient Maya Settlement in the Puuc Region, Yucatan, Mexico.* Monographs in World Archaeology, no. 15. Madison, WI: Prehistory Press.

Durnin, J. V., and R. Passmore. 1967. *Energy, Work and Leisure.* London: Heinemann.

Dyson, T., and M. Murphy. 1985. The onset of fertility transition. *Population and Development Review* 11(3):399–440.

Early, John D., and John F. Peters. 2000. *The Xilixana Yanomami of the Amazon: History, Social Structure and Population Dynamics.* Gainesville: University Press of Florida.

Easterlin, Richard A. 1978. The economics and sociology of fertility: A synthesis. In *Historical Studies of Changing Fertility,* ed. by C. Tilly, pp. 57–133. Princeton, NJ: Princeton University Press.

Easterlin, Richard A., and Eileen M. Crimmins. 1985. *The Fertility Revolution.* Chicago: University of Chicago Press.

Elder, G. H., J. Modell, and R. D. Parke. 1993. *Children in Time and Place: Developmental and Historical Insights.* Cambridge: Cambridge University Press.

Ellison, Peter T. 1990. Human ovarian function and reproductive ecology: New hypotheses. *American Anthropologist* 92(4):933–52.

———. 2001. *On Fertile Ground: A Natural History of Human Reproduction.* Cambridge, MA: Harvard University Press.

Ember, Carol R. 1983. The relative decline of women's contribution to agriculture with intensification. *American Anthropologist* 85:285–304.

Emerson, R. A., and J. H. Kempton. 1935. Agronomic investigations in Yucatan. *Carnegie Institution of Washington Yearbook* 34:138–42.

Emlen, Stephen T. 1978. The evolution of cooperative breeding. In *Behavioural Ecology: An Evolutionary Approach,* ed. by J. R. Krebs and N. B. Davies, pp. 245–81. Oxford: Blackwell Scientific.

———. 1982. The evolution of helping: An ecological constraints model. *American Naturalist* 119:29–39.

———. 1984. The evolution of cooperative breeding in birds and mammals. In *Behavioural Ecology: An Evolutionary Approach,* 2nd ed., ed. by J. R. Krebs and N. B. Davies, pp. 305–39. London: Blackwell Scientific.

———. 1991. Evolution of cooperative breeding in birds and mammals. In *Behavioural Ecology: An Evolutionary Approach,* 3rd ed., ed. by J. R. Krebs and N. B. Davies, pp. 301–37. London: Blackwell Scientific.

Emlen, Stephen, Hudson Reeve, Paul Sherman, and Peter Wrege. 1991. Adaptive versus nonadaptive explanations of behavior: The case of alloparental helping. *American Naturalist* 138(1):259–70.

Emlen S. T., and P. H. Wrege. 1991. Breeding biology of white-fronted bee-eaters at Nakuru. The influence of helpers on breeder fitness. *Journal of Animal Ecology* 60(1):309–26.

Eveleth, P. B., and J. M. Tanner. 1990. *Worldwide Variation in Human Growth.* Cambridge: Cambridge University Press.

Ewald, Paul W. 1994. *Evolution of Infectious Disease.* Oxford: Oxford University Press.

Fairbanks, L. 1990. Reciprocal benefits of allomothering for female vervet monkeys. *Animal Behavior* 40:553–62.

Fleagle, John G. 1999. *Primate Adaptation and Evolution,* 2nd ed. San Diego, CA: Academic Press.

Flinn, Mark V. 1988. Parent-offspring interactions in a Caribbean village: Daughter guarding. In *Human Reproductive Behavior: A Darwinian Perspective,* ed. by Laura Betzig, Monique Borgerhoff Mulder, and Paul Turke, pp. 189–200. Cambridge: Cambridge University Press.

Folbre, Nancy. 1986. Hearts and spades. Paradigms of household economics. *World Development* 14(2):245–55.

Foley, R. 1996. The adaptive legacy of human evolution: A search for the environment of evolutionary adaptiveness. *Evolutionary Anthropology* 4:194–203.

Fossey, D. 1979. Development of the mountain gorilla (*Gorilla gorilla beringei*): The first thirty-six months. In *The Great Apes,* ed. by D. A. Hamburg and E. R. McCown, pp. 139–86. Menlo Park, CA: Benjamin-Cummings.

French, Jeffery A. 1997. Proximate regulation of singular breeding in callitrichid primates. In *Cooperative Breeding in Mammals,* ed. by Nancy G. Solomon and Jeffery A. French, pp. 34–75. Cambridge: Cambridge University Press.

Fricke, Thomas. 1990. Darwinian transitions: A comment. *Population Development Review* 16(1):107–19.

Galdikas, B. M. 1985. Subadult male orangutan sociality and reproductive behavior at Tanjung Puting Reserve. *American Journal of Primatology* 8:87–99.

Galdikas, B. M., and J. W. Wood. 1990. Birth spacing patterns in humans and apes. *American Journal of Physical Anthropology* 83:185–91.

Gann, Thomas W. F. 1918. *The Maya Indians of Southern Yucatan and Northern British Honduras*. Bureau of American Ethnology, Bulletin 64. Washington, DC.

Godas Daltabuit, Alicia Rios Torres, and Fraterna Perez Plaja. 1988. *Coba: Estrategias Adaptativas de Tres Familias Mayas*. México DF: Universidad Nacional Autónoma de México.

Goldizen, Anne Wilson. 1987. Tamarins and marmosets: Communal care of offspring. In *Primate Societies*, ed. by Barbara Smuts, Dorothy Cheney, Robert Seyfarth, Richard Wrangham, and Thomas Struhsaker, pp. 34–43. Chicago: University of Chicago Press.

Goodall, Jane. 1986. *The Chimpanzees of Gombe: Patterns of Behavior.* Cambridge, MA: Harvard University Press.

Gould, Richard A. 1980. *Living Archaeology.* Cambridge: Cambridge University Press.

Greaves, Russell. n.d. Fishing strategies and technology. Ethnoarchaeological research strategies for Pumé foragers in Venezuela. Manuscript in preparation.

Grinnell, J., C. Packer, and A. E. Pusey. 1995. Cooperation in male lions: Kinship, reciprocity or mutualism? *Animal Behaviour* 49(1):95–105.

Gross, Daniel R. 1984. Time allocation: A tool for the study of cultural behavior. *Annual Review of Anthropology* 13:519–58.

Hames, Raymond. 1988. The allocation of parental care among the Ye'kawana. In *Human Reproductive Behavior,* ed. by Laura Betzig, Monique Borgerhoff Mulder, and Paul Turke, pp. 237–51. Cambridge: Cambridge University Press.

———. 1992. Time allocation. In *Evolutionary Ecology and Human Behaviour,* ed. by Eric Alden Smith and Bruce Winterhalder, pp. 203–35. New York: Aldine de Gruyter.

Hamilton, W. D. 1964. The genetical evolution of social behavior, parts I and II. *Journal of Theoretical Biology* 9:12–45.

Handwerker, W. Penn. 1986. The modern demographic transition: An analysis of subsistence choices and reproductive consequences. *American Anthropologist* 88:400–17.

Harcourt, A. H., K. J. Stewart, and D. Fossey. 1981. Gorilla reproduction in the wild. In *Reproductive Biology of the Great Apes,* ed. by C. E. Graham, pp. 265–79. New York: Academic Press.

Harvey, P. H., and T. H. Clutton-Brock. 1985. Life history variation in primates. *Evolution* 39:559–81.

Harvey, P. H., D. E. Promislow, and A. F. Read. 1989a. Causes and correlates of life history differences among mammals. In *Comparative Socioecology*, ed. by V. Standen and R. Foley, pp. 305–18. Oxford: Blackwell Scientific.

Harvey, P. H., A. F. Read, and D. E. Promislow. 1989b. Life history variation in placental mammals: Unifying data with theory. *Oxford Surveys in Evolutionary Biology* 6:13–31.

Hawkes, Kristen. 1992. Sharing and collective action. In *Evolutionary Ecology and Human Behavior*, ed. by Eric Alden Smith and Bruce Winterhalder, pp. 269–300. New York: Aldine de Gruyter.

Hawkes, Kristen, and N. G. Blurton Jones. 1997. Hadza women's time allocation: Offspring provisioning and the evolution of long postmenopausal life spans. *Current Anthropology* 38:551–77.

Hawkes, Kristen, and James O'Connell. 1981. Affluent hunters? Some comments in light of the Alyawara case. *American Anthropologist* 83:622–26.

Hawkes, Kristen, Kim Hill, Hillard Kaplan, and A. Magdalena Hurtado. 1987. Some problems with instantaneous scan sampling. *Journal of Anthropological Research* 43:239–47.

Hawkes, Kristen, James O'Connell, and Nicholas Blurton Jones. 1989. Hardworking Hadza grandmothers. In *Comparative Socioecology: The Behavioural Ecology of Humans and Other Mammals*, ed. by V. Standen and R. A. Foley, pp. 341–66. London: Blackwell.

———. 1995. Hadza children's foraging: Juvenile dependency, social arrangements, and mobility among hunter-gatherers. *Current Anthropology* 36(4):688–700.

———. 1997. Hadza women's time allocation, offspring provisioning and the evolution of long postmenopausal life spans. *Current Anthropology* 38(4):551–77.

Hawkes, Kristen, James O'Connell, N. Blurton Jones, H. Alvarez, and E. Charnov. 1998. Grandmothering, menopause and the evolution of human life histories. *Proceedings of the National Academy of Sciences*, 95:1336–39.

———. 2000. The grandmother hypothesis and human evolution. In *Adaptation and Human Behavior: An Anthropological Perspective*, edited by L. Cronk, N. Chagnon, and W. Irons, pp. 237–58. New York: Aldine de Gruyter.

Heath de Zapata, Andrews. 1980. *Vocabulario de mayathan. Diccionario Maya-English*. México DF: Mérida.

Heinsohn, R., and M. C. Double. 2004. Cooperative or speciate: New theory for the distribution of passerine birds. *Trends in Ecology and Evolution* 19(2):55–60.

Hewlett, Barry. 1991. Demography and childcare in preindustrial societies. *Journal of Anthropological Research* 47(1):1–37.

Higbee, E. 1948. Agriculture in the Maya homeland. *Geographical Review* 38:457–64.

Hill, Kim, and A. Magdalena Hurtado. 1991. The evolution of premature reproductive senescence and menopause in human females. *Human Nature* 2:313–50.

———. 1996. *Ache Life History*. New York: Aldine de Gruyter.

Hill, Kim, and Hillard Kaplan. 1988. Tradeoffs in male and female reproductive strategies among the Ache, Parts 1 and 2. In *Human Reproductive Behavior*, ed. by Laura Betzig, Monique Borgerhoff Mulder, and Paul Turke, pp. 277–305. Cambridge: Cambridge University Press.

———. 1999. Life history traits in humans: Theory and empirical studies. *Annual Review of Anthropology* 28:397–430.

Howell, Nancy. 1979. *Demography of the !Kung*. New York: Academic Press.

Hrdy, Sarah Blaffer. 1977. *The Langurs of Abu*. Cambridge, MA: Harvard University Press.

———. 1999. *Mother Nature*. New York: Pantheon.

———. in press. Evolutionary context of human development: The cooperative breeding model. In *Attachment and Bonding: A New Synthesis*, ed. by D. S. Carter and L. Ahnert. Cambridge, MA: MIT Press.

Hurtado, A. M., K. Hawkes, K. Hill, and H. Kaplan. 1992. Trade-offs between female food acquisition and child care among Hiwi and Ache foragers. *Human Nature* 3(3):1–28.

Instituto Nacional de Estadistica Geografia e Informatica (INEGI). 1991a. *XI Censo General de Población y Vivienda, 1990 Yucatan. Resultados Definitivos, tomo I*, Instituto Nacional de Estadistica Geografia e Informatica.

———. 1991b. *XI Censo General de Población y Vivienda, 1990 Estados Unidos Mexicanos, Resumen General*. México: Instituto Nacional de Estadistica Geografia e Informatica.

———. 1991c. *XI Censo General de Población y Vivienda, 1990 Campeche*. México: Instituto Nacional de Estadistica Geografia e Informatica.

Irons, William. 1983. Human female reproductive strategies. In *Social Behavior of Female Vertebrates*, ed. by Samuel K. Wasser, pp. 169–213. New York: Academic Press.

———. 1998. Adaptively relevant environments versus the environments of evolutionary adaptiveness. *Evolutionary Anthropology* 6:194–204.

Ivey, Paula K. 1993. Life-History Theory Perspectives on Allocaretaking Strategies among Efe Foragers of the Ituri Forest, Zaire. PhD dissertation, Department of Anthropology. Albuquerque: University of New Mexico.

———. 2000. Cooperative reproduction in Ituri Forest hunter-gatherers: Who cares for Efe infants? *Current Anthropology* 41(5):856–66.

Jamieson, I. G. 1989. Behavioral heterochrony and the evolution of birds' helping at the nest: An unselected consequence of communal breeding? *American Naturalist* 133:394–406.

Jamieson, I. G., and L. J. Craig. 1987. Critique of helping behavior in birds: A departure from functional explanations. In *Perspectives in Ethology*, vol 7, ed. by P. Bateson and P. Klopfer, pp. 79–98. New York: Plenum.

————. 1991. The unselected hypothesis for the evolution of helping behavior: Too much or too little emphasis on natural selection? *American Naturalist* 138(1):271–82.

Janson, Charles H. 1990. Ecological consequences of individual spatial choice in foraging groups of brown capuchin monkeys, *Cebus apella. Animal Behaviour* 40:922–34.

Janson, Charles H., and Carel P. van Schaik. 1993. Ecological risk aversion in juvenile primates: Slow and steady wins the race. In *Juvenile Primates,* ed. by M. E. Pereira and L. Fairbanks, pp. 57–74. Oxford: Oxford University Press.

Johnson, Allen. 1975. Time allocation in a Machiguenga community. *Ethnology* 14:301–10.

————. 1978. *Quantification in Cultural Anthropology.* Stanford, CA: Stanford University Press.

Johnson, Allen, and Clifford Behrens. 1989. Time allocation research and aspects of method and cross-cultural comparison. *Journal of Quantitative Anthropology* 1:313–34.

Johnson, Allen, and Timothy Earle. 2000. *The Evolution of Human Societies: From Foraging Group to Agrarian State,* 2nd ed. Stanford, CA: Stanford University Press.

Joseph, Gilbert M. 1980. Revolution from without: The Mexican revolution in Yucatan, 1910–1940. In *Yucatan: A World Apart,* ed. by Edward Moseley and Edward Terry, pp. 142–71. Tuscaloosa: University of Alabama Press.

Kaplan, Hillard. 1994. Evolutionary and wealth flows theories of fertility: Empirical tests and new models. *Population and Development Review* 20(4):753–91.

————. 1996. A theory of fertility and parental investment in traditional and modern human societies. *Yearbook of Physical Anthropology* 39:91–135.

————. 1997. The evolution of the human life course. In *Between Zeus and the Salmon: The Biodemography of Longevity,* ed. by Kenneth W. Wachter and Caleb E. Finch, pp. 175–211. Washington, DC: National Academy of Sciences.

Kaplan, Hillard, and John Bock. 2001. Fertility theory: Caldwell's theory of intergenerational wealth flows. In *International Encyclopedia of the Social and Behavioral Sciences,* vol. 8, ed. by Neil J. Smelser and Paul B. Baltes, pp. 5557–61. Oxford: Elsevier Science.

Kaplan, Hillard, Kim Hill, Jane Lancaster, and A. Magdalena Hurtado. 2000. A theory of human life history evolution: Diet, intelligence, and longevity. *Evolutionary Anthropology* 9(4):156–85.

Kaplan, Hillard S., and Jane B. Lancaster. 2000. The evolutionary economics and psychology of the demographic transition to low fertility. In *Adaptation and Human Behavior: An Anthropological Perspective,* ed. by Lee Cronk, Napoleon Chagnon, and William Irons, pp. 283–322. New York: Aldine de Gruyter.

Kaplan, Hillard, Jane B. Lancaster, John A. Bock, and Sara E. Johnson. 1995. Does observed fertility maximize fitness among New Mexican men? A test of an optimality model and a new theory of parental investment in the embodied capital of offspring. *Human Nature* 6(4):325–60.

Kasarda, John D. 1971. Economic structure and fertility: A comparative analysis. *Demography* 8:307–18.

Keckler, Charles N. W. 1997. Catastrophic mortality in simulations of forager age-at-death: Where did all the humans go? In *Integrating Archaeological Demography: Multidisciplinary Approaches to Prehistoric Populations,* ed. by Richard R. Paine, pp. 205–28. Center for Archaeological Investigations, Occasional Paper No. 24. Carbondale, IL: Southern Illinois University.

Kintz, Ellen R. 1990. *Life under the Tropical Canopy: Tradition and Change among the Yucatec Maya.* Fort Worth, TX: Holt, Rhinehart and Winston.

Koenig, A. 1995. Group size, composition, and reproductive success in wild common marmosets *(Callithrix jacchus). American Journal of Primatology* 35:311–17.

Koenig, A., and H. Rothe. 1991. Infant carrying in a polygamous group of the common marmoset *(Callithrix jacchus). American Journal of Primatology* 25:185–90.

Koenig, Walter, and Ronald Mumme. 1987. *Population Ecology of the Cooperatively Breeding Acorn Woodpecker.* Princeton, NJ: Princeton University Press.

———. 1990. Levels of analysis, functional explanations, and the significance of helper behavior. In *Interpretation and Explanation in the Study of Animal Behavior,* vol. 1, ed. by M. Bekoff and D. Jamieson, pp. 268–303. Boulder, CO: Westview.

Koenig, Walter, Frank Pitelka, William Carmen, Ronald Mumme, and Mark Stanback. 1992. The evolution of delayed dispersal in cooperative breeders. *Quarterly Review of Biology* 67(2):111–50.

Kozlowski, J. 1992. Optimal allocation to growth and reproduction: Implications for age and size at maturity. *Trends in Ecology and Evolution* 7:15–19.

Kozlowski, J., and R. G. Wiegert. 1986. Optimal allocation of energy to growth and reproduction. *Theoretic Population Biology* 29:16–37.

———. 1987. Optimal age and size at maturity in animals and perennials with determinant growth. *Evolutionary Ecology* 1:231–44.

Kramer, Karen L. 2002. Variation in juvenile dependence: Helping behavior among Maya children. *Human Nature* 13(2):299–325.

Kramer, Karen L., and James L. Boone. 2002. Why intensive agriculturalists have higher fertility: A household labor budget approach to subsistence intensification and fertility rates. *Current Anthropology* 43(3):511–17.

Kramer, Karen L., and Garnett P. McMillan. 1998. How Maya women respond to changing technology: The effect of helping behavior on initiating reproduction. *Human Nature* 9(2):205–23.

————. 1999. Women's labor, fertility and the introduction of modern technology in a rural Maya village. *Journal of Anthropological Research* 55(4):499–520.

Krebs, John, and N. B. Davies, eds. 1997. *Behavioral Ecology*, 4th ed. Oxford: Blackwell Scientific.

Lack, D. 1968. *Ecological Adaptations for Breeding in Birds*. London: Methuen.

Lancaster, Jane B. 1971. Play mothering: The relations between juvenile females and young infants among free-ranging vervet monkeys. *Folia Primatology* 15:161–82.

————. 1986. Human adolescence and reproduction: An evolutionary perspective. In *School-Age Pregnancy and Parenthood*, ed. by Jane B. Lancaster and Beatrix A. Hamburg, pp. 17–37. New York: Aldine de Gruyter.

————. 1991. A feminist and evolutionary biologist looks at women. *Yearbook of Physical Anthropology* 34:1–11.

————. 1997. An evolutionary history of human reproductive strategies and the status of women in relation to population growth and social stratification. In *Evolutionary Feminism*, ed. by P. A. Gowaty, pp. 466–88. New York: Chapman and Hall.

Lancaster, Jane B., and Chet Lancaster. 1983. Parental investment: The hominid adaptation. In *How Humans Adapt: A Biocultural Odyssey*, ed. by D. Ortner, pp. 33–66. Washington, DC: Smithsonian Institution.

————. 1987. The watershed: Change in parental-investment and family-formation strategies in the course of human evolution. In *Parenting across the Life Span*, ed. by Jane Lancaster, Jeanne Altmann, Alice Rossi, and Lonnie Sherrod, pp. 187–205. New York: Aldine de Gruyter.

Landa, Diego de. 1982 [1566]. *Relación de las cosas de Yucatan*. Mexico City, Editorial Porrua.

Lee, Robert B. 1979. *The !Kung San: Men, Women and Work in a Foraging Society*. Cambridge: Cambridge University Press.

Lee, Ronald D. 1994a. The formal demography of population aging, transfers and the economic life cycle. In *Demography of Aging*, ed. by Linda G. Martin and Samuel H. Preston, pp. 8–49. Washington, DC: National Academic Press.

————. 1994b. Population age structure, intergenerational transfer, and wealth. *Journal of Human Resources* 29(4):1027–62.

————. 1994c. Fertility, mortality and intergenerational transfers: Comparisons across steady states. In *The Family, the Market and the State in Ageing Societies*, ed. by John Ermisch and Naohiro Ogawa, pp. 135–57. Oxford: Oxford University Press.

————. 2000. A cross-cultural perspective on intergenerational transfers and the economic life cycle. In *Sharing the Wealth: Demographic Change and Economic Transfers between Generations*, ed. by Andrew Mason and Georges Tapinos, pp. 17–56. Oxford: Oxford University Press.

Lee, Ronald D., and Rodolfo A. Bulatao. 1983. The demand for children: A critical essay. In *Determinants of Fertility in Developing Countries,* vol. 1, ed. by R. A. Bulatao and R. D. Lee, pp. 233–87. New York: Academic Press.

Lee, Ronald D., and Karen L. Kramer. 2001. Demographic influences on resource alocation in Maya households. Paper presented at the annual meeting of the Population Association of America. Washington, DC.

———. 2002. Children's economic roles in the Maya family life cycle: Cain, Caldwell and Chayanov revisited. *Population and Development Review* 28(3):475–99.

Lee, Ronald D., Karen L. Kramer, and Hillard Kaplan. 2002. Children and the elderly in the economic life cycle of the household: A comparative study of three groups of horticulturalists and hunter-gatherers. Paper presented at the annual meeting of the Population Association of America. Atlanta.

Levine, Robert A. 1977. Child rearing as cultural adaptation. In *Culture and Infancy: Variations in the Human Experience,* ed. by Leiderman, S. R. Tulkin, and A. Rosenfeld, pp. 15–27. New York: Academic Press.

Levine R., P. M. Miller, and M. Maxwell West, eds. 1988. *Parental Behavior in Diverse Societies.* New Directions for Child Development, No. 40. San Francisco: Jossey-Bass.

Lewis, Oscar. 1951. *Life in a Mexican Village.* Urbana: University of Illinois Press.

Lindert, Peter. 1980. Child costs and economic development. In *Population and Economic Change in Developing Countries,* ed. by R. A. Easterlin, pp. 3–79. Chicago: University of Chicago Press.

———. 1983. The changing economic costs and benefits of having children. In *Determinants of Fertility in Developing Countries,* ed. by Rodolfo A. Bulatao and Ronald D. Lee, pp. 494–516. New York: Academic Press.

Linton, Ralph L. 1940. Crops, soils and culture in America. In *The Maya and Their Neighbors,* ed. by Clarence L. Hay, Ralph L. Linton, Samual K. Lothrop, Harry L. Shapiro, and George C. Vaillant, pp. 32–40. New York: Cooper Square.

Livi-Bacci, Massimo. 2001. *A Concise History of World Population,* 3rd ed. Oxford: Blackwell.

Low, B. S. 1989. Cross-cultural patterns in the training of children: An evolutionary perspective. *Journal of Comparative Psychology* 103:311–19.

———. 2000. *Why Sex Matters.* Princeton, NJ: Princeton University Press.

Low, B. S., and A. L. Clarke. 1992. Resources and the life course: Patterns through the demographic transition. *Ethology and Sociobiology* 13:463–94.

Low, B., A. L. Clarke, and K. Lockridge. 1992. Toward an ecological demography. *Population Development Review* 18:1–18.

Lundell, C. L. 1933. The agriculture of the Maya. *Southwest Review* 19(1):65–77.

Maler, T. 1902. Yukatekische Forschungen. *Globus* 82:197–230.

Matheny, R. T. 1978. Northern Maya water-control systems. In *Pre-Hispanic Maya Agriculture*, ed. by P. D. Harrison and B. L. Turner II, pp. 185–210. Albuquerque: University of New Mexico Press.

McKenna, James J. 1987. Parental supplements and surrogates among primates: Cross-species and cross-cultural comparisons. In *Parenting across the Life Span*, ed. by Jane Lancaster, Jeanne Altmann, Alice Rossi, and Lonnie Sherrod, pp. 143–84. New York: Aldine de Gruyter.

Minge-Kalman, Wanda. 1978. Household economy during the peasant-to-worker transition in the Swiss Alps. *Ethnology* 17:183–96.

Mitani, John C., and David Watts. 1997. The evolution of non-maternal caretaking among anthropoid primates: Do helpers help? *Behavioral Ecology and Sociobiology* 40:213–20.

Moehlman, P. D. 1986. Ecology of cooperation in canids. In *Ecological Aspects of Social Evolution: Birds and Mammals*, ed. by D. I. Rubenstein and R. W. Wrangham, pp. 64–86. Princeton, NJ: Princeton University Press.

Montgomery, Edward, and Allen Johnson. 1977. Machiguenga energy expenditure. *Ecology of Food and Nutrition* 6:97–105.

Moseley, Edward H. 1980. From conquest to independence: Yucatan under Spanish rule, 1521–1821. In *Yucatan: A World Apart*, ed. by Edward Moseley and Edward Terry, pp. 83–121. Tuscaloosa, University of Alabama Press.

Mueller, Eva. 1976. The economic value of children in peasant agriculture. In *Population and Development: The Search for Selective Interventions*, ed. by Ronald Ridker, pp. 98–153. Baltimore: Johns Hopkins University Press.

———. 1984. The value and allocation of time in rural Botswana. *Journal of Development Economics* 15:329–60.

Mumme, Ronald. 1997. A bird's-eye view of mammalian cooperative breeding. In *Cooperative Breeding in Mammals*, ed. by Nancy G. Solomon and Jeffery A. French, pp. 364–88. Cambridge: Cambridge University Press.

Munroe, Robert L., and Ruth H. Munroe. 1994 [1975]. *Cross Cultural Human Development*. Prospect Heights, IL: Waveland.

Munroe, Ruth, Amy Koel, Robert Munroe, Ralph Bolton, Carol Michelson, and Charlene Bolton. 1983. Time allocation in four societies. *Ethnology* 22:355–70.

Munroe, R. H., R. L. Munroe, and H. S. Shimmin. 1984. Children's work in four cultures: Determinants and consequences. *American Anthropologist* 86:339–79.

Nag, M., B. White, and R. Peet. 1978. An anthropological approach to the study of the economic value of children in Java and Nepal. *Current Anthropology* 19(2):293–306.

National Academy of Sciences. 1989. *Recommended Dietary Allowances*, 10th ed. Washington, DC.

Netting, Robert McC., Richard R. Wilk and Eric J. Arnould. 1984. *Households: Comparative and Historical Studies of the Domestic Group*. Berkeley: University of California Press.

Nicolson, N. A. 1987. Infants, mothers, and other females. In *Primate Societies,* ed. by B. B. Smuts, D. L. Cheney, R. M. Seyfarth, R. W. Wrangham, and T. T. Struhsaker, pp. 330–42. Chicago: University of Chicago Press.

Nicolson, Nancy, and M. W. Demment. 1982. The transition from suckling to independent feeding in wild baboon infants. *International Journal of Primatology* 3:318.

Nishida, T., H. Takasaki, and Y. Takahata. 1990. Demography and reproductive profiles. In *The Chimpanzees of the Mahale Mountains: Sexual and Life History Strategies,* ed. by T. Nishida, pp. 63–97. Tokyo: University of Tokyo Press.

O'Connell, J. F., Hawkes, K., and N. G. Blurton Jones. 1999. Grandmothering and the evolution of *Homo erectus. Journal of Human Evolution* 36:461–85.

Odell, Mary E. 1986. Price or production? Domestic economies, household structure and fertility in a Guatemalan village. In *Culture and Reproduction,* ed. by W. Penn Handwerker, pp. 125–43. Boulder, CO: Westview.

Pagel, Mark D., and Paul H. Harvey. 1993. Evolution of the juvenile period in mammals. In *Juvenile Primates,* ed. by M. E. Pereira and L. Fairbanks, pp. 28–56. Oxford: Oxford University Press.

Panter-Brick, C. 1989. Motherhood and subsistence work: The Tamang of rural Nepal. *Journal of Biosocial Science* 23:137–54.

Panter-Brick, Catherine, ed. 1998. *Biosocial Perspectives on Children.* Cambridge: Cambridge University Press.

Parsons, D. O., and C. Goldin. 1989. Parental altruism and self interest: Child labor among late-nineteenth-century American families. *Economic Inquiry* 27:637–59.

Patch, Robert W. 1993. *Maya and Spaniard in Yucatan 1648–1812.* Stanford, CA: Stanford University Press.

Pennington, Renee, and Henry Harpending. 1988. Fitness and fertility among Kalahari !Kung. *American Journal of Physical Anthropology* 77:303–19.

———. 1993. *The Structure of an African Pastoralist Community: Demography, History, and Ecology of Ngamiland Herero.* Oxford: Clarendon.

Pereira, M. E. 1993. Juvenility in animals. In *Juvenile Primates,* ed. by M. E. Pereira and L. Fairbanks, pp. 17–27. Oxford: Oxford University Press.

Pereira, M., and J. Altmann. 1985. Development of social behavior in free-living nonhuman primates. In *Nonhuman Primate Models for Human Growth and Development,* ed. by E. S. Watts, pp. 217–309. New York: A. R. Liss.

Pereira, M., and L. Fairbanks, eds. 1993. *Juvenile Primates.* Oxford: Oxford University Press.

Pingali, Prabhu L., and Hans P. Binswanger. 1987. Population density and agricultural intensification: A study of the evolution of technologies in tropical agriculture. In *Population Growth and Economic Development: Issues and Evidence,* ed. by D. Gale Johnson and Ronald D. Lee, pp. 27–56. Madison: University of Wisconsin Press.

Potts, Malcolm, and Roger Short. 1999. *Ever Since Adam and Eve.* Cambridge: Cambridge University Press.

Potts, Richard. 1998. Variability selection in hominid evolution. *Evolutionary Anthropology* 7:81–96.

Press, Irwin. 1975. *Tradition and Adaptation: Life in a Modern Yucatan Maya Village.* Westport: Greenwood.

Pusey A. E. 1983. Mother-offspring relationships in chimpanzees after weaning. *Animal Behaviour* 31:363–77.

———. 1990. Behavioural changes in adolescence in chimpanzees. *Behaviour* 115:203–46.

Ramakrishnan, P. S. 1992. *Shifting Agriculture and Sustainable Development: An Interdisciplinary Study from North-Eastern India.* Man and the Biosphere series. Paris: UNESCO.

Redfield, Robert. 1941. *The Folk Culture of Yucatan.* Chicago: University of Chicago Press.

———. 1950. *A Village That Chose Progress: Chan Kom Revisited.* Chicago: University of Chicago Press.

Redfield, Robert, and Alfonso Villa Rojas. 1934. *Chan Kom: A Maya Village.* Chicago: University of Chicago Press.

Reina, Ruben, and Robert Hill II. 1980. Lowland Maya subsistence: Notes from ethnohistory and ethnography. *American Antiquity* 45:74–79.

Restall, Matthew. 1997. *The Maya World: Yucatec Culture and Society, 1550–1850.* Stanford: Stanford University Press.

———. 1998. *Maya Conquistador.* Boston: Beacon.

Reynolds, Pamela. 1991. *Dance Civet Cat: Child Labour in the Zambezi Valley.* Athens: Ohio University Press.

Roff, D. A. 1986. Predicting body size with life history models. *Bioscience* 36:316–23.

Rogers, A. R. 1990. The evolutionary economics of human reproduction. *Ethology and Sociobiology* 11:479–95.

Rosetta, Lyliane. 1990. Biological aspects of fertility among Third World populations. In *Fertility and Resources,* ed. by J. Landers and V. Reynolds, pp. 18–34. Cambridge: Cambridge University Press.

———. 1995. Nutrition, physical workloads and fertility regulation. In *Human Reproductive Decisions: Biological and Social Perspectives,* ed. by R. I. M. Dunbar, pp. 52–75. London: Palgrave MacMillan.

Ross, C., and A. MacLarnon. 1995. Ecological and social correlates of maternal expenditure on infant growth in haplorhine primates. In *Motherhood in Humans and Nonhuman Primates: Biosocial Determinants,* ed. by C. Pryce, R. Martin, and D. Skuse, pp. 37–46. Basel: Karger.

———. 2000. The evolution of nonmaternal care in anthropoid primates: A test of the hypotheses. *Folia Primatology* 71:93–113.

Roys, Ralph L. 1943. *The Indian background of colonial Yucatan.* Carnegie Institution of Washington, Pub. 548. Washington, DC.

———. 1957. *The Political Geography of the Yucatan Maya.* Washington, DC: Carnegie Institution of Washington.

Russell, E. M., and I. C. R. Rowley. 1988. Helper contributions to reproductive success in the splendid fairy-wren (*Malurus splendens*). *Behavioral Ecology and Sociobiology* 22:131–40.

Ryder, James W. 1977. Internal migration in Yucatan: Interpretation of historical demography and current patterns. In *Anthropology and History in Yucatan*, ed. by Grant D. Jones, pp. 191–231. Austin: University of Texas Press.

Sabharwal, K. P., S. Morales, and H. Méndez. 1966. Body measurements and creatinine excretion among upper and lower socio-economic groups of girls in Guatemala. *Human Biology* 38:131–40.

Sabloff, J. A., P. A. McAnany, B. Fahmel Beyer, T. Gallareta, S. Larralde, and L. Wandsnider. 1984. *Ancient Maya Settlement Patterns at the Site of Sayil, Puuc Region, Yucatan, Mexico: Initial Reconnaissance, 1983.* Latin American Institute Research Series No. 14. Albuquerque: University of New Mexico.

Sabloff, J. A., and G. Tourtellot. 1991. *The Ancient Maya City of Sayil: The Mapping of a Puuc Region Center.* Middle American Research Institute Publication 60. New Orleans: Tulane University.

Sabloff, J. A., G. Tourtellot, B. Fahmel Beyer, P. A. McAnany, D. Christensen, S. Boucher, and T. Killion. 1985. *Settlement and Community Patterns at Sayil, Yucatan, Mexico: The 1984 Season.* Latin American Institute Research Series No. 17. Albuquerque: University of New Mexico.

Schülke, Oliver. 2003. To breed or not to breed—food competition and other factors involved in female breeding decisions in the pair-living nocturnal fork-marked lemur (*Phaner furcifer*). *Behavioral Ecology and Sociobiology* 55:11–21.

Sellen, D. W., and R. Mace. 1997. Fertility and mode of subsistence: A phylogenetic analysis. *Current Anthropology* 38:878–89.

Short, Roger. 1976. The evolution of human reproduction. *Proceedings of the Royal Society Series B* 195:3–24.

Sibly, R. M., and P. Calow. 1986. *Physiological Ecology of Animals.* Oxford: Blackwell Scientific.

Simpson, M. J. A., and A. E. Simpson. 1977. One-zero and scan methods for sampling behaviour. *Animal Behaviour* 25:726–31.

Sips, Richard. 1980. *Population Growth, Society and Culture.* New Haven, CT: HRAF.

Skoufias, Emmanuel. 1994. Market wages, family composition and the time allocation of children in agricultural households. *Journal of Development Studies* 30(2): 335–60.

Skutch, A. F. 1935. Helpers at the nest. *Auk* 52:257–73.

———. 1987. *Helpers at Birds' Nests: A Worldwide Survey of Cooperative Breeding and Related Behavior.* Iowa City: University of Iowa Press.

Small, Meredith. 1994. *Female Choices.* Ithaca, NY: Cornell University Press.

———. 1998. *Our Babies, Ourselves.* New York: Anchor Books.

———. 2001. *Kids.* New York: Doubleday.

Smith, C. C., and S. D. Fretwell. 1974. The optimal balance between size and number of offspring. *American Naturalist* 108:499–506.

Smith, Holly B. 1991. Dental development and the evolution of life history in Hominidae. *American Journal of Physical Anthropology* 86:157–74.

Smith, Holly B., and Robert L. Tompkins. 1995. Toward a life history of the Hominidae. *Annual Review of Anthropology* 24:257–79.

Smyth, Michael P. 1988. Domestic Storage Behavior in the Puuc Region of Yucatan, Mexico: An Ethnoarchaeological Investigation. PhD dissertation, Department of Anthropology. Albuquerque: University of New Mexico.

Solomon, Nancy G., and Jeffery A. French, eds. 1997. *Cooperative Breeding in Mammals.* Cambridge: Cambridge University Press.

Stacey, Peter B., and Walter D. Koenig, eds. 1990. *Cooperative Breeding in Birds.* Cambridge: Cambridge University Press.

Stearns, S. C., and J. Koella. 1986. The evolution of phenotypic plasticity in life-history traits: Predictions for norms of reaction for age- and size-at-maturity. *Evolution* 40:893–913.

Stecklov, Guy. 1997. Intergenerational resource flows in Côte d'Ivoire: Empirical analysis of aggregate flows. *Population and Development Review* 23(3):525–53.

———. 1999. Evaluating the economic returns to childbearing in Côte d'Ivoire. *Population Studies* 53:1–17.

Steggerda, Morris. 1932. *Anthropometry of Adult Maya Indians.* Washington DC: Carnegie Institution of Washington.

———. 1941. *Maya Indians of Yucatan.* Carnegie Institution of Washington, Publication 531. Washington, DC.

Stephens, John Lloyd. 1993 [1841]. *Incidents of Travel in Central America, Chiapas and Yucatan.* Washington, DC: Smithsonian Institution.

———. 1996 [1843]. *Incidents of Travel in Yucatan,* vols. I and II. Washington, DC: Smithsonian Institution.

Strassman, B. I. 1996. The evolution of endometrial cycles and menstruation. *Quarterly Review of Biology* 71(2):181–220.

Strassman, B. I., and Alice L. Clarke. 1998. Ecological constraints on marriage in rural Ireland. *Evolution and Human Behavior* 19:33–55.

Symons, D. 1979. *The Evolution of Human Sexuality.* New York: Oxford University Press.

Szreter, Simon. 1993. The idea of demographic transition and study of fertility change: A critical intellectual history. *Population and Development Review* 19(4):659–701.

Tanner, J. M. 1990. *Foetus into Man: Physical Growth from Conception to Maturity.* Cambridge, MA: Harvard University Press.

Tardif, Suzette D. 1997. The bioenergetics of parental care in marmosets and tamarins. In *Cooperative Breeding in Mammals,* ed. by Nancy G. Solomon and Jeffery A. French, pp. 11–33. Cambridge: Cambridge University Press.

Tardif, S. D., C. B. Richter, and R. L. Carson. 1984. Effects of sibling-rearing experience on future reproductive success in two species in *Callitrichidae. American Journal of Primatology* 6:377–80.

Thompson, J. Eric. 1930. *Ethnology of the Mayas of Southern and Central British Honduras.* Field Museum of Natural History Publication 274. Anthropology Series vol. 17(2). Chicago.

Tourtellot, G., J. A. Sabloff, P. A. McAnany, T. W. Killion, K. Camaren, R. Cobos, C. Dore, B. Fahmel Beyer, S. Lopez, Carlos Perez, S. Wurtzburg, with an appendix by M. P. Smyth. 1989. *Archaeological Investigations at Sayil, Yucatan, Medio, Phase II: The 1987 Field Season.* University of Pittsburgh Anthropological Papers, No. 2.

Trivers, Robert. 1972. Parental investment and sexual selection. In *Sexual Selection and the Descent of Man,* ed. by Bernard Campbell, pp. 136–79. Chicago: Aldine.

———. 1974. Parent-offspring conflict. *American Zoologist* 14:249–64.

———. 1985. *Social Evolution.* Menlo Park, CA: Benjamin Cummings.

Turke, Paul W. 1988. Helpers at the nest: Childcare networks on Ifaluk. In *Human Reproductive Behavior,* ed. by Laura Betzig, Monique Borgerhoff Mulder, and Paul Turke, pp. 173–88. Cambridge: Cambridge University Press.

———. 1989. Evolution and the demand for children. *Population and Development Review* 15(1):61–90.

———. 1991. Theory and evidence on wealth flows and old-age security: A reply to Fricke. *Population and Development Review* 17(4):687–702.

Ulijaszek, Stanley. 1995. *Human Energetics in Biological Anthropology.* Cambridge: Cambridge University Press.

United States Bureau of the Census. 1992. *Statistical Abstract of the United States: 1992.* Washington, DC.

van Schaik, C. P. 1989. The ecology and social relationships amongst female primates. In *Comparative Socioecology,* ed. by V. Standen and R. A. Foley, pp. 195–218. Oxford: Blackwell.

Vehrencamp, S. L. 1978. The adaptive significance of communal nesting in groove-billed anis *(Crotophaga sulcirostris). Behavioral Ecology and Sociobiology* 4:1–33.

Villa Rojas, A. 1945. *The Maya of East Central Quintana Roo.* Washington, DC: Carnegie Institution of Washington.

Vining, Daniel R. Jr. 1986. Social versus reproductive success: The central theoretical problem of human sociobiology. *Behavioral and Brain Sciences* 9:167–216.

Vlassoff, M. 1979. Labour demand and economic utility of children: A case study in rural Indian. *Population Studies* 33(3):415–28.

Voland, E., E. Siegelkow, and C. Engel. 1991. Cost/benefit oriented parental investment by high status families: The Krummhörn case. *Ethology and Sociobiology* 12:105–18.

Watts, D. P. 1991. Mountain gorilla reproduction and sexual behavior. *American Journal of Primatology* 24:211–26.

Watts, David P., and Anne E. Pusey. 1993. Behavior of juvenile and adolescent great apes. In *Juvenile Primates,* ed. by Michael E. Pereira and Lynn A. Fairbanks, pp. 148–67. Oxford: Oxford University Press.

Weil, Peter. 1986. Agricultural intensification and fertility in the Gambia. In *Culture and Reproduction,* ed. by W. Penn Handwerker, pp. 294–320. Boulder, CO: Westview.

Weisner, Thomas. 1982. Sibling interdependence and child caretaking: A cross-cultural view. In *Sibling Relationships: Their Nature and Significance across the Lifespan,* ed. by Michael Lamb and Brian Sutton-Smith, pp. 305–27. Hillsdale, NJ: Erlbaum.

———. 1987. Socialization for parenthood in sibling caretaking societies. In *Parenting across the Life Span,* ed. by Jane Lancaster, Jeanne Altmann, Alice Rossi, and Lonnie Sherrod, pp. 237–70. New York: Aldine de Gruyter.

Weisner, Thomas, and Ronald Gallimore. 1977. My brother's keeper: Child and sibling caretaking. *Current Anthropology* 18:169–90.

West, Robert C. 1964. Surface configuration and associated geology of Middle America. In *Handbook of Middle American Indians,* vol. 1, ed. by Robert C. West, pp. 33–83. Austin: University of Texas Press.

White, Benjamin. 1973. Demand for labor and population growth in colonial Java. *Human Ecology* 1:217–36.

———. 1975. The economic importance of children in a Javanese village. In *Population and Social Organization,* ed. by Moni Nag, pp. 127–46. The Hague: Mouton.

Whiting, B. 1983. The genesis of prosocial behavior. In *The Nature of Prosocial Development: Interdisciplinary Theories,* ed. by D. Bridgeman, pp. 221–42. New York: Academic Press.

Whiting, Beatrice Blyth, and Carolyn Pope Edwards. 1988. *Children of Different Worlds: The Formation of Social Behavior.* Cambridge, MA: Harvard University Press.

Whiting, J. W. M., and B. B. Whiting. 1975. *Behavior of Children in Six Cultures.* Cambridge, MA: Harvard University Press.

Wich, S. A., S. S. Utami-Atmoko, T. Mitra Setia, H. R. Rijksen, C. Schürmann, J. A. R. A. M. van Hooff, and C. P. van Schaik. Life history of wild sumatran orangutans *(Pongo abelii)*. Manuscript in review.

Wiley, R. H., and K. N. Rabenold. 1984. The evolution of cooperative breeding by delayed reciprocity and queuing for favorable social positions. *Evolution* 38:609–21.

Wilk, Richard R. 1983. Little house in the jungle: The causes of variation in house size among modern Kekehi Maya. *Journal of Anthropological Archaeology* 2:99–116.

Wilkie, James W., ed. 2002. *Statistical Abstract of Latin America,* vol 38. UCLA Latin American Center Publications. Los Angeles: University of California Press.

Willis, Robert. 1988. Life cycles, institutions, and population growth: A theory of the equilibrium rate of interest in an overlapping generations model. In *Economics of Changing Age Distributions in Developed Countries,* ed. by Ronald D. Lee, W. Brian Arthur, and Gerry Rodgers, pp. 106–38. Oxford: Clarendon.

Wilson, Chris, and Robert Woods. 1991. Fertility in England: A long-term perspective. *Population Studies* 45:399–415.

Wilson, Eugene M. 1980. Physical geography of the Yucatan Peninsula. In *Yucatan: A World Apart,* ed. by Edward Moseley and Edward Terry, pp. 5–40. Tuscaloosa: University of Alabama Press.

Winterhalder, B. 1983. Opportunity-cost foraging models for stationary and mobile predators. *American Naturalist* 122:73–84.

———. 1996a. Gifts given, gifts taken: The behavioral ecology of nonmarket, intra-group exchange. *Journal of Archaeological Research* 5:121–68.

———. 2001. Intra-group transfers of resources and their implications for hominid evolution. In *Meat Eating and Human Evolution,* ed. by C. B. Stanford and H. T. Bunn, pp. 279–301. Oxford: Oxford University Press, pp. 279–301.

Wiseman, F. 1978. Ecology of Maya lowlands. In *Pre-Hispanic Maya Agriculture,* ed. by P. D. Harrison and B. L. Turner II, pp. 63–115. Albuquerque: University of New Mexico Press.

Wood, James W. 1994. *Dynamics of Human Reproduction.* New York: Aldine de Gruyter.

Woolfenden, Glen E., and John W. Fitzpatrick. 1984. *The Florida Scrub Jay: Demography of a Cooperative-Breeding Bird.* Princeton, NJ: Princeton University Press.

World Health Organization. 1985. Energy and protein requirements. Report of a joint FAO/WHO/UNU expert consultations. *Technical Report Series 724.* Geneva.

Worthman, Carol M. 1993. Biocultural interactions in human development. In *Juvenile Primates,* ed. by Michael E. Pereira and Lynn A. Fairbanks, pp. 339–58. Oxford: Oxford University Press.

———. 1999. Evolutionary perspectives on the onset of puberty. In *Evolutionary Medicine,* ed. by Wenda Trevathan, E. O. Smith, and James J. McKenna, pp. 135–63. New York: Oxford University Press.

Yewoubdar, Beyene. 1989. *From Menarche to Menopause: Reproductive Lives of Peasant Women in Two Cultures.* Albany: State University of New York Press.

Zeller, A. C. 1987. A role for women [*sic:* grandmothers] in hominid evolution. *Man* 22:528–57.

− INDEX −

Ache, 217*n*10; mean age at first birth for, 211*n*4
Ache children: helping behavior of, 135; as net producers, x; participation in food production, 123
Adaptive behavior, helping as, 13
Adolescence, 213*n*16
Age: average, of consumption and production, 141, 200; body size and, 18; at death, 78; effect of laborsaving technology on female at first birth, 156–162; at first birth, 155–156; mean, at marriage, 79; at net production, 128–131, 135–136, 196; payback, for Maya children, 141–143; return rate and, 42; of sexual maturity, 14, 18, 19, 155–156, 161; water collection and, 43–44; work effort and, 131
Age patterning: in child care, 111–114; of children's work, 31, 34, 102–119; in domestic work, 105–111; in field work, 102–105; task difficulty and, 45; in total work, 114–119
Age/sex pyramid, 84–85
Age-specific fertility, 183
Age-specific surplus production balance, 128
Aging of population, 76–78
Agricultural children: cost of, to parents, 24; as hard workers, 123
Agricultural cycle, 62, 67–70, 94, 102, 103, 114
Agriculturalists: children's value for, xi; Egyptian, 141; fertility rates of, viii, ix; Indian, 141; number of children of, 140–141, 143; in Yucatan Peninsula, 52; Zimbabwe, 92. *See also* Subsistence agriculturalists
Agricultural tasks, 35–36, 102
Aguadas, 50, 213*n*1
Allomothering, 23; direct reproductive benefit and, 12; helpers in, 12
Almuchil, 55
Animal tending, 135
Arable land, availability of, for young couples, 163

Arcsine transformation, 207–208
Atole, 107
Australian Central Desert, tasks for children in, 31
Aztecs, 53

Bachelorhood, 80
Bangladesh, wage and nonwage labor in, 134
Bangladesh children: cumulative food consumption for, 143; net flow of wealth for, 140
Beekeeping, 34, 39, 63, 114, 135, 214*n*9
Behavioral ecology, 11; economic approaches to children's economic contributions, 11–17; relationship between resources and fertility and, 16–17
Best-fit model for probability of mother giving birth to first child, 200
Birth documentation, 214–215*n*2
Birth intervals, 144, 170, 183; length of, 9–10, 80–81, 167, 169; option of extending, 219*n*14
Body size: gains in, 31, 36; predation rates and, 19; return rate and, 42
Bolonchen Hills: Maya settlement of, 49; present-day Maya population in, 57–58; soils of, 66; tropical rain forest in, 65; water resources in, 50

Caloric consumption, 132
Caloric expenditures, 126–127; in domestic work, 125; in field work, 125; in ranking of task strength, 34
Calorie savings, laborsaving technology and, 160
Campeche (state), 49, 213*n*2
Capital: embodied, 37; human, 133
Cárdenas, Lázaro, 54–55
Carrying as focus of allomothering research, 12
Cash economy: Maya participation in, 124; purchase of goods in, 214*n*18
Caste War, 54